Jane Austen

By the same author

The Winter Queen
The Tudors
The Monarchs of Britain
The Vogue Bedside Book I
The Vogue Bedside Book II
Beaton in Vogue
Royalty in Vogue
Society in Vogue

Jane Austen

A COMPANION

Josephine Ross

Rutgers University Press
New Brunswick, New Jersey

First published in the United States 2003
by Rutgers University Press, New Brunswick, New Jersey

First published in Great Britain 2002
by John Murray (Publishers) Ltd,
50 Albemarle Street, London W1S 4BD

Library of Congress Cataloging-in-Publication Data and British Library
Cataloging-in-Publication Data are available upon request.

ISBN 0-8135-3299-X

Printed in Great Britain

Contents

Illustrations

Illustrations

The author and publishers would like to thank the following for permission to reproduce illustrations: Plate 1, National Portrait Gallery, London; 2 and 4, Private Collection (Jane Austen Memorial Trust); 3, 17, 26, 29, 32 and 37, Bridgeman Art Library, London/Private Collection; 5 and 44, Angelo Hornak Library; 6, The British Library, London (Add.59874 f.85v–86); 7 and 11, Bridgeman Art Library, London/Jane Austen's House, Chawton; 8, 9, 10, 13, 14, 15, 19 and 42, Jane Austen Memorial Trust; 12 and 28, Bridgeman Art Library, London/Victoria Art Gallery, Bath and North East Somerset Council; 21, © The British Library, London; 22, The Royal Collection © 2002 Her Majesty Queen Elizabeth II; 23, The British Library, London (Eger.3038 f.14v); 24 and 25, John Murray Archive; 30, Bridgeman Art Library, London/Museum of London; 31, Bridgeman Art Library, London/Fitzwilliam Museum, University of Cambridge; 33, Private Collection; 34, Bridgeman Art Library, London/Guildhall Library, Corporation of London; 36, Julia Brown Collection; 38, Bridgeman Art Library, London/The British Library; 39, Bridgeman Art Library, London/Louvre, Paris; 40, The British Library, London (P 2378); 41, Bridgeman Art Library, London/Wilberforce House, Hull City Museums and Art Galleries. Plates 16, 18, 20, 35 and 43 are from the author's collection.

Preface

When *Northanger Abbey* first appeared in 1817, published by John Murray, it contained a prefatory note by Jane Austen, informing her readers that 'this little work' had, in fact, been written long before. 'Thirteen years have passed since it was finished', the 'Authoress' explained; now, the public were 'entreated to bear in mind' that 'during that period, places, manners, books and opinions have undergone considerable changes'. Her doubts as to the enduring appeal of her fiction seemed, initially, to be justified. Though *Northanger Abbey*, printed in a 4-volume set with *Persuasion*, was well received, by 1821 demand had dwindled; and the last unsold copies were remaindered by John Murray, at the bargain price of 3*s* 1*d* a set.

The rest, of course, is history. Today, Jane Austen is one of the most famous and popular authors in the English language. *Northanger Abbey* and *Persuasion*, along with her other four completed novels, are literary classics: filmed and televised, studied in schools and universities – above all, read and enjoyed throughout the world.

Yet while her fiction now seems timeless, almost two centuries after her death some aspects of Jane Austen's world and work are, inevitably, unfamiliar to many modern readers. What, for example, was 'hartshorn'? How did Lizzy Bennet 'let down' her gown to hide her muddy petticoat? Why was it such a breach of etiquette for Mr Collins to introduce himself to Mr Darcy? And which Romantic writers gave

Marianne Dashwood her ideas? To answer questions such as these, and many more, is a prime aim of this little *Companion*.

It is not a biography; the recent Lives by such authorities as Claire Tomalin, David Nokes, Park Honan and Carol Shields (among others) have surely rendered further Jane Austen biographies superfluous for some time to come. Nor does it presume to offer a history of the period. Rather, it is intended to serve as a brief guide to the world of Jane Austen, as encountered in her letters and novels. Chapter 1 provides a short account of her life: subsequent chapters focus on specific topics, from fashion ('The Present Fashions') and literature ('The Subject of Books') to the day-to-day concerns of mealtimes, medicine and travel ('The Common Daily Routine'). Each is individually planned, and complete in itself, so that the *Companion* can be read in any sequence, or as a linked, continuous narrative.

If, in the process, it sheds any light on the 'places, manners, books and opinions' of Jane Austen's day, it will have served its purpose.

Acknowledgements

I have received a great deal of help and support in the preparation of this book. In particular, I am indebted to Fiona Sunley, of Godmersham, for her kind hospitality and expert guidance; and Mary-Blanche Ridge for introducing me to the taste of the Austens' apple butter and the beauties of Bath. I am also deeply grateful to Virginia Murray; to Grant McIntyre, Gail Pirkis and Caroline Westmore at John Murray; and to Ingrid Grimes, who copy-edited the manuscript. The picture research skills of Julia Brown were invaluable – as was the kind assistance of the Jane Austen Memorial Trust, at Chawton. The Librarian and staff of the London Library, and the staffs of the British Library, The Royal Photographic Society, Bath and Winchester Cathedral Visitor Centre, also provided much-appreciated help.

Finally, I should like to thank Robin Muir; Marie-Thérêse Caluori; David Roberts; my late parents; and my husband Jamie, whose patience, encouragement, support and advice were, quite simply, beyond words. This book is for him.

I

A Brief Life

'Pictures of perfection as you know make me sick and
wicked.'

Jane Austen, letter to her niece Fanny, 1817

About a hundred and fifty years ago, a gentleman visiting
Winchester Cathedral asked a verger to direct him to the grave
of Jane Austen. The verger pointed out the site, near the centre
of the north aisle, then enquired respectfully, 'Pray Sir, can you
tell me whether there was anything particular about that lady;
so many people want to know where she was buried?' His
ignorance was understandable. The dark marble memorial slab,
with its inscription to 'the youngest daughter of the late Revd
George Austen', made no mention of the deceased woman's literary career. Though it paid tender tribute to the 'extraordinary
endowments of her mind', it did not record that here lay the
author of such novels as *Sense and Sensibility* and *Pride and
Prejudice, Mansfield Park* and *Emma*. At the time of her burial, in
July 1817, the omission had seemed appropriate. Unlike such
famous writers of the age as Fanny Burney and Sir Walter Scott,
Jane Austen had not been a fashionable Regency figure; during
her lifetime her books had all been published anonymously, and
she had been at pains to keep her identity strictly concealed
from the general public. ('A Thing once set going in that way
– one knows how it spreads!' she had chided in 1813, when her
brother Henry revealed her authorship of *Pride and Prejudice* to
some aristocratic acquaintances.) Fifty years after her death, her

fiction no longer in wide demand, there was little reason why her name should be recognizable to the world at large.

Yet there was something 'particular about that lady', as the number of enquiries for her burial-place suggested; and after the appearance, in 1870, of the first full-length account of her life (in which the anecdote of the verger was related), there could be no more seclusion for Jane Austen. Written by her nephew, the Revd J. E. Austen-Leigh, *A Memoir of Jane Austen* was not an ambitious biography, but a fond portrait of a long-dead literary aunt, compiled from family reminiscences and papers; its influence, however, was to be far-reaching. Jane Austen's novels had always attracted a discerning, if select, readership. In her lifetime her admirers had ranged from eminent writers, such as Sheridan and Southey, to Lord Byron's future wife Annabella Milbanke (who thought the 'interest' of *Pride and Prejudice* 'very strong, especially for Mr Darcy'), and the Prince Regent himself, to whom, by flattering permission, *Emma* was dedicated. After her death, her distinguished devotees included Lord Macaulay, who talked of her in society, praised her in print, and proposed to reissue her complete novels, with a biographical preface by himself, to fund a fine new memorial in Winchester Cathedral. Macaulay's plans came to nothing, however; and in an age crowded with great and popular novelists, from Dickens, Thackeray and the Brontë sisters to Trollope and Mrs Gaskell, 'Miss Austen' remained a relatively shadowy figure from the past – until the success of her nephew's *Memoir*, at the beginning of the 1870s, brought the woman and her work to the attention of a new, and broad, range of Victorian readers. In their 'secret thoughts', the *Memoir* confided, the Austens had presumed to rank 'dear Aunt Jane' with her best-selling contemporaries, the great Fanny Burney and the romance-writer Maria Edgeworth: but by the end of the nine-teenth-century her reputation had far eclipsed theirs. As the *Dictionary of National Biography* of 1885 stated, Jane Austen had won the 'admiration, even to fanaticism, of innumerable readers'; and in the years that followed, amid a surge of articles, essays, critical studies and reprints of her novels, the unmarried daughter of a Georgian vicar, who had feared to be made 'a wild beast' by her contemporaries, was to become one of the best-known authors in the English language – her private correspondence pored over; her personal life exposed and anatomized. Like her own most romantically naive creation, Marianne Dashwood in *Sense and Sensibility*, Jane Austen, the great ironist, was 'born to an extraordinary fate'.

The world with which her name would become synonymous was that of the Regency of 1811–20: the effulgent era of high-waisted dresses and high-sprung phaetons; of John Nash terraces and Thomas Hope interiors: of the Princess of Wales's adultery scandals and Napoleon's defeat at Waterloo; of ballrooms, battlefields and Byronic heroes. The world into which she was born, however, on 16 December 1775, seemed a more orderly, less frenetic place. George III had then been on the British throne for fifteen years, and, at 37, was a stable and dutiful monarch – fond of agriculture and his ever-growing family, and showing as yet no sign of the insanity which, in the year of *Sense and Sensibility*'s first publication, would cause his unpopular heir, the Prince of Wales, to be appointed Prince Regent. In France, the frivolous new Queen Marie-Antoinette was indulging her extravagant whims at Versailles, unchecked by her stolid husband Louis XVI, or by any inkling of impending Revolution. The first battle of America's War of Independence had taken place in June 1775, near Bunker Hill; but at the time of Jane Austen's birth, six months later, the rebel colonists were still nominally subjects of King George, and in the words of the rousing patriotic song by James Thomson (a favourite Austen poet), Britannia still ruled the waves.

For the clever, playful daughter of a close-knit country vicar's family, it was a congenial age in which to be born.

There was as yet no threat from Bonaparte's armies in Europe to alarm uncomprehending children; and the theories of educationalists such as the pious Hannah More had yet to impinge on the nation's nurseries. The Austens of Steventon, in Hampshire, though Tory in their politics and staunchly Anglican in their religion, were comfortably easy-going in their ways; and Steventon Rectory, where Jane Austen grew up, was renowned as a 'pleasant and prosperous' household. The Revd George Austen, Jane's father, was descended from Kent clothiers who had become considerable landowners; his own father, however, had been a mere surgeon, a relatively low-ranking profession in Georgian society, and when he died young, in 1737, only the assistance of a rich relation secured a gentleman's education for the orphaned boy. Fortunately, at Tonbridge School and Oxford University George Austen proved an able scholar: he became a Fellow of his old college, St John's, and in 1764, after taking Holy Orders, he married a niece of the eminent Master of Balliol – Miss Cassandra Leigh. It was to be a largely happy union. George Austen (who was known at Oxford as 'the handsome Proctor') was a good-looking man, with fine hazel eyes; Cassandra Leigh, though less beautiful than her elder sister Jane, had an elegant, aquiline profile, a mind both clever and practical, and grander social connections than those of her husband – including, through her paternal grandmother, a duke. She was an unpretentious woman, however, who preferred country life to the bustle of fashionable London, which she thought 'a sad place'; above all, she had 'a lively imagination', a taste for writing poetry, and a sharp sense of humour. The Austen family set great store by wit. Puns and *bons mots* by friends and forebears were preserved in their household lore long after they had lost the power to amuse; and amid the general 'flow of spirits' at Steventon Rectory the children of George and Cassandra Austen were brought up to be not only 'good, amiable and sweet-tempered' (in her phrase), with 'a natural judgement of what is right' (in his), but also to be lively, entertaining company.

The birth of their second daughter, and seventh child, was announced by George Austen in a typically light-hearted letter to his half-brother's wife, Mrs Walter. Writing on the following day, 17 December 1775, he observed that the Walters must have 'wondered a little we were in our old age grown such bad reckoners ... for Cassy certainly expected to have been brought to bed a month ago'; however, he reported happily, 'We have now another girl, a present plaything for her sister Cassy, and a future companion. She is to be Jenny ...'. The homely pet name of Jenny, for Jane, was not heard of again; but on another point the letter proved prescient. Jane Austen and her sister – inevitably named Cassandra, after their mother – were to become devoted, lifelong companions. As the only girls in a family with five spirited sons, they were likely to see one another as natural allies in childhood; but the bond between them was to be exceptionally strong, and enduring. In looks and character they were not thought particularly alike; Cassandra (the prettier), who was described as 'prudent and well-judging', with a somewhat reserved manner, was said to resemble the third Austen son, steady, practical Edward, while Jane, who would be known for her 'sunniness of temper', had more in common with the fourth brother, charming, amusing Henry. Nevertheless, throughout her life Jane Austen looked up to Cassandra as a mentor and superior in every way – considering her not only 'wiser and better than herself', but funnier too. 'You are indeed the finest comic writer of our present age', she told her sister delightedly in 1798, in reply to a letter of Cassandra's which had made her almost 'die of laughter'.

As well as a sense of humour, the Austen sisters shared books, clothes, secrets and – even as adults – a bedroom. By the time Jane was born Steventon was becoming decidedly crowded. The second Austen son, George, born in 1766, had some mysterious, apparently mental, disability which caused him to be brought up away from home; beyond occasional references, such as a comment by Mrs Austen that her 'poor little George' had fits, he was scarcely ever mentioned. Besides George (who would outlive Jane by twenty years), there were seven healthy Austen children: James, born in 1765; Edward, born in 1767; Henry, born in 1771; then, between 1773 and 1775, a child a year, Cassandra, Francis and Jane; and finally, in 1779, Charles. Perhaps in response to such 'violently rapid' childbearing, in later life their mother would become a confirmed hypochondriac: Jane's letters were to be full of references to her tiresome, but transitory, ailments, from headaches, insomnia and indigestion to 'a very dreadful Cold', and – on one alarming occasion – 'An Asthma, a Dropsy, Water in her Chest and a Liver disorder'. Yet while her children were young Mrs Austen was evidently an energetic woman, who kept cows and ducks, gardened and mended, and ran her large household with the 'useful plain sense' and 'unaffected benevolence' of Catherine Morland's capable mother in *Northanger Abbey*, rather than the exhausted incompetence of Mrs Price, slipshod mother of the heroine Fanny (and seven others) in *Mansfield Park*.

The suggestion, familiar to novelists throughout history, that fictional characters must be based on real people was one which Jane Austen always rejected with courteous irritation. 'I am too proud of my gentlemen', she demurred on one occasion, 'to admit that they are only Mr A., or Colonel B.' After *Emma* was published, in 1815, she noted that a dissatisfied reader was 'convinced that I had meant Mrs and Miss Bates for some acquaintance of theirs – People whom I never heard of before'. Yet the temptation to draw parallels between her own childhood and that which she ascribes to Catherine Morland, in *Northanger Abbey*, is to many readers, irresistible. Like the good-natured clergyman who was Catherine's father, the Revd George Austen was comfortably-off, with the income from two church livings, or parishes; having been educated by one generous relation, his uncle Francis Austen, who presented him with the living of Deane, he later acquired the patronage of another kinsman – Thomas Knight, a cousin who owned extensive property (including the mansions of Godmersham and Chawton) in both Kent and Hampshire, and who gave him the living of Steventon, where Jane was born. There, in the simple, old-fashioned Rectory, with its bare, beamed ceilings and uncorniced interiors, she spent the first twenty-five years of her life. There, in grounds surrounded by sprawling Hampshire hedgerows, she played with her sister and brothers – perhaps like the rowdy young Morlands, at 'cricket, baseball, riding on horseback and running about the country'. There she learned the parlour games of spillikins and cup-and-ball at which she would be adroit as an adult; there – again like Catherine Morland – she discovered the boundless pleasures of reading, from the poetry of Pope and Gray, and the plays of Shakespeare, to the fun of lurid Gothic horror stories and ludicrous romances, teeming with swooning heroines and black-hearted villains. She might also – as Catherine did – have amused herself on fine days by 'rolling down the green slope at the back of the house'; as her nephew's *Memoir* recorded, there was a 'terrace of the finest turf' behind Steventon Rectory.

Despite enlargements and improvements, the Rectory can scarcely have seemed spacious when the whole family was present, as, in addition to his own children, the Revd George Austen took in boarding-pupils, to supplement his income. Among them were several sons of local grandees, including a future Earl of Portsmouth; the most notable, however, was a child whom the Austens cared for at the start of their married life – the infant son of Warren Hastings, the first Governor-General of India, who in 1788 would be impeached and tried at Westminster for misconduct (though eventually exonerated). Left motherless in 1769, little George Hastings was entrusted to the Austens through the offices of George Austen's sister Philadelphia Hancock, the wife of a surgeon in India, who knew the Governor-General well. Tragically, the boy died before Jane was born; but Warren Hastings always spoke warmly of the Austens' kindness to his child, and his relationship with the family remained cordial. At the time of Hastings's dramatic trial, when Jane was aged 12, the Austens were among his loyal supporters; some twenty-five years later, having retired to England, he was sent an early copy of *Pride and Prejudice*, which he evidently enjoyed. 'I long to have you hear Mr H.'s opinion of *P. & P.*' Jane wrote excitedly to Cassandra, in September 1813.

As an adult, Jane Austen was to speak of herself as having been a shy child; yet if not a romping tomboy, like the 'noisy and wild' Catherine Morland, she would seem to have been a cheerful small girl, who scribbled in the margins of her schoolbooks, took a keen interest in her elders' activities, and constantly made up verses and stories to amuse herself and her indulgent family. As a baby, she was apparently 'put out to nurse' in the village, and at the early age of 7 she was sent away to school, with her sister; but such partings did not seem to affect her equable nature. A copy of the French schoolbook *Fables Choisies*, inscribed at the front 'Miss Jane Austen 5th Decr 1783' survives – its back page enlivened with the bold signatures 'Jane Austen' and 'Francis Austen', and the poignant note, 'Mother's angry. Father's gone out', scrawled in a childish handwriting. 'Father' permitted his bright little daughter a certain licence even where Church business was concerned: in the parish register, where weddings were recorded, Jane was allowed to fill in sample entries, giving her own name as that of the bride, with imaginary grooms who ranged from 'Edmund Arthur William Mortimer of Liverpool' to the more prosaic 'Jack Smith'.

Marriage to some suitable Smith or Mortimer was no doubt expected to be the Austen sisters' destiny, just as Jane assumed it would be that of her beloved niece Fanny, to whom she wrote tenderly, in 1817, 'Depend upon it, the right man *will* come', adding ominously, 'Single Women have a dreadful propensity for being poor.' While a woman's prospects of a good marriage might be enhanced by accomplishments such as music, drawing and languages, to be over-educated might have the opposite effect. 'A woman,' Jane was to write acidly in *Northanger Abbey*, 'if she have the advantage of knowing anything, should conceal it as well as she can.' By the standards of the day, however, Jane Austen was well educated, for her sex. 'I think I may boast myself to be, with all possible vanity, the most unlearned and uninformed female who ever dared to be an authoress,' she declared with characteristic modesty in 1815, in a letter to the Prince Regent's humourless librarian; half a century later, in his *Memoir*, her nephew qualified the claim, describing her – somewhat condescendingly – as 'according to the ideas of the time, well educated, though not highly accomplished'. In fact, though she lacked the classical education bestowed, as of right, on her brothers, and claimed brightly to know nothing of 'science and philosophy', Jane Austen was better informed, and far better read, than most women of her day, having good French and some Italian, a love of history, considerable skill in both music and drawing, and an extensive, intelligent knowledge of some of the greatest writers in the English language, from Johnson, Richardson and Fielding, to Goldsmith, Hume and Crabbe. She might have said, as Lizzy Bennet does in *Pride and Prejudice*, when questioned on her education, 'Such of us as wished to learn, never wanted the means.'

The Austen boys (unlike their own sons) were not sent away to any of the great British public schools, but were tutored at home by their scholarly father until old enough to go to Oxford – or, in the case of the two youngest, Francis and Charles, to begin their naval training. It was decided that Cassandra should be sent to a boarding-school, however, at the age of 9; and because, as Mrs Austen remarked, 'If Cassandra were going to have her head cut off, Jane would insist on sharing her fate', Jane, then aged 7, duly went with her. Their initial experience was an unhappy one. The establishment chosen, in Oxford, was kept by a Mrs Cawley, sister-in-law to Mrs Austen's beautiful sister Mrs Cooper – whose own daughter, also named Jane, went there too. A daunting, uncommunicative woman, Mrs Cawley soon moved her pupils to Southampton, where both the Austen girls became seriously ill, possibly with diphtheria, and had to be removed from her care by their aunt, Mrs Cooper. The little girls recovered, but Mrs Cooper caught the disease and died. Despite the tragedy, in 1784 Cassandra and Jane Austen were sent away again, to a more cheerful school kept by Mrs La Tournelle, a widow with an artificial leg. The Abbey School, Reading, was housed by the gatehouse of an ancient abbey (no doubt to the satisfaction of the future author of *Northanger Abbey*), and its regime was lenient, consisting of a little instruction by tutors, and much companionable gossip and play. Memories of Mrs La Tournelle's were surely behind the description of Mrs Goddard's 'real, honest, old-fashioned Boarding-school' in *Emma*, to which girls such as the heroine's naive friend Harriet Smith were sent to 'scramble themselves into a little education', while being well and kindly cared for.

Most of Jane Austen's education was acquired, however, amid the books and clever conversation of Steventon, where she and Cassandra had returned for good by the late 1780s. By then George and Cassandra Austen had more time to devote to their daughters, as the boys were rapidly leaving home – even the two youngest, who, aged about 12, embarked on what were to be distinguished careers in the navy, by entering the Royal Naval Academy at Portsmouth. While James and Henry Austen followed their father's footsteps to St John's College, Oxford, Edward (regarded, in the absence of the disabled George, as second in age) left Steventon for a new life, as the adopted heir to a wealthy, childless couple who could offer him great prospects. Edward's benefactor was Thomas Knight of Godmersham in Kent, son of the kinsman who had presented the Steventon living to the Revd George Austen. The unofficial adoption of children for social advantage – so strange to twenty-first-century sensibilities – was by no means uncommon in Jane Austen's time: in her own fiction it would be central to the plot in two of her six novels, with Fanny Price being sent to live with the haughty Bertrams, in *Mansfield Park*, and Frank Churchill becoming the adopted heir of his rich aunt in *Emma*. In Edward Austen's case, the arrangement worked well. Less bookish than his brothers and sisters, but steady, amiable and 'quite a man of business', in Mrs Austen's words, he became a typical Georgian squire and – to the benefit of his mother and sisters, in later years – man of property. Like other heirs to fortunes and estates, he was sent on the Grand Tour of Europe: in 1791 he made a good marriage to a baronet's beautiful daughter, Elizabeth Bridges: eventually, in 1812, he changed his surname officially from Austen-Knight to 'Knight' alone. ('I must learn to make a better "K"', was Jane Austen's dry response to the news.) Yet Edward remained deeply attached to his natural family, in particular his sister Cassandra, who stayed with him constantly at Godmersham. On one of her own, much rarer, visits there, in 1808, his other sister wrote to Cassandra that it felt 'odd' to have a vast and splendid bedroom – 'The Yellow Room' – all to herself, adding wistfully, 'To be at Godmersham without you also seems odd.'

The room which they slept in at Steventon was, by contrast, cramped; but it had the benefit of an adjoining dressing-room which, in such a masculine household, provided the sisters with a welcome retreat of their own. As well as a flowered, chocolate-brown carpet, a painted cupboard and a looking-glass, the room was furnished with their favourite possessions, from Cassandra's drawing equipment and Jane's piano to a sewing-basket, a writing-desk, and well-stocked bookshelves. The Austen sons were enthusiastic sportsmen, who hunted and shot and – particularly in Francis's case – had a good eye for a horse, from boyhood; but though Jane could drive a donkey-carriage, and she and Cassandra were 'desperate walkers', their chief pleasures, even as children, were artistic and creative. Cassandra drew excellently. She had a particular talent for caricatures, which revealed the sly wit which Jane so loved, but which her reserved air tended to conceal from others. It was fittingly ironic that the only certain, authentic, full-face portrait of Jane Austen to have survived should be a droll sketch by Cassandra, dating from about 1810. Almost a caricature – round-cheeked, beady-eyed, and looking askance – it evidently caught the sitter so well that, however unflattering, it was carefully preserved.

Significantly, Jane Austen's earliest-known writings, dating from about 1787, when she was 11 or 12, were all parodies and satires. Even as a child she was an astute observer of social and literary conventions – and in particular, those of trashy popular fiction: the elopements and lurid deathbeds; the improbably rediscovered rich relations and fainting, virtuous heroines. Prefaced with grand dedications to her family and friends, these juvenile works varied from childish fragments, such as *The Adventures of Mr Harley* ('a short but interesting Tale . . . with all imaginable respect inscribed to Mr Francis William Austen Midshipman on board his Majesty's ship the Perseverance'), to productions as elaborate as the hilarious *Love and Freindship* [*sic*], 'a novel in a series of Letters', written when she was about 15. If some of the comedy was sheer nonsensical fun – the heroine of *The Beautifull* [*sic*] *Cassandra* punches a pastrycook and shoplifts a bonnet; the Johnsons in *Jack and Alice* were 'a family of Love . . . though a little addicted to the Bottle and the Dice' – much of it was skilful, pre-cocious, and intensely funny. Her family clearly relished, and encouraged, Jane's early writing: although the originals have disappeared, three manuscript volumes survive into which, in the 1790s, she carefully copied out her *Juvenilia* – some 90,000 words in all.

Among them were several short dramatic pieces, which reflected the Austens' enthusiasm for reciting and acting. As a family they often read aloud to one another; Jane's correspondence mentioned such instances as her brother James reading Walter Scott's *Marmion*, and herself reading aloud Southey's *Espriella's Letters*, 'by candlelight'. When *Pride and Prejudice* was published, in 1813, Mrs Austen read one of the first copies aloud – though unfortunately not well: her 'too rapid way of getting on', and inability to vary her voice for the characters, rather spoiled its author's enjoyment of her masterpiece. Others in the family had more acting talent, however; and from 1782, when Jane was about 7, they put on plays at Steventon – first in the dining-room, later in a converted barn. In these her high-minded eldest brother showed his less solemn side, writing prologues and epilogues for the productions, as well as taking part. Though an academic and a clergyman, James Austen had a taste for entertaining: as well as writing poetry, while at Oxford he edited *The Loiterer*, a magazine in the style of *The Spectator*, to which he, his undergraduate brother Henry, and possibly, under a pen-name, his schoolgirl sister Jane, were contributors. James and Jane Austen were very different characters, and in later years there would be considerable friction between them. 'His Chat seems all forced, his Opinions on many points too much copied from his Wife's and his time here is spent . . . in walking about the House and banging the doors, or ringing the bell for a glass of water', Jane wrote vexedly to Cassandra in 1807, after one of James's disruptive visits. As a child, however, she had revered him; and rather as her fictional Edmund Bertram would do for his naive cousin Fanny Price, in *Mansfield Park*, he evidently acted as her unofficial tutor, discussing books with her and encouraging her early writing. Though too young to take part herself, she would surely have been an eager spectator at the dramas enacted at the Rectory in the 1780s.

'My uncle's barn is fitting up quite like a theatre, and all the young folks are to take their part', Jane's half-cousin Philadelphia Walter reported in 1787. That Christmas, the production at Steventon was a Restoration comedy, *The Wonder! A Woman Keeps A Secret*, by Susannah Centlivre, and among the 'young folks' taking part was another Austen cousin, the flighty and fascinating Eliza de Feuillide, daughter of the Revd George Austen's sister, Philadelphia Hancock, who had been sent out to India to find a husband. Born in Calcutta in 1761, and married, aged 20, to a French aristocrat, Eliza was a more exotic creature than most of the sedate Hampshire gentry among whom Jane grew up, and her effect on the Rectory party was not unlike that of the alluring, unsettling Mary Crawford on the Bertrams in *Mansfield Park*. To add to her importance, Eliza was the god-daughter of the great Warren Hastings – some whispered, the daughter. (A letter from Jane to Cassandra, soon after Eliza's death in 1813, included the enigmatic statement, 'Mr Hastings never *hinted* at Eliza, in the smallest degree', in reply to an unknown question.) Whatever the truth behind the rumours, certainly Hastings made generous provision for his god-daughter; and the beautiful Mrs Hancock was living in Europe with Eliza, and not with her elderly surgeon-husband in India, at the time of Mr Hancock's death in 1775.

Pretty, shallow and vain, Eliza was in her element in pre-Revolution Paris, where her doting mother introduced her into fashionable society in the late 1770s. The elegance of French clothes and customs, and the splendour of attending Court functions at Versailles, in the presence of Queen Marie-Antoinette, were central topics in Eliza's letters to her half-cousin Philadelphia Walter – and no doubt of her conversation when she visited her country cousins at Steventon. In 1781 she acquired a new source of self-congratulation, when she married a titled French army officer, the Comte de Feuillide. 'He literally adores me', she confided sweetly to the increasingly resentful 'Phila' Walter. George Austen, who was fond of his giddy niece, was evidently 'much concerned' by her marriage to a Catholic, and a foreigner – and with good reason, as history would show; but the carefree Countess continued to visit England and the Rectory, and even the birth of her only child (a sickly son, named Hastings), in 1786, did not deter her pursuit of amusement.

Play-acting became a craze at Steventon when Eliza was staying, and the 12-year-old Jane was clearly struck by what she witnessed. She tried her own hand as a dramatist, producing such gems as *The Mystery*, 'An Unfinished Comedy', which gleefully exposed such absurd conventions as the stage whisper and the *sotto voce* revelation. (Act One begins masterfully, 'Enter *Corydon. Cory*: But Hush! I am interrupted. Exit *Corydon*.') Some thirty years later, when she was writing *Mansfield Park*, with its vivid scenes of amateur theatricals, Jane Austen must have recalled these childhood experiences – the bustle of 'arrangements and dresses, rehearsals and jokes'; and – more potently – the rivalries and sexual tensions liable to develop when young people were freed from strict social codes to address, and even caress, one another, while uttering open endearments. 'Phila' Walter, like Fanny Price, virtuously declined to act, but Eliza lost no opportunity to display her charms, on or off-stage; and to differing degrees both James and Henry Austen – though four and ten years her junior – fell under her spell. Before returning to France with her 2-year-old son, in 1788, she visited them at Oxford, where she was 'mightily taken' with all she saw, from the gardens of their college to the sight of Henry himself, grown tall and handsome, with his hair powdered and dressed 'in a very *ton*ish style'.

For all her faults and follies, Eliza brought a valuable glimpse of the wider eighteenth-century world into Jane Austen's sheltered early life. She had been to Court, both at Versailles and St James's, danced at Almack's, the exclusive London night-club, and paraded at the theatre in Tunbridge Wells; she could talk knowledgeably of the scenery in India and the fashions in Paris. When her titled husband went to the guillotine, in 1794, the newspaper reports of the horrors of the French Revolution became shocking reality for the Steventon family; and when, in 1797, the dashing 36-year-old widow married Jane's 26-year-old brother Henry, after a tentative flirtation with James, the stuff of romantic novels, such as the Austens loved to read aloud by candlelight, became startling fact. Eliza's 'racketing' way of life was one to which Jane Austen herself never aspired; her preferred society was that of the polite, agreeable, rural gentry and clergy – the '3 or 4 Families in a Country Village' which she once recommended as the ideal basis for a novel. Yet the legacy of this coquettish cousin and sister-in-law would often be discernible in her fiction. Whether or not (as family tradition held) the buccaneering Mary Crawford was indeed inspired by Eliza, *Love and Freindship*, Jane Austen's juvenile parody of fashionable female silliness, was gaily dedicated 'To Madame La Comtesse de Feuillide'; and from the 'resolutely stilish' Isabella Thorpe, in *Northanger Abbey*, to the ignorant flirt Lydia Bennet in *Pride and Prejudice*, many of the less estimable women in Jane Austen's novels would evoke echoes of Eliza and her half-knowing, half-naive brand of self-seeking feminine charm.

'Our neighbourhood was small, for it consisted only of your mother', Letter 4th of *Love and Friendship* began succinctly. The neighbourhood around Steventon was, fortunately, not so restricted: though Cassandra and Jane did not make their debut in London society (unlike Eliza), they seemed to find no shortage of amusement within their own circle. Apart from relations whom they visited further afield – Edward and his adoptive parents, the Knights, at Godmersham; Francis Austen, the Revd George Austen's first benefactor, at Sevenoaks; Mrs

Austen's brother and sister-in-law, the Leigh-Perrots, at Bath – there were numerous local families with whom the Austens were on dancing and dining terms, and who kept Jane supplied with material for jokes and speculation. Names which featured in her correspondence included the Jervoises and the Terrys ('the former of whom were apt to be vulgar, the latter noisy', she recorded ruefully after one dance in 1799); the Digweeds, who rented Steventon Manor; and the well-to-do, agreeable Bigg family of Manydown, with whom Jane and Cassandra often stayed after attending the monthly public balls at the Assembly Rooms in Basingstoke. The three Bigg girls, whose father and brother took the surname Bigg-Wither, in token of an inheritance, were particular friends of the Austen sisters; closer still, however, were Mary and Martha Lloyd, whose clergyman father briefly occupied the parsonage house at Deane, George Austen's subsidiary living. The Misses Lloyd were not beauties, having been scarred by smallpox in childhood; but they were 'very sensible and good-humoured' (in Eliza's faintly condescending words), and the elder, Martha, shared the Austens' love of good jokes and bad novels. The Austen and Lloyd girls came to regard each other almost as sisters – 'She is the friend and sister under every circumstance', Jane once wrote tenderly of Martha. When the Lloyds left the house at Deane in 1792, to make way for the new incumbent, James Austen, and his bride, Anne Mathew, Jane gave Mary a characteristic parting-gift – a miniature, home-made sewing-kit, containing needles, thread and a verse in minute writing, entreating her to 'recollect your friend'. The sentiment was in the style of the popular enamel patch-boxes and souvenir trinkets of the day; the tiny, wittily conceived and exquisitely made object was wholly in the style of Jane Austen.

The idealized view of his aunt expressed by James's son, J. E. Austen-Leigh, in his *Memoir*, was not shared by all who knew her. Philadelphia Walter, meeting her female Austen cousins for the first time in 1788, much preferred Cassandra: Jane, she thought 'not at all pretty and very prim, unlike a girl of twelve', adding that she seemed 'whimsical and affected'. A somewhat different report, later circulated by the novelist Mary Russell Mitford, whose mother had known the Austens at Steventon, claimed that Jane was 'the prettiest, silliest, most affected husband-hunting butterfly' – a charge which Austen-Leigh indignantly rebutted, pointing out that Jane had been under 8 years old when Mrs Mitford knew her. It may be that having been a quaint, precocious child Jane Austen passed though a giggling, flirting stage of adolescence; certainly Eliza approvingly described her and Cassandra, in the early 1790s, as 'perfect beauties' who 'of course gain hearts by the dozens'. Allowing for Eliza's exaggerations, and the fact that Cassandra was the more 'regularly handsome' of the two, Jane Austen clearly grew into an attractive young woman, taller than average, with a slim figure, curly brown hair, a small nose and mouth and her father's bright hazel eyes. Round, rosy cheeks – 'a little too full' – were her only defect, according to one childhood acquaintance, the novelist Sir Egerton Brydges; but this un-heroinelike feature did not prevent her from attracting the romantic interest of several eligible young men – including, most importantly, Sir Egerton's own handsome kinsman by marriage, Tom Lefroy.

The beginning of Jane Austen's treasury of surviving letters, written over a period of twenty-one years, largely to Cassandra, dates from January 1796, at which time she was just 20 years old: at work, privately, on an early version of the first of her great novels, *Sense and Sensibility*, and at the height of a half-serious, half-teasing relationship with the 'very gentlemanlike, good-looking, pleasant' young nephew of her much-loved friend Mrs Lefroy. The wife of the Rector of Ashe, near Steventon (and Sir Egerton Brydges's sister), Anne Lefroy had a deep affection for Jane, who thought her in return an 'Angelic woman', and after her death in 1804 wrote a heartfelt poem in her memory. Tom Lefroy, a 20-year-old

Irishman, was staying at Ashe when he met Jane Austen in 1795; the attraction between them rapidly became obvious enough to cause gossip in the neighbourhood and earn Jane a reproof from her ever-correct sister. 'You scold me so much', Jane responded happily, the day after a local dance, 'that I am almost afraid to tell you how my Irish friend and I behaved. Imagine to yourself everything most profligate and shocking in the way of dancing and sitting down together.' She used the same joking tone for every reference to her 'friend', from the colour of his coat – 'too light' – to the teasing he had to endure about her at Ashe. Dramatically, she confided that she was expecting a proposal of marriage from him – yet in the same letter she mentioned him airily as 'Mr Tom Lefroy, for whom I do not care sixpence'. At the end of his visit she wrote, mock-tragically, 'The day is come on which I am to flirt my last with Tom Lefroy. . . . My tears flow as I write at the melancholy idea.' The true extent of her feelings for this youthful admirer was to remain concealed, from both her sister and history. After Jane's death, Cassandra sifted zealously through her correspondence and destroyed all intimate, or indiscreet, references, especially those concerning love-affairs; the fact that she left intact so much about this romance suggests that she, at least, thought it insignificant. Tom Lefroy returned to Ireland and embarked on a distinguished legal career, rising eventually to become Lord Chief Justice of Ireland; Jane Austen resumed her daily round of visits and shopping, family duties and social life – and by the end of that year, had embarked on the first draft of what would eventually become one of the greatest novels in the English language: *Pride and Prejudice*.

Her original title for the work was *First Impressions*, a reference to a passage in her own favourite novel, Samuel Richardson's *Sir Charles Grandison*. Even in its early (now vanished) form, before being 'lop't and crop't' into the immortal *Pride and Prejudice*, the manuscript delighted the few confidants to whom Jane showed it; as millions in later generations would do, they read and re-read it avidly. 'I do not wonder at your wanting to read *First Impressions* again, so seldom as you have gone through it', Jane teased Cassandra in January 1799; later in the year she wrote jokingly, 'I would not let Martha read *First Impressions* again upon any account ... she means to publish it from memory, and one more perusal must enable her to do it.' In fact, an attempt was indeed made to publish *First Impressions*. Three months after its completion, in November 1797, the Revd George Austen wrote to the London firm of Cadell, offering 'a manuscript novel, comprising 3 vols., about the length of Miss Burney's *Evelina*', and enquiring how much they might 'venture to advance for the property of it', if, 'on perusal', it were 'approved of'. It was a timelessly, touchingly inept approach on behalf of an aspiring author, and Cadell had no hesitation in declining – by return of post – even to look at the manuscript which was the forerunner of *Pride and Prejudice*.

The lack of immediate publishing prospects did not deter Jane Austen from writing enthusiastically during this period. The spurned *First Impressions* was rapidly followed, in 1797, by *Sense and Sensibility* – according to Cassandra's recollections, a reworking of the earlier novel in letters, *Elinor and Marianne*, which had apparently involved 'something of the same story and characters'. By 1799 she had also produced *Susan*, the first draft of *Northanger Abbey*. Three major works of English literature had been conceived and drafted in three years, an astonishing achievement; yet, as ever, Jane Austen seemed bent on keeping her literary activities as private as possible. Her letters during this period were filled with details of her daily life, from news of family and friends and comments on dances, books and fashions, to funny, tart asides such as 'I was as civil to them as their bad breath would allow'; but they included no mention of her own work in hand. Her niece Anna, James Austen's first child, remembered in old age how, staying at Steventon as a small girl, she once overheard her aunts Jane and Cassandra laughing together over a passage of Jane's writing, and was sternly warned never to speak of it to anyone else.

The events which mainly concerned Jane Austen during the busy 1790s were family ones: the births, marriages, career advancements and deaths which were taking place in the real world, while she was bringing into fictional being Mrs Jennings and Marianne Dashwood, plotting Mr Darcy's exchanges with Elizabeth Bennet, and conjuring up Catherine Morland's Gothic terrors. The year 1793 saw the births of the first of her beloved nieces and nephews – Anna to James and Anne Austen, and Fanny to Edward and Elizabeth Austen-Knight. Tragically, James's wife died two years later; as a result, the motherless Anna became especially close to her aunts Cassandra and Jane, and remained so even after acquiring a stepmother, in 1797. James's second wife was Mary Lloyd, the Austen sisters' good friend, and at first the match seemed ideal. Miss Lloyd, despite her bad complexion, had not only acquired a highly respectable husband, but had also regained her old home, the parsonage at Deane, which her family had vacated for James and his previous wife. (Intriguingly, *Pride and Prejudice*, then being drafted as *First Impressions*, would echo this situation, with the clergyman Mr Collins proposing to marry one of the Bennet sisters in order to restore her to her old home, of which he was the heir.) Jane Austen's mother was overjoyed by her eldest son's remarriage, telling Mary, with fond egotism, 'I look forward to you as a real comfort to me in my old age, when Cassandra is gone into Shropshire, and Jane – the Lord knows where.' Behind her happiness lay barely concealed relief that James was not marrying his seductive cousin, Eliza de Feuillide. The widowed Countess had other plans, however. She had made it clear – as the fictional Mary Crawford was to do – that she had no wish to become a clergyman's wife; and so it was the younger and more dashing Austen son, Henry (who, on leaving Oxford, had joined the militia and not the Church), who became Eliza's second husband, at the end of 1797.

If the Austens were shocked by the handsome, talented Henry's marriage to a racy widow ten years his senior, it was a minor disappointment compared with the tragedy which befell Cassandra earlier in the same year: the death of her clergyman fiancé, Thomas Fowle. A former pupil of the Revd George Austen, Thomas, like Edward Ferrars in *Sense and Sensibility*, fell in love with his tutor's pretty daughter – but unlike the ensnared Edward he chose well, and he and Cassandra became discreetly engaged in 1795. He had the prospect of a modest Church living, in Shropshire; but to improve his financial situation before marrying, he agreed to accompany his influential kinsman, Lord Craven, to the West Indies, as a regimental chaplain. There, in February 1797, at Santo Domingo, he died – like so many of the British troops – of Yellow Fever. 'Jane says her sister behaves with a degree of resolution and propriety which no common mind could evince in so trying a situation', Eliza wrote soberly, early in May. For all her exemplary fortitude, reminiscent of Elinor Dashwood's self-command, Cassandra seems never to have considered marriage again – despite occasional hints from her family that she should. 'My father and mother made the same match for you last night, and are very much pleased with it. *He* is a beauty . . .', Jane wrote encouragingly, two years later, in May 1799.

Significantly, none of her letters from the period of her sister's bereavement has survived; but those dating from the following autumn onwards were as full of news and fun as ever. They could be caustic, as when she wrote of a Mrs Hall who, 'owing to a fright', had delivered a stillborn child, adding with heartless wit, 'I suppose she happened unawares to look at her husband.' Yet in general her tone was playful and self-mocking. 'Whenever I fall into misfortune, how many jokes it ought to furnish to my acquaintance in general, or I shall die dreadfully in their debt for entertainment,' she once mused penitently. Where her own family – the children in particular – were concerned, her tone was almost invariably tender, sympathetic and warm; and in writing of her mother's exaggerated ailments she showed remarkable loyalty and patience. What could not be concealed, from Cassandra at least, was her mounting irritation with James and his second wife. Once such a close friend, Mary became humourless and mean-spirited after her marriage, though James seemed devoted to her, and wrote frequent unremarkable verses in her praise. By contrast, every mention of the sailor Austens, Francis and Charles, conveyed their sister's glowing affection. In these arduous years of war against Napoleon at sea, 'our dear Frank' and 'our own particular little brother', Charles, were sources of constant concern and pride to Jane; she peppered her letters with loving references to sloops and frigates, names of ships they served in, such as *Petterel* and *Endymion*, and news of promotions and prize money – the bounty for capturing enemy vessels, by which a successful officer might make his fortune, as Captain Wentworth would in *Persuasion*. In December 1798, having told Cassandra the great news of Frank's promotion to Captain, she wrote exultantly, 'There! I may now finish my letter and go and hang myself, for I am sure I can neither write nor do anything which will not appear insipid to you after this.' The origins of Fanny Price's pride in her gallant midshipman brother, and Anne Elliot's unquenchable love for her erstwhile naval fiancé, in her two most serious novels, are not hard to trace.

The year 1800 marked a turning-point in Jane Austen's life. She was then 25; and while she might not, as yet, have 'felt her approach to the years of danger', as did the ambitious, 29-year-old spinster Elizabeth Elliot, in *Persuasion*, the years of promise, which might have led her 'the Lord knows where', were inexorably drawing to an end. Another semi-serious romance, in 1798, had ended without a proposal, though this suitor – a jovial 27-year-old Fellow of Emmanuel College, Cambridge, the Revd Samuel Blackall – had hinted to Mrs Lefroy of his hopes of 'a nearer interest' with the Austen family. In 1813, on hearing of his marriage, Jane wrote fondly, 'I should very much like to know what sort of a Woman she is. He was a piece of Perfection, noisy Perfection himself which I always recollect with regard.' Marriage without love was, for her, unthinkable – 'anything is to be preferred or endured', she once stated vehemently; yet she was acutely conscious of the dangers of old age for the single woman with no fortune. Her own dependent situation as a spinster daughter was harshly underlined, late in 1800, when Mrs Austen suddenly announced to her and Cassandra, 'It is all settled. We are to leave Steventon and go to Bath.' For the Revd George Austen, now almost 70, and ready to retire and hand over the Steventon living to James, it was an understandable decision, but for Jane the shock was so great that, according to one account, she fainted.

She loved Steventon and its surrounding countryside, prided herself on being a 'Hampshire-born Austen', and disliked Bath; but that busy, commercial, newly built city, with its shifting population and fading claims to fashion, was to be her home. With her usual good sense and good humour, she tried to make the best of the situation: by January 1801 she was writing optimistically of her plans for removing, or disposing of, books and furniture, and the progress of their Bath house-hunting, adding, 'I get more and more reconciled to the idea of our removal. We have lived long enough in this Neighbourhood...there is something interesting in the bustle of going away, & the prospect of spending future summers by the Sea or in Wales is delightful.' Such Christian cheerfulness could not alter her real aversion to the move, however; and there would be little solace in the company of Mrs Austen's brother and sister-in-law, the Leigh-Perrots, with whom the Austens lodged on arrival, at their town-house, No. 1 Paragon.

The elegant, but self-centred, Mrs Leigh-Perrot − a rich woman in her own right − had recently been involved in a drama worthy of Jane Austen's juvenile fiction: a Bath shop-keeper had accused her of stealing a parcel of lace, and she had spent eight months in squalid prison lodgings, awaiting trial. Her dutiful husband had shared her confinement, and was ready to sell his property and accompany her, should she be convicted and transported. Fortunately she was found innocent, in March 1800, and restored to her former respectability. Under the Leigh-Perrots' aegis, Jane was introduced, in the spring of 1801, into the polite world of Bath; and a new phase of her life began.

There was little real gaiety in her letters now, as she reported on her sedate round of engagements: walks with her uncle to drink the medicinal waters; visits to uninspiring friends and acquaintances; disappointing public dances at the Assembly Rooms. 'Another stupid party last night', she complained openly, on 13 May. Perhaps to keep her mind occupied, she became intensely concerned with matters of dress, referring constantly to what she and others wore, and describing in detail clothes being made for her. A more pressing topic was the family's search for a house to rent; after ruling out 'putrifying Houses' in Green Park Buildings and cramped lodgings in Seymour Street, the Austens eventually settled − to Jane's relief − at No. 4 Sydney Place, overlooking the leafy pleasure-grounds of Sydney Gardens.

Marriage and an establishment of her own must have seemed more desirable than ever to Jane Austen now; but two last opportunities came to nothing. In 1801, the Austens went on holiday to the West Country; while staying at a seaside resort, possibly Sidmouth, they encountered a charming gentleman, with whom Jane apparently fell deeply in love. There is a long break in her correspondence at this period, and exactly what took place − even his name and occupation − is uncertain. But according to her great-niece, a happy marriage for Jane Austen seemed imminent – until a letter reached her containing news of the young man's death. It was surely a measure of her grief, and despondency at her situation, that when she received a proposal from another quarter, just over a year later, her first instinct was to accept it. This suitor, Harris Bigg-Wither, had much to recommend him: he was the young brother of Jane's and Cassandra's close friends, the Bigg sisters, and heir to the delightful estate of Manydown, near Steventon. It was while staying at Manydown, in November 1802, that Jane received young Harris's offer, and agreed to marry him. But at 21 he was six years her junior – and she did not love him. Early next morning she told him she had changed her mind, and she and Cassandra left the house unceremoniously. It was the only proposal of marriage she was ever recorded as receiving, and in society's eyes a good one; yet 'without Affection' she could not marry him, however disagreeable the alternatives.

Even her writing brought Jane Austen little but disappointment during this period. She began a novel entitled *The Watsons*, about a young woman in unhappy family circumstances, but abandoned it after writing some 17,500 words; still more frustratingly, in 1803 she actually sold a novel to a publisher for the first time, only to wait in vain for it to appear in print. The publisher, Crosby, paid her £10 for the work, entitled *Susan*, and even advertised it; but 'the business proceeded no further', Jane recalled resentfully, when preparing the manuscript for its eventual publication, in 1817, as *Northanger Abbey*. After thirteen years, and four published novels, that early disappointment still rankled.

Though Jane's mother (who would live to be 87) claimed to be constantly ailing, it was her father who became seriously ill, and died, in January 1805. For Jane his loss was a second blow: a month earlier, on her own twenty-ninth birthday, her much-loved friend Mrs Lefroy had been killed in a riding accident. She would miss her father's intelligent presence and 'sweet, benevolent smile'; nevertheless, as she would later write of the fictional Elinor Dashwood, 'still she could struggle, she could exert herself' – informing Frank, on board HMS *Leopard*, of the death, consoling her self-centred mother, and supervising the affairs of their diminished household. With contributions from Jane's brothers, and a legacy from Cassandra's late fiancé, Mrs Austen and her daughters – like the widowed Mrs Dashwood and hers – were left with an income of about £500: just sufficient for their needs. The Austens had recently moved house, to be nearer the health-giving waters of the Pump Room, for Jane's father; now they moved again, to smaller lodgings, first in Gay Street, then in Trim Street; finally, in the summer of 1805, they left Bath altogether – 'with what happy feelings of Escape!' Jane would later exclaim to Cassandra.

From a brief residence in the fashionable resort of Clifton, outside Bristol, and an agreeable, extended visit to some elegant relations of Mrs Austen's, the Leighs of Stoneleigh Abbey in Warwickshire, the Austen females settled in Southampton, in 1806, in a house at No. 4 Castle Square, which they rented with Frank and his new wife. There they were joined by Jane's dear friend Martha Lloyd, whose mother had recently died. After the smoky city air and vapid society of Bath, quiet domesticity in a naval town suited Jane's tastes. She involved herself happily with the housekeeping – 'You know how important the purchase of a sponge-cake is to me', she joked to Cassandra – and planned improvements to the garden, proposing 'Currants and Gooseberry Bushes', and mentioning her 'particular desire' for syringa and a laburnam, as praised in a verse by Cowper – one of her favourite poets. Above all, she had the pleasure of Frank's company. He was now Captain Austen, and rising steadily in the navy; to his chagrin, he had missed the glorious victory of Trafalgar in 1805, having been dispatched to Gibraltar for supplies; but early in 1806 he saw action in the West Indies, and returned home in triumph to marry his fiancée, Miss Mary Gibson of Ramsgate. Though devoutly religious, and a stickler for discipline, he was also fair-minded and good-humoured, and when on leave busied himself making wooden toys for the growing brood of Austen children, or knotting 'very nice fringe for the Drawing-room Curtains' at Castle Square, as Jane reported with pleasure. She approved of his wife, who revealed a proper liking for novels, unlike 'the other Mary', James's prim and parsimonious wife, who – to crown her faults – seemed to enjoy no books at all.

'The very quiet way in which we live', as Jane summed up their Southampton existence, was tragically interrupted, in the autumn of 1808, by the death of another sister-in-law, Edward's beautiful Elizabeth. A few months before, Jane had visited her amid the 'Elegance & Ease & Luxury' of Godmersham, where she was expecting her eleventh child. Early in October, after giving birth to a healthy boy, she suffered a sudden 'seizure', and died. Their grief drew the Austens still closer together. While Cassandra supervised the bereaved household at Godmersham, Jane had Edward's two eldest sons, 14-year-old Edward and 13-year-old George – who were both now Winchester schoolboys – to stay at Southampton; ever-sensible, as well as compassionate, she not only comforted their tears and guided their prayers, but energetically cheered them up with books, outings and endless games, from 'bilbocatch, at which George is indefatigable', (she wrote) to 'spillikins, paper ships, riddles, conundrums and cards'. The widower's gratitude to his devoted sisters took a practical form. Before the end of the year Jane was writing, with unfeigned joy, of another 'approaching removal': not to Kent – as was briefly mooted – but back to her beloved Hampshire. Close to one of Edward's larger properties, Chawton Manor, was a cottage which he now offered, rent-free, to his mother and sisters. It was a modest, brick-built house on a main road, which had been a farm steward's dwelling; but to Jane Austen it represented a settled home at last. Before leaving Southampton she attended a last ball at the Assembly Rooms where she had originally danced fifteen years earlier. 'I thought it all over', she confided to Cassandra; '& in spite of the shame of being so much older, felt with thankfulness that I was quite as happy now as then.'

Early in July, 1809, 'our dear trio', as Henry Austen called his mother and sisters, moved to Chawton, together with the indispensable Martha Lloyd; three weeks later, in a verse-letter to Frank, Jane wrote gaily,

> Our Chawton home, how much we find
> Already in it to our mind,
> And how convinced that, when complete,
> It will all other Houses beat.

The house, known today (though not in Jane Austen's time) as Chawton Cottage, stood so close to the busy London-to-Winchester road that the occupants of passing mail-coaches and carriages could glimpse the family seated at meals, and see Mrs Austen gardening in a sturdy green smock; to give his tenants some privacy, Edward blocked off the main downstairs front window, replacing it with one in a side wall, and cultivated a high, screening hedge. Jane seemed unperturbed by the traffic, however; she was delighted with the shrubbery walk, the orchard and the kitchen garden, and was gratified that, though the rooms were small, there were six bedchambers. Mrs Knight, Edward's formidable adoptive mother, who lived nearby, evidently indulged in some speculation worthy of Emma Woodhouse about a possible match between Jane Austen and the local vicar: 'She may depend upon it', was Jane's gleeful response, 'I *will* marry Mr Papillon, whatever may be his reluctance, or my own.' More practically, she resolved to buy a new pianoforte, telling Cassandra that she would practise country dances, 'that we may have some amusement for our nephews and nieces, when we have the pleasure of their company'. At the age of 33, she seemed to be resigning herself to a future as a devoted aunt, rather than a wife and mother.

There was another role, however, which Jane Austen was determined now to fulfil: that of professional writer. Before leaving Southampton, in April 1809, she had sent a somewhat peremptory letter to the firm of Crosby, who had bought her novel *Susan* six years earlier, requesting that they should publish it with 'no farther delay', or else permit her to offer it elsewhere. Mr Richard Crosby's reply was uncompromising. She might buy back her manuscript for the £10 he had paid; otherwise, if it appeared in print he would take immediate legal action. There, for the time being, matters rested; but Jane Austen's literary ambition had been rekindled. In the new-found security of her 'Chawton home' she looked out the old manuscripts from Steventon days, and settled to work once more – revising, editing, rewriting. The novel which finally marked her publishing debut was thus not the disputed *Susan*, but a rewritten version of a still earlier work, originally called *Elinor and Marianne*, and composed (according to Cassandra's recollections) as a series of letters. Now, over a dozen years after its conception, it emerged into the world as an ironic, engaging romance, centred on a widow with two adult daughters, living with genteel economy in a country cottage provided by a kindly, landowning kinsman.

Sense and Sensibility, 'A Novel in Three Volumes, By A Lady' appeared in November 1811, published by T. Egerton of The Military Library, Whitehall, and priced at 15 shillings the set. The first edition was small, consisting of only some 750–1,000 copies; but Jane Austen's delight at seeing her work in print at last was intense. In April 1811, while correcting her first proofs, she wrote joyfully to Cassandra, 'I am never too busy to think of *S. & S.* I can no more forget it, than a mother can forget her sucking child.' Yet she had no expectation that the book would be well received. Under her publishing contract, she was to reimburse T. Egerton if sales did not cover the printing costs, and according to Henry Austen, now a London-based banker and businessman, who acted as her agent, 'she actually made a reserve from her very moderate income to meet the expected loss'. In fact, *Sense and Sensibility* met with a modest success. Reviewers thought it 'a genteel, well-written novel', and 'a pleasing narrative'; while the ageing society beauty Lady Bessborough (mother of Lord Byron's future mistress, Lady Caroline Lamb) told a correspondent that some of her aristocratic friends were 'full of it', adding, 'Tho' it ends stupidly, I was much amused by it'. Even the Prince Regent's 15-year-old daughter and heir, the sadly unacademic Princess Charlotte, was impressed: '*Sense and Sencibility* [*sic*]', she enthused, was 'interesting, and you feel quite one of the company'. Within twenty months the first edition was sold out, and Jane Austen had made 'a clear profit' of about £140.

She was now a professional (albeit anonymous) author, and for all her reticence, began to enjoy the role. She still regarded her writing as something of a private pleasure, to be discreetly fitted in between family duties, social calls, piano practice and needlework; but she now spent as much time as possible at her little mahogany writing-desk in the front parlour at Chawton – writing on small, separate leaves of paper which could be hidden under a blotter if she was interrupted. Reputedly, the house had a creaking door; it was said that Jane refused to have the creak silenced, as it gave her warning when anyone was approaching. Concealment was still highly important to her; even such a close relation as James's son Edward – who, as James Edward Austen-Leigh, was to write the celebrated *Memoir* of his aunt, sixty years later – was not told of her authorship of *Sense and Sensibility* or *Pride and Prejudice* until some time after both had been published. Despite working under such constraints, during 1812 Jane finished revising the manuscript begun at Steventon in the 1790s as *First Impressions* for publication as *Pride and Prejudice*, and embarked on an entirely new novel – *Mansfield Park*. By the end of the year *Pride and Prejudice* had been sold to Egerton for £110 ('I would rather have had £150, but we could not both be pleased', Jane commented); and by 29 January 1813, the first copy of the novel which she called 'my own darling child' had arrived at Chawton, and had been read aloud to the family and Miss Benn, a neighbour – who, astonishingly, remained quite unaware of its authorship. 'She really does seem to admire Elizabeth', Jane reported with pleasure. She herself claimed to have had some initial 'fits of disgust' with it, partly because Mrs Austen's reading did not do justice to the characters, and partly, she told Cassandra, as if to excuse their mother, because the work was 'too light, and bright, and sparkling'. It needed 'shade', she mused, tongue-in-cheek: 'a long chapter of sense', or else of 'solemn specious nonsense', about 'something unconnected with the story', such as 'a critique on Walter Scott, or the history of Buonaparté, or anything that would . . . bring the reader with increased delight to the playfulness and epigrammatism of the general style'. She rounded off the joke, 'I doubt your quite agreeing with me here. I know your starched notions.'

In fact, as both she and Cassandra were happily aware, *Pride and Prejudice* was a triumph. It brought its reclusive author neither fame (which she did not want), nor fortune (which she did); but other great writers of the day, from Sheridan to Scott himself, were delighted by it, and the public apparently concurred. The first edition of about 1,500 copies had sold out by July 1813, and a second appeared in November – at the same time as a reprint of the slower-selling *Sense and Sensibility*. 'I have now therefore written myself into £250, which only makes me long for more', Jane informed Frank in early July. With her usual modesty, she added dismissively, 'I have something in hand – which I hope on the credit of *P. & P.* will sell well, tho' not half so entertaining.'

That 'something' was *Mansfield Park*, her first newly conceived novel since the fallow Bath years, when *The Watsons* had
been abandoned. With its theme of ordination, and timid,
poor-relation heroine, Fanny Price, '*M.P.*' was to represent 'a
complete change' from the buoyant comedy of the previous
novels; but the mature Jane Austen of this second writing
phase was a less light-hearted creature than the carefree young
woman of the 1790s. *Pride and Prejudice* would remain a
favourite with its author and her circle, as with future generations; in two lists of 'Opinions' which she drew up after the
publication of *Mansfield Park* and *Emma*, reader after reader
confessed to a preference for '*P. & P.*' – while Mr and Mrs
Leigh-Perrot owned endearingly that 'Darcy and Elizth. had
spoilt them for anything else'. Jane Austen herself considered
Elizabeth Bennet 'as delightful a creature as ever appeared in
print'; on a visit to Henry in London, in May 1813, she
reported that she had looked for a good likeness of her heroine
at the fashionable exhibitions of paintings, but had been disappointed – concluding, straight-faced, 'I can only imagine
that Mr D. prizes any Picture of her too much to like it should
be exposed to the public eye.' From the captivating Elizabeth
Bennet, who said 'I dearly love a laugh', to shrinking Fanny
Price, who considered herself 'graver than other people',
was a bold creative step; but despite its author's misgivings,
Mansfield Park was accepted without hesitation by Egerton,
who 'praised it for it's [*sic*] Morality', and the first edition of
some 1,250 copies, published in May 1814, sold out within
six months.

Henry Austen, on whose artistic judgement Jane greatly
relied, thought *Mansfield Park* was '*extremely interesting*'. If he
recognized aspects of his own wife, Eliza de Feuillide, in
worldly, self-seeking Miss Crawford, his pleasure in the novel
was unaffected. Eliza had died a year before, in April 1813;
characteristically, Henry's grief – though acute – had been
short-lived. 'His Mind is not a Mind for affliction', Jane gently

reminded Cassandra. The most charming and amusing of the Austen brothers, Henry was also the most volatile – regularly changing employment, moving house and losing his heart; yet Jane never lost her affectionate faith in him. In the summer of 1813, when the flutter of public interest in *Pride and Prejudice* was at its height, it was he who, defying her well-known desire not to be made a 'wild beast' by the world, betrayed the secret of her authorship, in circles where it was likely to spread. 'Henry heard *P. & P.* warmly praised in Scotland, by Lady Robt. Kerr and another Lady; – & what does he do . . . but immediately tell them who wrote it!', Jane fretted to Frank, in a letter of 25 September 1813. Loyally, she attributed their brother's indiscretion to 'affection and partiality'; but she thanked Frank, with emphasis, for his 'superior kindness . . . in doing what I wished'. She briefly considered abandoning any further attempt at anonymity, and trying rather to make 'all the Money than all the Mystery I can' from her next novel; but the desire to protect what remained of her privacy was too strong. 'After all,' she concluded philosophically to Frank, 'what a trifle it is in all its Bearings, to the really important points of one's existence even in this World!'

A really important point of her and the Austen family's existence, in that autumn, was the engagement of her niece Anna, James's daughter from his first marriage, to Benjamin Lefroy – son of Jane's dear, late friend Mrs Lefroy of Ashe (and cousin of her own long-ago admirer, Tom). From a child-hood clouded by her mother's death and an uncongenial step-mother, Anna had grown into an elegant, agreeable, but headstrong young woman, who delighted and alarmed the Austen family by turns. By 1813 she had already had one broken engagement; and though Ben was 'sensible, certainly very religious, well-connected' and destined for the Church, Jane had doubts about the match, citing 'some queerness of temper on his side and much unsteadiness on hers'. When Ben refused a most suitable curacy, soon afterwards, she decided

'He must be maddish', adding, 'It cannot last.' In the event, the engagement lasted for over a year; and on 8 November 1814, at Steventon, the 21-year-old Anna became Mrs Ben Lefroy in a wedding which her half-sister Caroline (who was a bridesmaid, aged 9, in a white frock and straw bonnet) recalled, years later, as 'the extreme of quietness'.

Until domesticity and successive pregnancies intervened, Anna had been working on a novel which she sent in instalments to her aunt Jane, for her professional opinion. Jane Austen's responses were illuminating. With generous thoroughness – though immersed in writing *Emma* at the time – the author of *Pride and Prejudice* offered the would-be author of *Enthusiasm*, or *Which Is the Heroine?*, a judicious mixture of praise, criticism and sound technical advice, from the need for consistency in characterization, to the banality of clichés such as 'a Vortex of Dissipation'. ('I do not object to the Thing', this sporting aunt explained, 'but . . . it is such thorough novel slang, and so old, that I dare say Adam met with it in the first novel he opened.')

Anna's pleas for literary guidance were succeeded, at the end of 1814, by requests for advice on her love-affairs from another favourite niece, Edward's eldest daughter, Fanny Knight. Like Anna, Fanny was motherless, and thus specially close to her childless Chawton aunts; but unlike Anna, she had grown into a steady, prudent young woman, whom Jane dotingly described as 'almost another sister'. Which suitor to accept, and how to judge her own feelings, were questions of Fanny's which elicited some of Jane Austen's most revealing and deeply felt letters. 'There are such beings in the World . . . as the Creature You and I should think perfection, Where Grace and Spirit are united to Worth, where the Manners are equal to the Heart and Understanding, but such a person may not come in your way . . .', she wrote in November 1814. She might have had in mind the hero of her novel-in-progress, *Emma* – the 'unaffected, gentlemanlike' Mr Knightley.

If Mr Knightley was the embodiment of an ideal, Emma Woodhouse herself decidedly was not. 'I am going to take a heroine whom no one but myself will much like', Jane had stated: and in the 'handsome, clever and rich', but domineering, matchmaker Emma, she created a central character whom some readers (including Fanny Knight) 'could not bear'. Yet this ironic masterpiece – completed in the glorious year of Waterloo – was to bring Jane Austen the greatest recognition and distinction of her brief life.

'People are more ready to borrow and to praise than to buy', she complained, late in 1814; and though she added, 'which I cannot wonder at', the lack of financial reward for her writing clearly rankled. When Egerton proved reluctant to 'hazard' a second edition of *Mansfield Park*, she decided to change her publisher – and this time, she boldly opted for the best and most fashionable of the day. In the summer of 1815, the recently-completed *Emma* was offered to John Murray of Albemarle Street, whose illustrious list of authors ranged from Scott and Southey to the literary cult-hero Lord Byron. There was no certainty that the great Byron's 'dear Murray' would take on a work of popular fiction by an anonymous 'Authoress': before committing himself, the publisher sent the manuscript for evaluation by another leading man of letters, William Gifford, editor of the influential *Quarterly Review* (which John Murray published). Gifford's response was encouraging. He had thought *Pride and Prejudice* 'a very pretty thing'; of *Emma*, he had 'nothing but good to say'. On 17 September 1815, Jane wrote happily to Cassandra, 'Mr Murray's letter is come. He is a rogue, of course, but a civil one.' The offer, of £450, to include the copyrights of both *Mansfield Park* and *Sense and Sensibility*, was disappointing; yet such were Murray's charm and reputation that after some bargaining – handled with considerable ineptitude by Henry – a deal was agreed. John Murray would publish *Emma* and reprint *Mansfield Park*, in return for 10 per cent of all profits.

Financially, it would prove an unsatisfactory arrangement for Jane Austen, with her initial profits on *Emma* being offset against a loss on *Mansfield Park*; professionally, however, the change of publisher brought notable benefits. *Emma* was handsomely produced, in a larger and more expensive edition than her previous works; and the involvement of Murray and Gifford secured her a favourable notice in the *Quarterly Review* for May 1816. The anonymous critic who praised the anonymous 'authoress' was none other than the great Sir Walter Scott; to Jane Austen, however, he was simply, and delightedly, 'so clever a Man as the Reveiwer [*sic*] of *Emma*'.

Although she was unaware of her encounter with one pre-eminent Regency figure, she was all too conscious of her dealings with another - the most august of all, HRH the Prince Regent himself. The connection between the Prince and the novelist began at the time of *Emma*'s sale to John Murray, when Jane was staying with her brother Henry in London. Henry became alarmingly ill, and was tended by a physician who moved among the most fashionable households – the Prince's town residence of Carlton House among them. On finding that the loving sister at Mr Austen's bedside was none other then the author of *Pride and Prejudice* – one of His Royal Highness's favourite novels – the medical man duly carried the news from Hans Place to Carlton House. The upshot was a historic communication from the Prince's librarian, the Revd James Stanier Clarke, to Miss Jane Austen, inviting her to visit the palace, where she would be shown round the library and apartments, and paid – on the Regent's instructions – 'every possible attention'. Though a Tory, and inherently loyal to the Crown, Jane Austen was no supporter of the raffish, extravagant Regent, who was estranged from his troublesome (but popular) wife, Princess Caroline: 'I shall support her as long as I can', she had declared in 1813, 'because she *is* a Woman, & because I hate her Husband.' Royal favour was not to be trifled with, however; and on 13 November 1815, the historic visit of Jane Austen to Carlton House took place. No record of the occasion survived; but in a letter to the librarian, dated 15 November, she mentioned that, among other 'flattering attentions', he had given her the Regent's permission to dedicate a future work to 'HRH The PR'. It was an honour which caused Jane Austen considerable discomfiture. She felt obliged to reassure herself, through Mr Clarke's offices, that the royal offer was in earnest – and to reassure her friend Martha Lloyd, in a letter to Cassandra, that in accepting it she would be 'influenced . . . by nothing but the most mercenary motives'. A reply of hilarious pomposity from her Carlton House correspondent brought confirmation; and so when *Emma* appeared, on 12 December 1815, it bore a fulsome dedication to the Prince, by his 'Dutiful and Obedient Humble Servant, The Author', which must, to Jane's intimates, have recalled the comically grand dedications of her *Juvenilia*.

The business of directing the printers over the inscription, and arranging for a presentation copy to be specially bound for the Prince Regent, brought Jane Austen into increasingly friendly contact with John Murray, who gave her important advice, lent her books and contributed, she wrote gratefully, to her 'Convenience and Amusement'. By contrast, Mr J. S. Clarke, who had evidently been slightly smitten by her, became increasingly tiresome, interspersing compliments on her 'Genius' and 'Principles' with pressing suggestions that her next novel should feature a heroic English clergyman exactly like himself – 'Fond of, & entirely engaged in Literature – no man's Enemy but his own'; opposed to parish tithes and obliged to bury his own mother, 'as I did . . . I have never recovered the Shock'. Jane delicately declined, protesting that so 'unlearned and uninformed' a female as herself would be unequal to portraying so erudite a man; but the librarian was undeterred. When, in March 1816, the Regent's only child Princess Charlotte became engaged to Prince Leopold of Saxe-Cobourg, Mr Clarke proposed that Miss Austen should publish a 'historical romance, illustrative of . . . the august House of Cobourg'. Jane's reply was a masterpiece of ironic tact. Declaring that she could write 'a serious romance' for no other motive than to save her life, and even then would undoubtedly be hanged before finishing a chapter, she concluded decisively, 'No, I must keep to my own style and go on in my own way; and though I may never succeed again in that, I am convinced that I should totally fail in any other.' There the exchange evidently ceased, but it had a postscript, in the form of a document entitled 'Plan of a Novel, according to hints from various quarters'. A glorious burlesque synopsis, in the style of her early skits, it included, as the heroine's father, a clergyman 'of a very literary turn'; deeply opposed to tithes; and 'nobody's Enemy but his own'.

The Austen family needed some amusement, in the spring of 1816, as the hapless Henry had become bankrupt. In the aftermath of the Battle of Waterloo, Britain's economy had slumped, and Henry's latest business – a bank, with a branch at Alton, near Chawton – was one of many which failed. Among those who lost money in the bank were Jane's uncle Mr Leigh-Perrot, and her brother Edward; she herself lost £13, and Henry's loyal housekeeper, Mme Bigeon, much of her savings. Yet nothing depressed Henry for long, and within months, aged almost 45, he had embarked on a new career: that of clergyman, for which he had originally been destined before Eliza and other ambitions intervened. 'Uncle Henry writes very superior sermons', Jane informed her nephew and future biographer, James's son Edward.

Her antipathy to James and his second wife Mary never impinged upon her relationship with their children, Edward and Caroline. Both – like their half-sister Anna – had literary leanings, which she encouraged. Caroline's attempts at short stories were warmly received at Chawton ('I wish I could finish Stories as fast as you can', Jane complimented her in December 1815); in Edward she saw the makings of a professional writer, 'in a style, I think, to be popular'. When a section of his 'extremely clever' novel went missing, late in 1816, Jane obligingly joked that she might have been suspected of stealing it. 'What should I do with your strong, manly, spirited Sketches?', she teased. 'How could I possibly join them on to the little bit (two Inches wide) of Ivory on which I work with so fine a Brush, as produces little effect after much labour?'

In that difficult year – the last full year of her life – the gloom of Henry's bankruptcy was compounded, for the Austen family, by anxiety for Charles, whose ship, HMS *Phoenix*, was lost in February. Though all on board were saved, and Charles himself was exonerated after the obligatory court-martial, it was a dramatic reminder of the perils of naval command, even in peacetime. Fittingly, the novel on which Jane Austen's fine 'Brush' was then engaged gave expression to her heartfelt admiration for the Royal Navy, its officers and their ways. According to her nephew's *Memoir*, one family friend thought the heroine, Anne Elliot, was a portrait of Jane herself, remarking, 'Her enthusiasm for the navy, and her perfect unselfishness, reflect her completely.' The author would surely have disagreed. 'You may *perhaps* like the heroine', she told Fanny Knight, 'as she is almost too good for me.' Nevertheless, this last complete novel, which would be published after Jane Austen's death as *Persuasion*, contained unmistakable, elegiac traces of autobiography – not least in the robust treatment of self-pity and imaginary illness. While she was writing it, between August 1815 and the summer of 1816, her own health had begun to fail. The fatigue, stomach disorders and skin discolouration which twentieth-century medicine would recognize as symptoms of Addison's Disease had set in, making daily life increasingly burdensome; but years of tending her hypochondriac mother had taught her to make light of her own ill-health. 'Sickness is a dangerous Indulgence at my time of life', she wrote jokingly to Fanny, in March 1817.

Writing remained Jane Austen's solace, while her strength allowed. On finishing *Persuasion*, in July 1816, she was weak and uncharacteristically depressed, and the ending, in which her hero and gentle heroine were reunited, seemed 'tame and flat'. By August, however, her spirits had revived, and she wrote a new denouement. Chapter X of the final volume was cancelled, and replaced by two new chapters, which included Anne Elliot's impassioned claim for the female sex, 'of loving longest, when existence or when hope is gone'. By a curious irony, while writing, and revising, the autumnal *Persuasion*, Jane was also preparing for publication a novel dating from the spring of her career – the sparkling, youthful, horror-fiction burlesque, originally known as *Susan*, which would appear after her death under a new title, *Northanger Abbey*. The early version had finally been bought back from the obstructive Mr Crosby by Henry – who took great pleasure in revealing, once the manuscript was secured, that it was by the same 'Lady' as *Pride and Prejudice* and *Emma*. This book – alone among Jane Austen's works – would contain a prefatory note, 'By the Authoress', describing its sale and non-publication thirteen years before, and entreating readers to 'bear in mind . . . that during that period, places, manners, books and opinions have undergone considerable changes'. It would also, tragically, include a posthumous 'Biographical Notice' by Henry Austen, telling the world for the first time of his sister's identity and brief life; for by the time *Persuasion* and *Northanger Abbey* finally appeared, in December 1817, 'the hand which guided that pen', as Henry floridly, but lovingly, wrote, 'was mouldering in the grave'.

At the beginning of 1817 Jane Austen had seemed to be rallying. She wrote cheerfully of taking walks, and dosing away her illness; she asked her old friend Alethea Bigg for the recipe for some 'excellent orange wine', and amused her niece Cassy, Charles's daughter, by sending her a letter entirely written backwards, dated 'Notwahc, Naj 8' and including such titbits as 'Ew deef eht Nibor yreve gninrom'. She even started work on a new novel, set in a seaside resort called Sanditon: as the dates on the surviving manuscript show, she wrote (and revised) some 24,000 words between 27 January and 18 March of that year, when the work was abandoned. Sketchy, and very different in power from her earlier fiction, *Sanditon* held little promise of greatness, but its author admitted to her beloved niece Fanny, on 23 March, 'I have not been well for many weeks.' Her decline was hastened by a severe blow in April: her rich, childless uncle James Leigh-Perrot died, leaving his entire fortune to his temperamental wife; only on her death would a substantial legacy devolve upon James Austen, and the relatively small sum of £1,000 each upon his brothers and sisters. His own sister, the widowed, impecunious Mrs Austen, was omitted entirely from the will. 'I am ashamed to say that the shock of my Uncle's Will brought on a relapse', Jane wrote to her brother Charles, adding apologetically, 'a weak Body must excuse weak Nerves'. She was now almost bedridden; when she ventured downstairs, she lay on a makeshift arrangement of several chairs pushed together, to leave the only sofa free for her mother's use.

In a final attempt at a cure, Jane Austen left her 'Chawton home' for the last time in May, and accompanied by her 'tender, watchful, indefatigable nurse' Cassandra, journeyed to Winchester, where she could be cared for by an eminent local surgeon, Mr Lyford. Somehow she retained her customary humour and spirit, expressing pleasure in her 'very comfortable' lodgings in College Street, which had a 'neat little Drawing room with a Bow-window', and keeping up a valiant flow of jokes with her correspondents. Beneath the cheerfulness, however, there was a deepening note of reflection and resignation. 'If I live to be an old Woman, I must expect to wish I had died now; blessed in the tenderness of such a Family, & before I had survived either them or their affection', she told her friend Miss Sharp, before leaving Chawton; from Winchester, a week later, she wrote of the 'anxious affection' of her family, saying, 'I can only cry over it, and pray God to bless them more and more.' It was her last known letter. At half-past four in the morning of 18 July 1817, with her head pillowed against Cassandra's lap, Jane Austen died, aged 41.

In a detailed, and deeply moving, account of her sister's last hours, Cassandra told Fanny Knight, 'She was the sun of my life, the gilder of every pleasure, the soother of every sorrow . . . it is as if I had lost a part of myself.' The loss to literature was not mentioned; the loss to Jane Austen's family and friends was all. Several of the brief notices of her death which appeared in the local and London press made no reference to her writing – even after the Austens' own announcement, in *The Courier*, had, for the first time, publicly acknowledged her authorship of the four novels then in print; in September, one periodical merely noted the event, with the titles of her works, under the heading 'Provincial Occurrences'. By then, Jane Austen had been buried for almost six weeks. The funeral, on 24 July 1817, was so quiet and private that Cassandra – who, as was customary for women at the time, did not attend – had to be 'upon the listen' to know when the cortege departed. 'I watched the little mournful procession the length of the street', she wrote to Fanny Knight, until 'it turned from my sight, and I had lost her for ever.' Respecting to the last Jane's well-known wish for privacy, the gravestone in Winchester Cathedral honoured the deceased not for her literary genius, but for 'her charity, devotion, faith and purity'.

Her last two completed novels were published at the end of the year, by John Murray, in a 4-volume set, priced at 24s. The 'Authoress's' fears that the work due to be published thirteen years before, as *Susan*, might since then have become dated seemed, at first, unfounded; retitled *Northanger Abbey*, this early, Gothic-romance burlesque and its mature, elegiac companion, *Persuasion*, sold briskly during 1818. By 1820, however, times – and tastes – were changing; and the appeal of Jane Austen's fiction for the general public appeared to be waning. In January of that year, the old, blind, deranged King George III died, and the Regency decade came to an end with the succession of his florid heir as King George IV. Just a year later, remaindered copies of Jane Austen's *Emma* and *Mansfield Park* were advertised by John Murray, at the bargain prices of 2*s* and 2*s* 6*d*. It was, indeed, the end of an era.

'Tho' I like praise as well as anybody, I like what Edward calls *Pewter* too', Jane had written ruefully in 1814; even she, with her fondness for imagining 'impossible contingencies', could not have dreamed of the quantities of both praise and pewter which her 'pictures of domestic life in country villages' would one day generate. In her lifetime, her writing had earned her less than £1,000; by the end of the twentieth century she would have become one of the best-selling authors of all time, her novels endlessly reprinted, translated, and dramatized; her 'Chawton home', as well as her discreet grave in Winchester Cathedral, places of literary pilgrimage. She would always have her detractors, from her contemporary Mme de Staël (who thought her 'vulgaire'), to Mark Twain, who regarded her with 'an animal repugnance'. Yet millions of others – E. M. Forster, Winston Churchill and Vladimir Nabokov among them – would appreciate and treasure the genius of the woman whom Rudyard Kipling called 'England's Jane'. They, like the first of her great enthusiasts, Sir Walter Scott, could only read and re-read her works, with the reflection, 'What a pity such a gifted creature died so early!'

2

'The Common Daily Routine'

'Composition seems to me Impossible, with a head full
of Joints of Mutton and doses of rhubarb.'
Jane Austen, letter to Cassandra, 1816

'Where shall I begin? Which of all my important nothings shall
I tell you first?' Jane Austen wrote to her sister Cassandra in
June 1808. She proceeded to set down a typically entertaining
account of a journey to Godmersham on the previous day,
beginning with her departure at 'half after seven' in the
morning from the Bath Hotel ('very dirty, very noisy, and very
ill-provided'), and culminating with a description of her arrival
in the entrance hall of their brother's great Georgian mansion
– including, en route, news of the family's health, mention of
the evening's dinner-party, comments on her accommodation
in the 'Yellow' bedchamber, and a regretful note on their pretty
niece Anna's fashionably unbecoming new 'crop' hairstyle. To
her contemporaries, such details might indeed have seemed
'nothings'; but to the modern reader they offer 'important', and
fascinating, glimpses into the day-to-day life of one of Britain's
greatest writers. 'I can command very little quiet time at
present', she wrote ruefully to her niece Fanny Knight in 1814;
and reading her correspondence, today, with its accounts of
cookery and housekeeping, travelling and dancing, music-
practice, entertaining and games-playing, it seems remarkable
that she ever found any 'quiet time' at all in which to concen-
trate on the composition of her six great novels.

Like most English gentlewomen of her day, Jane Austen was brought up to be a competent mistress of a household, conversant with the price of food, the preparation of dishes, and the niceties of producing meals, from light suppers to formal dinners. Many women of her class, while instructing household servants and collecting recipes, did not actually do any cooking themselves: Mrs Bennet in *Pride and Prejudice* is clearly offended when asked by Mr Collins – obviously with an eye to his future wife – which of his 'fair cousins' is responsible for the dinner, retorting that 'her daughters had nothing to do in the kitchen'. Jane Austen herself may have done no cooking, but she took a keen, and knowledgeable, interest in the whole process of food-preparation, from the rearing of animals and growing of vegetables, to the purchase of commodities such as tea, coffee and sugar, and the choice of dishes for the family table. Certainly, she enjoyed her victuals; in her juvenile romantic spoof-novel *Love and Freindship*, when the fatuous hero demands, in a 'most nobly contemtuous [*sic*] Manner' whether there is 'no other support for an exalted Mind' than the 'mean and indelicate employment of Eating and Drinking', his sensible sister replies firmly, 'None that I know of, so efficacious'. A self-destructive disinclination for food was as much a hazard for young women in the Regency as now: Lord Byron's overwrought mistress Lady Caroline Lamb seems to have suffered from the self-starvation complaint classified in modern times as anorexia nervosa, just as Jane Austen's fictional 17-year-old Marianne Dashwood, despairingly disappointed in love, neglects to eat, and wastes away to the point where she becomes dangerously vulnerable to physical illness, and almost dies. Jane herself seemed to experience no such troubles, but while evidently remaining slim, enjoyed her food and drink. She must have known of, and encouraged, her dear friend Martha Lloyd's delight in collecting recipes, which resulted in a leather-bound book, containing over a hundred carefully preserved 'receipts' for every aspect of household cookery and home care, from meat and soup dishes and sauces, to jellies, pickles, and preserves, along with dubious-sounding health remedies and simple beauty products, such as cold cream and lavender water. One witty recipe, 'A Receipt for a Pudding', was provided by Jane's mother; characteristically it is written in rhyme.

Growing up at Steventon, Jane had the benefit of a wholesome, home-produced diet, with fresh milk, butter and cheese from her mother's Alderney cows, pork products from the family pigs, and plentiful local fruit and vegetables. Throughout her life she retained a taste for simple, nourishing food; in one of her first surviving letters, of 1796, she mentioned sharing a nursery supper with some of her small relations, at which she enjoyed 'souse' – homely portions of pig, such as ears and cheek, pickled in brine. 'Caroline, Anna and I have just been devouring some cold souse, and it would be difficult to say which enjoyed it most', she wrote cheerfully. In 1798, a year in which her mother suffered from various prolonged (if undefined) illnesses, she wrote that Mrs Austen's medical adviser, Mr Lyford, had arrived during dinner, and had been invited to share the family meal, which included 'some pease-soup, a sparerib, and a pudding', along with some of 'my father's mutton . . . the finest that was ever ate'. Plain fare as it was, mutton was a staple of the Georgian and Regency diet, so that 'to eat one's mutton' become a standard term for any form of dining. By that year, when Jane was 23, she was increasingly taking on the running of the Austen household: 'My mother desires me to tell you', she wrote importantly to Cassandra, 'that I am a very good housekeeper', adding, teasingly, 'I really think it my particular excellence.' On that occasion, she particularly congratulated herself on the tenderness of some boiled fowls, from her parents' farmyard.

Though she was at this time drafting the original versions of *Sense and Sensibility*, *Pride and Prejudice* and *Northanger Abbey*, the 'peculiar excellence' of Jane Austen's writing had frequently to take second place, while she busied herself with domestic duties. 'I carry about the keys of the Wine and Closet, & twice since I began this letter have had orders to give in the Kitchen', she wrote in October 1798. To be a good 'housekeeper' was a housewifely duty and virtue which each of her heroines would clearly possess, in their widely different married lives. Elinor Dashwood's modest estimate of £1,000 as 'wealth', compared with her sister Marianne's assertion that 'two thousand a year is a very moderate income', shows how prudently she will administer her country parsonage home; Fanny Price, in *Mansfield Park*, with her conflicting experiences of her mean, but competent, Aunt Norris and her hopelessly inept mother at Portsmouth, is clearly destined to create, on marrying Edmund, a well-managed 'home of affection and comfort'. Catherine Morland's down-to-earth mother, in *Northanger Abbey*, fears that her daughter will prove 'a sad, heedless young housekeeper'; but the reader is left to infer that this reformed tomboy heroine, who has already proved her inner strength by making a difficult journey home on her own, in a post-chaise, will be more than equal to the task. And Elizabeth Bennet in *Pride and Prejudice*, though she has grown up with 'nothing to do in the kitchen', makes a good start as future mistress of Pemberley by striking up a cordial relationship with the senior household retainer, Mrs Reynolds, and the trusty gardener who shows her round the grounds. Mrs Elton, in *Emma*, may claim credit, affectedly, for having been 'half an hour this morning shut up with my housekeeper', but the well-bred heroine Emma herself is continually shown putting good 'housekeeping' principles into practice, as when she supervises the curing of a pig, and arranges the distribution of delicate cuts of the carcass to their needy neighbours, the Bateses. Tactfully, she also ensures that, despite her father's health-fads, his friends are allowed to eat and drink well at his table. For all her faults, Emma can say, with truth, 'I hope I am not often deficient in what is owing to guests.'

An essential aspect of housekeeping was the business of keeping budgets and comparing prices – as the dual sense of the word 'economy' (also 'oeconomy') used in Jane Austen's day to signify household administration, as well as the practice of frugality, suggests. On leaving the largely self-sufficient Steventon for Bath, where all the family's food and provisions had to be shopped for, Jane noted details of prices with keen interest. 'Meat is only 8*d* per pound, butter 12*d* and cheese 9½*d*', she reported in 1801; salmon, however, seemed to her expensive, at '2*s* 9*d* per pound the whole fish'. The high cost of this luxury item could, she decided, be attributed to the presence, at the time, of HRH the Duchess of York and her entourage in the city. It was not in Jane's character to be wasteful, and she was quick to spot an inferior product: before one of Cassandra's visits to their close friend Catherine Hill, née Bigg, who now lived with her husband at Streatham, Jane teased, 'I suppose you will be going to Streatham, to . . . eat very bad Baker's bread', implying either that the Hills' bread was not home-made, and fresh, or (worse), that it was supplied by a baker who adulterated his product with a substance such as powdered chalk. Nevertheless, while checking on prices and quality herself, she despised meanness masquerading as good housekeeping; and few characters in her fiction are as odious as Mrs Norris in *Mansfield Park*, who is for ever 'making a small income go a long way' by saving pence, at the expense of the put-upon heroine Fanny Price's happiness, and even health. Mrs Norris is incensed by the liberality with which her successor Mrs Grant runs the Mansfield Parsonage: complaining that 'a fine lady in a country parsonage was quite out of place', she fulminates against the cook's high wages, the fact that Mrs Grant is 'scarcely ever seen in her offices' (meaning the kitchen regions) and the 'quantity of butter and eggs that were regularly consumed in the house'. Yet while pandering to a husband who was 'very fond of eating', and living in some style, Mrs Grant is, it emerges, a capable housewife, who makes the most of home-grown produce, from turkeys, geese and local game, to apricots grown in her garden. When, during a highly symbolic conversation in the Parsonage garden, her worldly sister Mary makes it plain that she intends to live a wealthy, indulged life, preferably in London, buying her bedding plants and her food from 'the nurseryman and the poulterer', Mrs Grant teasingly reminds her of the 'remoteness and unpunctuality' and 'exorbitant charges and frauds' of such tradesmen. 'A large income is the best receipt for happiness' is Miss Crawford's rejoinder – playing neatly on the word 'receipt', with its contemporary double sense of 'recipe'. Fanny Price may be shocked by such worldly attitudes; but even she, experiencing her mother's slovenly home-management at Portsmouth, is obliged to allow some truth to the statement, as she contemplates the milk, 'a mixture of motes floating in thin blue', and endures the ministrations of half-trained, underpaid servants, who dish up ill-cooked 'hashes' – concoctions of chopped meat in gravy or sauce – so that Fanny is obliged to make her 'heartiest meal of the day' on biscuits or buns, bought in from local shops by her brothers. Good, classic, plain cooking was evidently what Jane liked best: 'Good apple pies are a considerable part of our domestic happiness', she confided to Cassandra in 1815; and a decade earlier she mentioned a supper of toasted cheese which a young kinsman ordered, 'entirely on my account'. However, she appreciated elegant living to the full, as her letters from Godmersham constantly showed, and she was always ready to pick up tips: after one visit, in 1798, she decided to have an ox-cheek cooked at Steventon, adding, 'And I mean to have some little dumplings put into it, that I may fancy myself at Godmersham.' Fifteen years later, the pleasures of luxury had not palled. 'I have no occasion to think of the price of Bread or Meat where I am now', she wrote from Godmersham in 1813; 'let me shake off vulgar cares & conform to the happy Indifference of East Kent wealth'.

For innocent Catherine Morland, brought up in a country vicarage, the Tilneys' way of life in *Northanger Abbey* is a revelation: even taking breakfast with them, in Bath, she marvels, 'Never before had she beheld half such variety on a breakfast-table.' Jane Austen's mother left an admiring description of the lavish breakfasts served at her cousins' country house, Stoneleigh Abbey, reporting, during a visit in 1806, that they included 'Chocolate, Coffee, Tea, Plumb Cake, Pound Cake, Hot Rolls, Cold Rolls, Bread, butter' and (characteristically) 'dry toast for me'. Though Catherine, in *Northanger Abbey*, is wakened at 8 a.m., Jane Austen herself apparently rose at 7 a.m.; while some of her contemporaries might then have taken a cup of tea or chocolate, it was customary not to have breakfast until about 10 a.m., by which time a good many activities might have been carried out, from writing letters and shopping, to visiting. The hour at which the main meal of the day, dinner, was taken became later and later in Jane Austen's lifetime: 'We dine now at half after Three, & have done dinner I suppose before you begin', she wrote from Steventon to Cassandra at Godmersham, in 1798; but as the fashion for later dining spread through society, she reported in 1808, 'We never dine now till five.' In upper-class circles, six-thirty was the approved time. Emma Watson, heroine of her unfinished novel *The Watsons*, is embarrassed to be visited by young Lord Osborne and his would-be fashionable friend, Tom Musgrave, at five to three, when the family dinner is about to be served: 'You know what early hours we keep', her sister explains to the grand visitors, with 'honest simplicity'. Though Jane Austen herself seems to have had little more than tea with rolls and butter for breakfast, this meal could be a substantial affair, as the 'cold pork bones and mustard' and 'broken egg-shells' left from the breakfast after the ball in *Mansfield Park* suggest; but as the time till dinner lengthened, some intervening refreshment became increasingly necessary, and luncheon developed from a selection of light items, such as cold meat, laid out on a sideboard, from which family and guests could help themselves, or refreshments served on a tray, to a more structured repast, which after Jane Austen's era would become known as 'lunch'. Callers at any time of day would be offered refreshments, ranging, at the upper end of the social scale, from the 'beautiful pyramids of fruit' which Mr Darcy's sister, in *Pride and Prejudice*, offers to her visitors at grand Pemberley, to the passed-on leftover cake from a friend's party which the poor, but hospitable, Miss Bates, in *Emma*, eagerly shares with some callers at her cramped lodgings.

A formal dinner, such as that to which Mrs Bennet invites Mr Bingley, 'on whom she had such anxious designs' as a husband for her daughter, would have run to two full 'courses', involving a first spread of dishes, including meat, poultry and fish, along with vegetables, pies and puddings. This – in elegant circles – would then give way to another full serving, featuring 'made' dishes, from savoury fricassées to sweet syllabubs, which, in turn, would be succeeded by a selection of light 'dessert' items, such as nuts, olives and dried fruits, for the guests to toy with. At a sign from the hostess, the ladies would withdraw, to drink tea or coffee and discuss children, fashion and local affairs, while the gentlemen might linger for an hour over the port, talking of politics, sport and other such great matters. Making tea was a ritual of some importance: a precious commodity, imported in Jane Austen's day from China, it was stored under lock and key in decorative 'caddies', and spooned out to the required strength by the hostess or a trusted family member. 'She always makes tea you know', is Lady Bertram's plaintive reason for not wishing to part with Fanny Price for an evening, in *Mansfield Park*. The London tea merchant Thomas Twining – based then, as now, in the Strand – was the supplier from whom Jane Austen bought the family tea. 'I do not mean to pay Twining until later in the day, when we may order a fresh supply', she wrote in 1814, while staying with her brother Henry in London. Preferences in hot drinks, as today, varied, however: while General Tilney, in *Northanger Abbey*, insists on hot chocolate, Jane Austen's own rich, indulged brother Edward evidently opted for coffee: 'The coffee-mill will be wanted every day while Edward is at Steventon', Jane warned Cassandra in 1799.

From tea and coffee to pork spare-ribs, pound cake and fresh fruit, much of the food enjoyed by Jane Austen, her contemporaries and her characters, is familiar to the modern reader; yet other dishes popular in the Regency era require explanation today. 'White soup', a staple of elegant entertainment in her day, was served regularly at ball suppers; though the recipe varied, the result generally involved veal stock, cream and almonds, sometimes thickened with rice or breadcrumbs. Mr Bingley in *Pride and Prejudice* promises to hold a ball 'As soon as Nicholls' (his cook) 'has made white soup enough.' When Jane Austen herself, with her friend Martha Lloyd, gave a party, in 1808, 'black butter' was on the menu. Unfortunately, this delicacy, involving apple puree and sugar, was not always a success: Jane and Martha decided that theirs had not been boiled enough – but they finished off the leftovers, with relish, 'in unpretending privacy'. Another feature of party nights, well known to Jane Austen, was negus – a fortifying, spicy drink concocted from calves-foot jelly, along with lemon and wine, served hot. In *The Watsons*, the would-be man-about-town Tom Musgrave finds himself about to end the evening, after a ball at an inn, by helping the landlady serve negus to the remaining dancers; in *Mansfield Park*, a tired Fanny Price makes her way to bed after her first ball, 'feverish with hopes and fears, soup and negus'.

Excessive drinking was clearly thought highly comic by the young Jane Austen and her family. Several passages in her juvenile writings poke fun at Georgian attitudes to drunkenness, from her satire on the virtuous pretence of feminine abstemiousness, in *The Visit* – 'Sir Arthur never touches wine', declares Lady Hampton, turning the convention on its head, 'but

Sophy will toss off a bumper with you' – to the dramatic climax of Chapter 4 of *Jack and Alice*: 'The Bottle being pretty briskly pushed about . . . the whole party . . . were carried home, Dead Drunk.' Without indulging as freely as the fictional Sophy or Alice, Jane Austen clearly enjoyed good wine: in 1800 she apologized for writing with a shaky hand, which she attributed to having drunk too much the night before; in later life she commented that one of the 'Douceurs' (sweeteners) of ageing was that she was now given a place at parties 'on the Sofa near the Fire & can drink as much wine as I like'. One of the pleasures of staying at her brother Edward's mansion of Godmersham was the excellence of the 'French wine' served there. While Britain and France were at war, and blockades were in place, new supplies of claret became hard to obtain, and the wines of Spain and Portugal, Britain's allies, grew in popularity; the fortified wine Madeira became increasingly fashionable, and appears both in Jane's letters and in her novels. At a great house such as Godmersham, however, a well-stocked cellar would continue to provide a selection of fine claret; so that Jane, while staying there in 1808, could report with delight, 'I shall eat Ice & drink French wine' – though she added hastily that the cheerful companionship and 'unreserved Conversation' of more informal Chawton, on her return, would 'make good amends for Orange Wine'. In fact, such home-made alcoholic drinks were produced in many well-to-do households, including Manydown (owned by Jane's friends the Bigg-Wither family), and her fictional Hartfield, home of rich Emma Woodhouse. In one of her last letters, dated January 1817, Jane asked Alethea Bigg for the recipe for 'some excellent orange wine . . . made from Seville oranges': this may be the 'receipt' involving 'the chop't pieces of 33 Seville oranges' copied by Martha Lloyd into her cookery book. In *Emma*, the ambitious clergyman Mr Elton carefully takes down the recipe for spruce beer which he has encountered at Hartfield. Essence of spruce, like

Spanish oranges, could not be home-grown, unlike the currants for currant wine, and the honey for mead – but even these familiar crops could fail: in 1811 Jane complained of 'fewer currants' in the Chawton garden than expected, adding, 'We must buy currants for our Wine', and in 1816 she wrote, 'There is to be No Honey this year. Bad news for us.' On moving to Bath in 1801, Jane had worried about finding a suitable site for Cassandra's beehives; and even amid the 'Elegance & Ease & Luxury' of a Godmersham visit, in 1813, she told her sister tenderly, 'I find time in the midst of Port & Madeira to think of the 14 Bottles of Mead very often.'

The connection between diet and health was one which Jane herself made regularly. She noted approvingly that a new acquaintance, like herself, took 'no cream in her coffee'; and in *Mansfield Park* there is clear inference that the 'bon vivant' parson Dr Grant's sudden death may be attributed to his over-indulgence in rich food and drink, an excess of 'butter and eggs' in particular. The pampered hypochondriac Arthur Parker, in Jane Austen's last, unfinished novel *Sanditon*, is shown – against better advice – insisting on strong, fatty cocoa and thickly buttered toast, while resisting all attempts to make him take exercise. 'The more Wine I drink,' he declares, 'the better I am'; and when pressed to enjoy the fresh air, he refers feebly to the benefits of standing by an open window. Faced with the entire Parker family, whose 'unfortunate turn for Medecine [*sic*] especially quack Medecine' had left them prey to 'various Disorders', the heroine Charlotte Heywood emerges as a champion of modern medical common sense; as when, asked what the effects of 'strong Green tea' might be, she responds coolly, 'Keep you awake perhaps all night.' Jane Austen herself took a robust view of health problems and medical care. Years of pandering to her self-involved mother, whose constant ailments did not prevent her living to be 88 years old, left her decidedly unimpressed by imaginary illnesses – her own, far more serious, symptoms included. She believed in the importance of fresh air and exercise: '(We are) desperate walkers', she wrote on one occasion, of herself and Martha; and even in her latter days she tried the remedy of donkey-riding to build up strength – rather as Fanny Price, in *Mansfield Park*, is expected to improve her health by regular riding, first on an 'old poney' from the great house, and later on a docile mare specially bought for her benefit by her champion and hero, Edmund. Even towards the end of her short life, while vacating the family sofa at Chawton for her more demanding but less needy mother, Jane Austen joked about her own weaknesses. 'I am a poor Honey at present', she confessed lightly to her niece Caroline, shortly before her death.

Towards others' ailments, however, she was deeply compassionate – whether the problem was a wasting illness, or a whitlow on the finger. Though such indispensable elements of modern medicine as anaesthetics and antibiotics had yet to be discovered, some aspects of eighteenth- and early nineteenth-century health care were based on sound enough principles. The common practice of blood-letting, used for almost every condition from fevers to fractures, might now seem archaic, but the application of blood-sucking leeches – referred to more than once in Jane Austen's correspondence – still has a place in medical science; and today, as in her time, patients with gout are warned against drinking red wine, and advised to take plenty of water (though not necessarily at Bath). 'Magnesia' – powdery magnesium carbonate – remains a homely remedy for mild stomach disorders, in its unpleasant-tasting form as 'Milk of Magnesia'. The opiate-based substance laudanum, which Jane, among her responsibilities as housekeeper, was allowed to dispense to her mother, would not now be kept (even under lock and key) in any family medicine-cupboard; yet its calming effects on a highly-strung person, such as Mrs Austen, anticipated the twenty-first-century use of tranquillizers, and sleeping-pills. Other

Regency remedies, however – including some of the potions listed in Martha Lloyd's household book – ranged from the ineffectual to the downright dangerous. Calomel, which appeared to bring relief to a friend of the Austens in 1813, was derived from poisonous mercury, while the popular substance hartshorn – made from shavings of deers' antlers, boiled down to produce a form of ammonia – would have brought little benefit when taken internally, as liquid spirit, or reduced to a jelly. Hartshorn might, perhaps, have had some effect as an ingredient in pungent smelling-salts, such as those which quick-thinking Anne Elliot offers to Louisa Musgrove, after her dangerous fall on the Cobb at Lyme in *Persuasion*; but strong-smelling lavender drops, as applied to Marianne Dashwood, in her distressed state in *Sense and Sensibility*, could only have been of mild restorative use to a hysterical, or fainting, person.

One major medical advance which occurred in Jane Austen's day, and which she referred to in passing, in her correspondence, was the development of vaccination, pioneered by the great Dr Jenner, as a protection against the ravages of contagious disease. During an evening with friends, in 1800, she mentioned that, among other diversions, 'Dr Jenner's pamphlet on the cow pox' had been read aloud to the company. Inoculation, initially brought to England by Lady Mary Wortley Montagu, became a fashionable cause, taken up by the royal family and leading members of the aristocracy. For the great advances in anaesthesia, however, the world would have to wait for some fifty years after Jane Austen's death. Her female friends and relations had scant relief during the agonies of childbirth; battlefield and shipdeck surgery were carried out without effective painkillers; and even the minor miseries of earache or toothache had to be stoically borne, unless such unscientific curatives as the application of a boiled onion (to the former), or oil of sweet almonds (to the latter) might prove helpful. Though the need to clean and conserve teeth was well recognized – rubbing with a cloth, rather than brushing, being the favoured method – toothache was a regular hazard of Jane Austen's day. The misery of an extraction, without modern anaesthesia, is reflected in her juvenile work *Catharine*: to the heroine's 'violent' bout of 'toothake' [*sic*], her shallow, silly friend Camilla responds, 'You wo'nt [*sic*] have it out, will you?', adding, unhelpfully, 'I had rather undergo the greatest Tortures in the World than have a tooth drawn.' Several references in Jane's letters underline the hazards of contemporary dentistry: a Mr Spence, in London, tending her nieces in 1813, found much to do – to his own financial benefit, Jane suspected. She could accept that Lizzy, her brother Edward's second daughter, had 'a very sad hole between two of her front teeth', so that, at a second appointment, they had to be 'filed and lamented over again'; it was even reasonable that 'poor Marianne had two taken out' – an operation which, overheard by Jane, Fanny and Lizzy from an adjoining room, involved 'two sharp hasty Screams', to their distress. When it came to her beloved Fanny, however, Jane clearly had reservations about the treatment of her teeth. 'Pretty as they are, Spence found something to do to them,' she noted, 'putting in gold and talking gravely'. With typical Austen irony she concluded, 'I think he must be a Lover of Teeth & Money & Mischief . . . I would not have had him look at mine for a shilling a tooth & double it.'

Since treatment in a public hospital was not then an option for the well-to-do, Jane and her family were always (like her fictional characters) nursed at home through any illness, however severe. At Steventon, Mrs Austen's doctor Mr Lyford was a frequent visitor; in Henry Austen's London household the young physician Charles Haden became a guest and family friend, as well as medical adviser. Having first mentioned him to Cassandra as 'an Apothecary' Jane became anxious to correct this description, with its somewhat lowly associations of the dispensing chemist; in a letter of 15 November she described him, jokingly, as 'something between a Man & an Angel', and commended his 'good Manners & clever conversation'. She recorded his comments on *Mansfield Park* ('he prefers it to *P. & P.*'), and encouraged a very public flirtation between him and her niece Fanny, who were seen at one of Henry's parties in two chairs ('I *believe* at least they had *two* chairs'), immersed in conversation. In her novels, medical men are relegated to a minor social role: the heroine of *Emma* is keen to snub the pretensions of Mr Perry, who plans to 'set up his carriage' like a gentleman; and in *Sense and Sensibility* the ageing, man-hunting spinster Anne Steele, whose amorous interests are generally confined to down-at-heel clerks and the like, sets her sights on a dull-sounding local doctor. Mr Haden was evidently aware of the potential social limitations of his calling, but, Jane wrote approvingly, 'He never does appear in the least above his Profession, or out of humour with it.' In fact, it was a medical attendant on the Prince Regent himself, with a certain influence behind the scenes in London sickrooms and drawing-rooms who, in 1815, let it be known to his royal patient that the author of *Pride and Prejudice* was then in town – with the result that Jane Austen received her historic invitation to the palace of Carlton House.

One of Mr Haden's attractions as a guest was his musical ability. Jane and he had an amusing exchange on the subject, in 1815, during which she attempted, unsuccessfully, to counter 'his firm belief that a person *not* musical is fit for every sort of Wickedness'. More helpfully, that evening, while Fanny played he 'sat & listened & suggested improvements'. Jane Austen's attitude to the highly-rated social skill of music was decidedly ambivalent. She had a deep personal appreciation of music; she enjoyed playing the piano herself, rising early at Chawton to practise, so as not to disturb the household, and encouraging others to study as much as possible. (To her little niece Caroline, in 1815, she recommended the use of her piano, while writing, on a gentle note of warning, that nothing heavy should be placed on the delicate instrument.) It was during Jane's lifetime that the pianoforte, with its mechanism of strings struck by hammers, rather than plucked by 'jacks', took over from the less resonant harpsichord and spinet of early Georgian times. Only on a pianoforte could Marianne Dashwood, in *Sense and Sensibility*, have pounded out so powerfully 'a very magnificent concerto' – perhaps one of Beethoven's masterly works for the instrument, published in 1795. Jane Austen had every respect for true musical skill; in 1811 she wrote warmly of a Miss Harding, who had 'flowers in her hair and music at her fingertips', but in this, as in everything, she was impatient of pretentiousness. The affectation of musical taste, such as Mrs Elton displays in *Emma*, particularly annoyed her: far more acceptable is the honest ignorance of Mrs Cole, in the same novel, who hopes her small daughters may learn to play. The Cole family's newly acquired, expensive piano, is, naturally a grand; that which Jane Fairfax receives, perhaps like Jane Austen's own, is 'a very elegant-looking . . . large sized square pianoforte', in the older tradition. The arrival, in mysterious circumstances, of this instrument, sent down from the famous firm of John Broadwood in London, provides an intriguing plot-twist in this great novel of symbols, metaphors, games and double-dealings.

Among the selection of music which the giver of Jane Fairfax's piano thoughtfully sends with it are works by the contemporary German composer Cramer, and some 'Irish airs'. The latter choice represents a subtly naughty allusion by the donor, Frank Churchill, for the heroine, Emma, to pick up, to their secret joke (which Emma takes seriously) that Jane is in love with a friend's Irish husband; however, Irish songs were much in vogue in the Regency, so their inclusion among any young lady's repertoire would not seem strange. Jane Austen herself included such light popular songs among her own collection of music – some printed, some copied out by her own hand, with the staves carefully, if laboriously, ruled: a task which Willoughby in *Sense and Sensibility* devotedly undertakes for Marianne. For a contemporary of Beethoven, Mozart and Haydn, Jane Austen had surprisingly unambitious musical tastes: though her own selection, still preserved today, includes compositions by Handel, Gluck and Haydn, she seemed chiefly to have been attracted to dance tunes and popular ballads – 'simple old songs', as her nephew (and first biographer) James Austen-Leigh recorded. Like her self-effacing, last heroine, Anne Elliot in *Persuasion*, she was evidently more concerned to play for others' enjoyment than her own pleasure. Anne – though a truly gifted performer – is always content to submerge her own talent in providing dance-music so that younger members of the company may enjoy 'an unpremeditated little ball'. On moving to Chawton, in 1808, Jane assured Cassandra that she would acquire a piano, no matter how great the expense, adding, 'And I will practise country dances, that we may have some amusement for our nephews and nieces.'

Dancing was one of her own favourite activities, which she indulged in, during her youth, at every possible opportunity. The monthly public assemblies held in Basingstoke were an important feature of her life at Steventon: what she wore, who was present, and whom she danced with, were mentioned frequently in her letters. Anticipating a ball, and holding a gossipy post-mortem on the following day, seemed to give her almost as much pleasure as the event itself. One of the games with which she amused her little nieces, in later years, was imagining a conversation between them, 'supposing we were all grown up, the day after a ball'. The small private dance which Emma Woodhouse and Frank Churchill organize in *Emma*, at the Crown Inn, must owe a good deal to the gatherings of Jane Austen's Hampshire youth at the Angel Inn (now demolished), in Basingstoke. The custom of ending an evening at home with some impromptu dancing for the younger members of the company is, similarly, reflected in such fictional scenes as the party at the Coles's house in *Emma*, and the mention of 'many an unpremeditated little ball' at the Musgroves' cottage in *Persuasion*, and the Middletons' mansion in *Sense and Sensibility*. In a house without a ballroom, finding enough space to dance in could pose a problem at this time when, rather than taking to the floor as separate couples, the pairs of participants all formed up together – either in round or square 'sets', for a cotillion or a quadrille, or, more commonly, in long lines, with the gentlemen facing their partners, for the popular 'country dances'. The waltz, in which couples twirled in pairs, had been introduced into England by the early 1800s, but was, in the Regency era, still largely confined to fashionable circles, and was frowned upon by some – inspiring Lord Byron to write a mocking poem on the subject. *Emma's* former governess, Mrs Weston, strikes up 'an irresistible waltz' for the company at the Coles' party, in *Emma*, but the young guests form up for a country dance, performed in the standard style, 'Longways for as many as will'. Favourite dances such as the 'Boulangères', mentioned in *Pride and Prejudice*, could allow for a certain amount of conversation between the partners as they waited to progress down the line: Catherine Morland and Henry Tilney have a delightful exchange, comparing the manoeuvres and duties of marriage and dancing; but this is cut short as the 'demands of the dance' become 'too importunate for a divided attention'.

Further opportunities for conversation (and flirtation) in a Regency ballroom occurred between dances, when it was the gentleman's duty to usher his partner back to her chaperone, or escort her to the tea-room, where he was expected to sit with her family and friends, rather than she with his – a point of social behaviour which Emma Watson, in Jane's unfinished novel *The Watsons*, points out to the little boy whom she has kindly partnered at a local ball. Unattached male guests might saunter about the room, greeting friends and surveying the proceedings, as Mr Darcy does, with a supercilious air, in *Pride and Prejudice*; it was not unusual for one of these 'lookers on' to stand behind a dancer in the line and chat, while he or she waited to move up the couples to perform the well-practised steps of skips, turns and 'hands-across'. Such conversations are, however, generally carried on by the more ill-bred, or self-centred, characters in Jane Austen's fiction, notably John Thorpe in *Northanger Abbey* and young Lord Osborne in *The Watsons*. The delightful Henry Tilney resents John Thorpe's intrusion, complaining – in his analogy between married couples and dancing partners – 'Nobody can fasten themselves on the notice of one, without injuring the rights of the other.'

For many unengaged gentlemen – and ladies – at a ball, the card-room would provide a refuge from music and chatter. During Jane Austen's era fortunes were gambled away, by both sexes; but in her fiction card-playing is, in general, shown merely as a popular pastime. Attitudes to cards are subtly used to denote character: the reprobate Wickham in *Pride and Prejudice* is, among his other vices, a gamester; greedy, sensuous Lydia Bennet, after a merry evening playing lottery-tickets (in which mother-of-pearl fishes were used as chips), can talk of little else but 'the fish she had lost and the fish she had won', while foolish, servile Mr Collins, having taken part in the round game of whist at the same party, admits to having 'lost every point', to the tune of some five shillings. When two more worldly gentlemen are invited to join in a 'rubber' of whist, in *Mansfield Park*, the stakes are likely to be as high as half-guineas. None of Jane's characters is interested in playing for high stakes. All her novels feature card-games, from whist and cassino, loo and lottery-tickets, to speculation, cribbage and piquet; but a rare brush, for a heroine, with gambling occurs in *Pride and Prejudice*, when Elizabeth Bennet, staying with Mr Bingley's house-party, is invited to join them at cards, but, suspecting they may be 'playing high', chooses instead to busy herself with a book. ('Do you prefer reading to cards?' enquires a surprised fellow guest.) In *Sense and Sensibility* the romantic rebel Marianne Dashwood somewhat rudely declines to join a whist-table, because (tellingly) she 'never would learn the game' – just as she refuses to join in so many of society's formal games of rules and decorum and polite deception. Jane Austen herself showed no great attraction to cards, though in her letters she frequently mentions taking part in many of the popular games, from cassino – played, in her novels, in such grand houses as Osborne Castle, in *The Watsons*, and Lady Catherine de Bourgh's mansion, Rosings, in *Pride and Prejudice* – to brag, an early form of poker (which she particularly enjoyed, recommending it, enthusiastically, over another favoured game, speculation), while staying at Godmersham. Her favourite entertainments tended to involve word-play, from conundrums, riddles and charades, to making up silly rhymes, but she was also fond of amusements which involved manual dexterity: cup-and-ball, and spilli-kins, in particular, according to her nephew's *Memoir*. (Her own pretty cup-and-ball set, carved from ivory, is still pre-served today.) Some of her pleasures were more physically demanding: in 1805, staying at Godmersham, she wrote of 'playing at Battledore & Shuttlecock with William', her 7-year-old nephew, adding impressively, 'we have kept it [the feather-flighted shuttlecock] up three times & once or twice *six*'.

For young people, and their more spirited aunts and elders, boisterous activities were part and parcel of Regency social life, as the scene of Christmas at the Musgroves' house in *Persuasion* demonstrates, with its depiction of 'chattering girls, cutting up silk and gold paper', and 'riotous boys holding high revel' beside tables 'bending under the weight of brawn and cold pies', while the head of the family can hardly make himself heard 'from the clamour of the children on his knees'.

The Bennet sisters' Aunt Phillips prefaces a supper-invitation with the promise of 'a nice comfortable noisy game of Lottery Tickets'. The 'domestic hurricane' of the Musgroves' cottage is not entirely to the taste of Anne Elliot, and certainly does not suit her snobbishly elegant friend Lady Russell; but quieter activities could be found in other households. The card-game quadrille, played by Lady Catherine de Bourgh and her guests at Rosings in *Pride and Prejudice*, was evidently much in favour with well-mannered, older people: it is to 'tea and quadrille' that kindly old Mr Woodhouse invites his coterie of dull female friends, in *Emma*, 'to win or lose a few sixpences by his fireside'. Backgammon, played with counters on a board or specially designed table, could also be enjoyed by two demure ladies; reporting from Godmersham in 1813, Jane Austen mentioned 'a grown-up musical young Lady who played backgammon with Fanny'. For men of all ages, tastes and temperaments, a game of billiards was usually inviting. 'The Comfort of the Billiard Table . . . draws all the Gentlemen to it whenever they are within', she noted, during the same visit.

When seeking recreation out-of-doors, rather than 'within', Jane Austen's male contemporaries were assumed to have in common a taste for sporting pursuits, as though it were a natural attribute of masculinity to shoot, fish or hunt, both for pleasure and for the pot. Her fictional heroes, from mild Edmund Bertram to arrogant Mr Darcy, enjoy field sports – as do her villains, Willoughby in particular. Ladies were not expected to join the guns or the chase; Jane was joking when she wrote, in 1796, that there was such a 'prodigious number of birds' that season that she might bag a few herself. Presents of game, from hares and rabbits to partridges, were always a welcome adjunct to the larder for a lady; an invitation to shoot, or fish, an agreeable compliment to a gentleman. Mr Gardiner is flattered and pleased when invited by Mr Darcy to fish in his river at Pemberley. It is, however, a mark of Mrs

Bennet's embarrassing ignorance when she urges Mr Bingley – 'When you have killed all your own birds' – that he should come and 'shoot as many as you please' on her husband's manor.

If women were considered ill-suited to almost any sporting activity beyond walking, riding, driving and a little sea-bathing, one field in which they were 'universally acknowledged' to be superior to men was in their 'talent for writing agreeable letters', as Henry Tilney teasingly points out to Catherine Morland in *Northanger Abbey*. Though Catherine (and, tacitly, the author) questions this notion, certainly Jane Austen herself spent many hours during her brief life writing letters, both for duty and for pleasure, resulting in the extraordinary, entertaining and revealing, witty and moving treasury of correspondence which survives to delight her readers today. 'I have now attained the true art of letter-writing', she remarked to Cassandra in 1801, 'which . . . is to express on paper exactly what one would say to the same person by word of mouth.' She would often begin a letter in the morning, before breakfast, and continue it in instalments, over several days, keeping family and friends abreast of all that was going on in her life, from details of shopping, visits and gossip, to occasional snippets of news about the progress of her novels and their publication. Each of her major works incorporates at least one letter to the heroine, quoted verbatim; the extent of some shows how long a single letter could be. To save space, and justify the cost of postage, it was customary to cram the paper as full as possible; Jane once complimented Cassandra on having fitted forty-two lines on to a page. She herself used abbreviations whenever she could, such as '&'; 'Yr.'; 'Wd.' for 'would'; 'Morn^g' for 'morning', and so on. It was also usual, when the sheet was full, to turn it sideways and write crossways over the existing lines – creating, as Miss Bates remarks fondly of a letter from Jane Fairfax, in *Emma*, 'all that chequerwork'. A large square of space had to be left blank, however, so that when the writer had finished, the foolscap could be folded in half, with the blank area now central in what had become the fourth page; the address would be written in this gap, and the edges tucked round to form an envelope, which would be sealed with a gum 'wafer', or coloured wax, impressed with the sender's personal device.

In town a letter might be delivered by hand, by a servant, saving time and cost; those fortunate enough to be familiar with a Member of Parliament might have letters 'franked' by him, enabling them to be sent free of charge. 'I cannot spare Mr Lushington' (MP for Canterbury) 'because of his frank', Jane joked of a fellow-guest at a Godmersham house-party in 1813; in *Mansfield Park*, Edmund Bertram encourages timid Fanny Price to write to her brother, assuring her, 'As your uncle will frank it, it will cost William nothing.' The cost of posting a letter had to be paid by the recipient, and by 1813 when *Mansfield Park* was completed, this was considered high, at four pence for up to 15 miles, and as much as seventeen pence for 700 miles. It was, however, considered an excellent service, as Jane Fairfax attests, in *Emma*, when she declares 'The post-office is a wonderful establishment', adding, 'If one thinks of all that it has to do . . . it is really astonishing!' Though such present-day factors as stamps and pillar-boxes had yet to be introduced, the service advanced greatly during Jane Austen's lifetime, developing from the earlier network of mounted postboys to a nationwide system of well-regulated mail-coaches (manned by armed guards for protection from highway robbery), which by 1811 covered distances of over 10,000 miles every day, between London and the regions, with 'seldom' – in Jane Fairfax's words – 'any negligence or blunder'. It was fortunate for her that the local post-office at Highbury was within walking-distance, so that she could collect her letters in person; had anyone else done so on her behalf, and recognized that Frank Churchill was writing to her, the secret of their engagement would have been out, since by convention, outside the family circle, an unmarried gentleman and lady could not write to one another under any other circumstances – which is why Elinor Dashwood, seeing Marianne send a letter to Willoughby 'by the two-penny post' in *Sense and Sensibility* takes it as proof that they are engaged.

Passengers as well as letters could travel speedily in mail-coaches, as Edmund Bertram does when journeying to Portsmouth in *Mansfield Park*. For ladies, modes of transport had to be governed by a concern for propriety, as well as convenience. The more old-fashioned, and economical, stage-coach was particularly frowned on, so that Miss Steele in *Sense and Sensibility* is anxious to inform her 'more grand relations' on arriving in London, that she and her sister had come in a hired post-chaise, while Jane Austen herself wrote, with amusement, in 1796, '*I* want to go in a Stage Coach, but Frank will not let me.' The business of stopping at different stages, or posts, on a long journey to change tired horses for a fresh team, which might involve paying a post-boy, supervising luggage and ordering refreshment, made it important that a respectable lady should not travel alone, and the insult to young Catherine Morland when, in *Northanger Abbey*, she is sent home unceremoniously from the Tilneys' to fend for herself on an 11-hour journey in a 'hack post-chase', is 'unforgivable'. It would have been courteous to send her, for the first stage, in the family's own carriage, with an attendant servant to accompany her thereafter in hired, private chaises.

For a short journey, a gentleman alone would often choose to ride; as Mr Weston points out, in *Emma*, a fit young man such as Frank Churchill could cover nine miles in an hour on horseback. 'But what is distance, Mr Weston, to people of large fortune?' exclaims the would-be elegant Mrs Elton – and for once, the haughtily well-bred Mr Darcy in *Pride and Prejudice* might have shared her view, since he comments, 'What is fifty miles of good road? Little more than half a day's journey . . .

a *very* easy distance.' At a time when carriages had iron-rimmed wheels, and roads were liable to be rutted in the country, or cobbled in a town, travelling at speed could be uncomfortable, and the high-springing of a light, sporty vehicle such as a curricle or phaeton was designed for smoothness of ride, as well as elegance of appearance.

In all, about a dozen different types of carriage appear in Jane Austen's novels, from the Dowager Mrs Rushworth's stately 'chariot' and Lady Bertram's postilioned 'chaise-and-four' in *Mansfield Park*, to silly Mr Collins's one-horse gig, in *Pride and Prejudice*, and the 'very pretty landaulette' which Anne Elliot drives (to her sister's envy) after her marriage in *Persuasion*. Yet no scene of travel could be more evocative of the spirit of the Regency than that in which the young heroine of *Northanger Abbey* finds herself riding high beside Henry Tilney in his curricle. 'His hat sat so well, and the innumerable capes of his great-coat looked so becomingly important', Jane Austen writes, that Catherine, 'convinced . . . that a curricle was the prettiest equipage in the world', concludes 'To be driven by him, next to being dancing with him, was certainly the greatest happiness in the world.'

In a detailed letter of May 1813, having mentioned, in rapid succession, the price of sugar, a purchase of gloves, and a journey from Guildford, Jane wrote, half-apologetically, 'I hope somebody cares for these minutiae.' Yet to her readers today, such minutiae are among the principal pleasures of both her letters and her great novels.

3

'The Present Fashions'

'Mrs Bennet was ... on one hand collecting an account of the present fashions from Jane, who sat some way below her, and on the other retailing them all to the younger Miss Lucases.'

Jane Austen, *Pride and Prejudice*, 1813

'I am amused by the present style of female dress', Jane Austen wrote from London to her friend Martha Lloyd, in September 1814. 'It seems to me a more marked *change* than one has lately seen.' She was then almost 39 years old, a middle-aged, unmarried, country gentlewoman who had never been a beauty; but she remained fascinated by fashion, in all its seductive details. The first of her surviving letters, dated January 1796, refers to purchases of silk stockings, white gloves and pink 'persian' fabric; the last, written just before her death in 1817, jokingly mentions 'longer petticoats' which she hopes – 'since the fashion allows it' – some ungainly acquaintances will adopt. In the years between, her correspondence maintained a regular, lively commentary on the dress of late Georgian and Regency England – from the changes in waistlines, hemlines and sleeves, to the colour of gentlemen's coats and the price of muslins. 'Dress is at all times a frivolous distinction, and excessive solicitude about it often destroys its own aim', she wrote with mock-severity in *Northanger Abbey*; and specific references to clothes are strikingly rare in her fiction. Yet when she chooses to mention a detail of dress – such as the 'glossy spots' on demure Fanny Price's best gown, or brash Isabella Thorpe's taste for red 'coquelicot ribands' — she does so with a deft assurance which reflects her own love and knowledge of the subject.

During the era spanned by Jane Austen's novels, from the late 1790s to her death in 1817, fashion had settled into a period of relative stability, characterized by high 'Empire' waists, light, soft fabrics and a classical simplicity for women, and an austere, ultra-masculine elegance for men. Since her birth in 1775, however, the dress of both sexes — like so much else — had undergone a revolution. In the mid-1770s, artifice and show had been in vogue. Stiff, ornate silks, worn over cumbersome hooped undergarments, had restricted women's freedom of movement, while gentlemen strutted in long-skirted coats, rich satin waistcoats and a profusion of velvet and embroidery. Feminine hairstyles reached a height of absurdity, with the hair strained up high over pads, then teased into curls, powdered, pomaded and decked with ribbons, fruit, flowers and even glass ornaments. Taking the excesses of the Seventies still further were the 'Macaronis' — young men of leisure who sought to outrage the public by the absurdity of their costume, flaunting vast wigs topped by tiny hats, tight waist-coats adorned with immense buttons and bows, and such effeminate fripperies as reticules, parasols and shoes with high, red, 'Louis' heels. Though no such figure of fun would have prinked its way into a Hampshire vicarage, the popular prints of the day, which mocked the Macaronis with relish, might have been seen in a country library or shop window by the sharp-eyed young Jane Austen; and she certainly knew Sheridan's classic comedy *The Rivals*, in which the 'Monkeyrony' fashions were satirized, as it was one of the plays put on at Steventon by her drama-loving family when she was 8 years old.

By the 1780s — as her frivolous cousin Eliza de Feuillide's letters from Paris attested — great 'changes in the toilette' were taking place. The influence of Jean-Jacques Rousseau's writings, which emphasized the importance of nature, and the growing popular taste for landscape and the 'picturesque' led, in fashion, to a new mood of naturalness and simplicity. Yellow straw hats, such as haymakers wore in the fields, were 'universally adopted', Eliza reported. Queen Marie-Antoinette (whom Eliza found 'exceedingly handsome at all times') built herself a charming little show-farm at Versailles, visited Rousseau's tomb, and sat for her portrait in a new style of 'chemise' dress – soft, white, gauzy, loosely sashed, and flatteringly pastoral. She presented a similar gown to the reigning English beauty Georgiana, Duchess of Devonshire (whose sister, Lady Bessborough, was to be an early admirer of *Sense and Sensibility*, some three decades later); when the influential Duchess wore it to the theatre in London, in 1784, she set British fashion's formal seal of approval on the informal new mode.

Throughout Jane Austen's childhood, the trend towards simplicity and ease in dress gathered pace. Improved methods of producing and printing cotton textiles – from Crompton's fine-spinning 'Mule' of 1779, to Cartwright's power-loom of 1785 – had contributed to the growth of cotton-manufacture as a mechanized industry, rather than a cottage craft; and as the 'dark Satanic mills' of Lancashire burgeoned, so too did the appeal of cotton, as a lighter, cheaper, more practical and less ostentatious alternative to the old stiff silks. In keeping with the new mood, women's towering hairstyles were lowered, softened, and fluffed out wide; pads at the hips and rump gave a gentle, Gainsborough-esque bustle to filmy gowns; waists rose higher; the female silhouette grew slimmer. At the same time, men's clothes were also moving towards a simpler, plainer mode. The French, often teased by the British for their love of finery and preference for Court over country life, nevertheless had a certain admiration for the English gentleman's taste for sturdy, unaffected garb, and tendency to appear in hunting and shooting clothes whenever possible – even in town. Though France would be the ultimate source of most women's fashions in Jane Austen's time, in men's clothing it was the country-sports-derived 'style Anglais' which came to dominate the mode.

The French Revolution of 1789, when Jane Austen was almost 14, brought rapid – and radical – changes to fashion, for both sexes. Extravagance and ostentation, hallmarks of the corrupt, decadent old nobility, became utterly outmoded. In Britain, those idealists and intellectuals who, like Wordsworth, briefly thought it 'Bliss . . . in that dawn to be alive', displayed their revolutionary sympathies in varying degrees of under-dressing: the brilliant Whig politician Charles James Fox (who had been an ardent Macaroni in his youth) now cultivated an unshaven and dishevelled appearance; while the pioneering feminist Mary Wollstonecraft was said to dress like 'a philo-sophical sloven'. Her fellow-radical (and husband) William Godwin evidently followed suit: in 1801 Jane Austen wrote gleefully, from Bath, that an acquaintance was 'as raffish in his appearance as I would wish every Disciple of Godwin to be'. Though France's Reign of Terror brought disillusionment, in the republican climate of the 1790s a new set of sartorial prin-ciples became established. Artifice, over-decoration and the parade of wealth were vulgar. True elegance lay in under-statement, and an air (however contrived) of neo-classical simplicity. And, as Marianne Dashwood would artlessly affirm in Jane Austen's first published work, *Sense and Sensibility*, 'Of all manly dresses, a shooting-jacket was the most becoming.'

As France advanced from Terror towards stability and the tri-umphs of the Napoleonic era, Englishmen's country dress was taken up as a liberated, rakish uniform by the group of politi-cal hotheads known as the 'Incroyables'. Involving theatrical boots, over-styled, dark cloth coats, and collars and neck-cloths worn so high as almost to conceal the wearer's face, the look was wildly exaggerated; but it reflected the general direction of men's fashion. Jane Austen's first surviving letter, written in January 1796, when she was just 20, mentioned that her 'Irish friend', Mr Tom Lefroy, with whom she was conducting a delightful flirtation, had 'but *one* fault'; his morning coat was 'a great deal too light'. She generously attributed this lapse of taste to his liking for the fictional hero Tom Jones, who had worn a white coat; but Fielding's classic novel had been written almost fifty years earlier, and by the mid-1790s a gentleman's coat should have been a sober, countrified shade of dark blue, green or brown. She could not marry this admirer, she declared firmly, 'unless he promises to give away his white coat'. It was a sentiment which the great arbiter of style George Brummell would have applauded.

Brummell was rising to prominence in London society, and fashion history, during the later years of the 1790s, while Jane Austen was at work on the early drafts of three of her mature novels: *Pride and Prejudice*, *Sense and Sensibility* and *Northanger Abbey*. These two great figures of their age moved in different worlds, and assuredly never met; yet they shared a philosophy both of manners and modes. Brummell, far from being the affected fop of later misconceptions, was a dandy: ironic, fastidious, and as opposed to all forms of vulgar excess as was Jane Austen herself. To Brummell, as to the creator of Mr Darcy, true elegance involved understatement. It was Brummell who persuaded the obese, extravagant Prince Regent to abandon gaudy waistcoats, pink satin suit-linings and jewel-studded buttons in favour of simple, dark clothes which depended for their effect on a perfection of cloth, cut and fit. Brummell deplored both the Tory affectation of dressing like a coachman, and the Whiggish cult of slovenliness; along with immaculate tailoring, he advocated scrupulous washing and freshly laundered linen. Though a master of the cutting remark, when called for, he was never gratuitously rude; and many of the insulting 'put-downs' attributed to him, on the subject of others' appearances and habits, were clearly invented

– or intended as self-caricature. One statement which did, however, have the true Brummell stamp was his famous style dictum: 'If John Bull' – the contemporary term for the British man-in-the-street – 'turns to look at you, then you are not well dressed.'

John Bull would almost certainly not have turned to look at Jane Austen. Though her nephew wrote in his *Memoir* that 'in person she was very attractive', both he and his sister Caroline recalled her as decidedly demure in her appearance – 'remarkably neat', rather than obviously 'regardful of the fashionable, or the becoming'. Such an assessment might not have displeased their aunt, fashion-conscious as she was. Though her letters regularly reported what was said about her dress and looks, she seemed content with faint praise: in November 1800, aged 24, she told Cassandra that their sister-in-law, James's wife Mary, 'said that I looked very well last night ... my hair was at least tidy, which was all my ambition'; and in 1811, when she was almost 36, she was 'very well-satisfied' to be called 'a pleasing-looking young woman', adding wistfully, 'that must do: – one cannot pretend to anything better now'. At an early age she took to the matronly fashion of wearing a light muslin cap over her curly brown hair, which, she explained, saved her 'a world of torment as to hairdressing', but which her nephews and nieces considered, regretfully, 'the garb of middle age'.

The slender, shift-shaped gown which had become the basis of the female wardrobe by 1800 was potentially the most erotic of dress-styles. Based on the clinging draperies of classical statuary, the *robe-en-chemise* left the wearer's arms bare, emphasized the breasts and outlined the figure – giving rise to the belief that some daring women actually dampened their garments to make them more revealing. Jane Austen clearly did not approve of the more indecent contemporary fashions. In a letter of 1798, from Godmersham, she criticized a fellow guest as being 'at once expensively and nakedly dressed'; and two years later, in Bath, she censured a Miss Langley for her 'fashionable dress and exposed bosom'. She reported in 1814 – when she was 38 – that she had 'lowered the bosom' of a gauze gown, 'especially at the corners', and 'plaited black sattin [*sic*] ribbon round the top'; but such a discreet *décolletage* was evidently modest, compared with what the *Ladies Monthly Magazine* condemned, in March 1803, as 'the nakedness of the mode . . . as much a hazard of health as it was trespass against modesty'.

At a time when most clothes (apart from accessories, such as gloves and shoes) could not be bought ready-to-wear, but had to be made individually, by a dressmaker, fashion magazines were valuable sources of information, as well as entertainment. They were still something of a novelty in Jane Austen's early adulthood, and do not feature in her novels, but she must surely have seen them from time to time. Heideloff's *Gallery of Fashion*, published in London from 1794 by a refugee from the Terror in Paris, brought British women their own new monthly magazine, containing sumptuous, hand-coloured illustrations, at a moment when the all-important French fashion industry had ceased to function: despite its cost and exclusivity, Heideloff's publication was so successful that others followed. The Piccadilly print-seller Ackermann launched, in 1809, his *Repository of Arts, Literature, Commerce, Manufactures, Fashions and Politics*; and from 1806 *La Belle Assemblée*, subtitled *Bell's Court and Fashionable Magazine*, appeared every month, costing 2s 6d, or 3s 6d with hand-coloured plates. Though they covered a wide range of topics, and *La Belle Assemblée* liked to flatter 'the British Fair' with worthy articles on hydraulics, Mme de Sévigné's prose style and Napoleon's political strategy in Europe, their chief appeal lay in the enticing illustrations of the 'New Spencer Walking Dress with the Incognita Hat', or the 'Most Fashionable Full Dress of the Month', included in every issue. Such pictures could be shown to a skilled dress-maker or home-needlewoman, and re-created – not always successfully. Jane Austen was, regretfully, 'obliged to alter' a white dress made for her by a Mrs Mussell; and in 1798, after what she described as 'a dreadful epoch of mantua-making', she complained to Cassandra, 'I cannot determine what to do about my white gown. I wish such things were to be bought ready-made.'

On that occasion she proposed to consult their clothes-conscious friend Martha Lloyd: as her novels showed, it was often through well-informed friends that fashion news was passed on. When the Bennet sisters' 'amiable, intelligent, elegant aunt', Mrs Gardiner, arrives from London, in *Pride and Prejudice*, 'the first part of her business ... was to distribute her presents and describe the newest fashions'; and on Jane Bennet's return from town, her mother's typically boisterous conversation at dinner consists of 'collecting an account of the present fashions from Jane' and relaying the details down the table, across the other diners, to some avid young female guests. Jane Austen's letters from London and Bath constantly informed her sister of what was being worn, and mentioned purchases which she had made on Cassandra's behalf. From Bath, in 1799, she sent news of the latest trimmings for hats: 'Flowers are very much worn, & Fruit is still more the thing ... I have seen Grapes, Cherries, Plumbs and Apricots.' Seeing, as ever, the funny side, she added, 'there are likewise Almonds & raisins, french Plumbs and Tamarinds at the Grocers, but I have never seen any of them in hats'; then, acknowledging the innate importance of the topic, she concluded, more seriously, 'My aunt has told me of a very cheap [shop] near Walcot Church, to which I shall go in quest of something for you.' Staying in the elegant society of Godmersham, in 1813, she mentioned a Miss Chapman, who 'had a double flounce to her gown', and advised her sister earnestly, 'You really must get some flounces' to lengthen and update some of her 'large stock of white morning gowns'.

Adding a flounce to a dress, or reviving a hat by retrimming it, was the sort of sewing which a woman of Jane Austen's class and income would have been expected to do for herself. When Elizabeth Bennet makes her first appearance in *Pride and Prejudice* she is 'employed in trimming a hat'; and later in the novel her spoilt, spendthrift sister Lydia buys a bonnet which she neither needs nor even likes, but acquires for the sheer pleasure of shopping, with the airy excuse, 'When I have bought some prettier-coloured satin to trim it with fresh, I think it will be very tolerable.' Even a feckless Lydia Bennet could sew, in Regency England. As the charming schoolgirl samplers of the period show, stitchcraft and embroidery were considered indispensable skills for a gentlewoman – whether she was born to wealth, like Mrs Jennings's daughter Charlotte, in *Sense and Sensibility*, whose sole schoolroom achievement appeared to be 'a landscape in coloured silks', or to an uncertain future, like Fanny Price in *Mansfield Park*, who has to turn her hand to all kinds of needlework, from making her cousins' theatrical costumes to hemming linen for her sailor brothers. 'Working', for young women in Jane Austen's novels, meant working with the needle. It was considered undesirable for a female to sit idly about; and in any house-hold of women a communal work-basket was generally to hand, containing garments to be made up for the poor, cravats or shirts to be hemmed for the men of the family, and mending. The last was not, however, a task to be done in elegant company: in 1804, while on holiday at Lyme, Jane mentioned visiting a Miss Armstrong, whose ungenteel mother 'sat darning a pair of stockings during the whole of my visit'. Prudently, with their own uninhibited mother in mind, she added, 'I do not mention this at home, lest a warning should act as an example.'

Jane Austen herself sewed beautifully. Unlike her tomboy heroine Catherine Morland, in *Northanger Abbey*, she enjoyed needlework; according to her nephew's *Memoir*, 'some of her merriest talk was over clothes which she and her companions were making, sometimes for themselves, sometimes for the poor'. Making up linen for a nephew, in 1799, she noted with satisfaction, 'I am the neatest worker of the party.' Satin-stitch was her speciality, and among the examples of her work preserved today is a white India-muslin shawl, decorated with a trellis design in exquisite satin-stitch. Patterns for such decorative embroidery were a popular feature of the early nineteenth-century fashion magazines: *La Belle Assemblée*'s monthly attractions included full-page diagrams of 'new and elegant embroideries' for items such as caps, flounces and handkerchiefs, which readers (or their seamstresses) could pull out and work from. Ready-printed dressmaking patterns were not generally available in Jane Austen's day, but she – and many of her female characters – were adept at taking patterns from existing garments, to be used as the model for new ones. In *Emma*, the heroine's protégée Harriet buys the fabric for a new dress, only to remember that she has left her 'pattern gown' at Emma's house; in *Sense and Sensibility*, the conniving Steele sisters seek both to flatter, and profit from, their self-satisfied hostess Lady Middleton by 'taking patterns from some elegant new dress, in which her appearance the day before had thrown them into unceasing delight'. Writing of her beloved niece Fanny Knight, in 1813, Jane reported that they had both been shopping for new caps, but added, 'Fanny is out of conceit with hers already, she finds that she has been buying a new cap without having a new pattern, which is true enough.'

While caps and cloaks could be bought ready-made, or enjoyably created at home, for her gowns Jane Austen employed the services of a series of dressmakers. The sewing-machine was not invented until the 1840s, over twenty years after her death; and women such as Mrs Mussell of Bath, whom Jane engaged to make Cassandra 'a dark gown' in 1801, or Miss Burton, in London, who obligingly charged 'only 8 shillings' for making her a pelisse in 1811, worked every tiny, even stitch by hand. Instructing a dressmaker as to the precise details of a new gown could be an exacting process; even the robustly unfashionable Mrs Croft, in the cancelled chapter of *Persuasion*, was observed by her husband to have been 'shut up together this half-hour' with 'her mantua-maker'. In a letter to Cassandra from Bath, in 1801, Jane Austen devoted over two hundred words to a minute description of the new 'round gown' which Mrs Mussell was making for her, including a small sketch of the bodice back – 'quite plain in the form $\bigvee$, and the sides equally so'. Within the basic 'Empire' silhouette, with its high bosom, low neck and slim skirt, endless variations were possible, from the length and shape of the sleeves, to the structure of the dress itself, which might be a one-piece 'round gown', fastening at the side, or have an 'apron front'. In this construction, a long slit in each side-seam, about half-way down, allowed the upper part of the skirt to be pulled up and fastened around the waist, exposing the petticoat, which was not an item of underclothing, but a secondary layer of the dress. (In December 1798 Jane mentioned turning an old 'coarse spot' gown into a petticoat.) It was in a dress of this easy, becoming style that Elizabeth Bennet set off across the fields to Netherfield Park, in *Pride and Prejudice*, 'jumping over stiles and springing over puddles' on the way, to arrive mud-splashed, windblown and glowing: 'her petticoat six inches deep in mud . . . and the gown which had been let down to hide it, not doing its office', according to her jealous rival for Mr Darcy's affections, Miss Bingley. Of all the fleeting references to clothes and appearances in Jane Austen's fiction, none is more effective than this vivid vignette. It expresses at once the character of Elizabeth herself – lively, spirited and self-assured – and the liberating nature of Regency women's dress. In the heavy brocades of her Georgian predecessors, or the strict corsets of her Victorian successors, a Lizzy Bennet could not have gone striding so freely over muddy fields, to arrive unconcernedly looking 'almost wild' in a grand household. But in Jane Austen's day, when prominent women such as Mme de Staël, Lady Caroline Lamb and Lady Hester Stanhope were making their mark on literature, society and even politics as never before, the clothes they wore expressed a social (as well as sartorial) freedom which their sex would not enjoy again until the twentieth century.

The light cottons and muslins of the period were practical, as well as becoming: Lizzy Bennet's mud-splashed petticoat would probably have been as easy to wash as her dirty ankles. The care of clothes was a subject of some importance to Jane Austen. She kept Cassandra informed of changes in the servants who washed for them (commenting of one, in 1798, 'She does not look as if anything she touched would ever be clean, but who knows?') and mentioned problems with cleaning and dyeing her gowns: 'I am sorry to say that my new coloured gown is very much washed out, though I charged everybody to take great care of it', she lamented in September 1796. The elegant, intelligent heiress Miss Tilney, in *Northanger Abbey*, is sufficiently concerned with 'the subject of muslins' to have discussed it with her delightful brother, Henry; as a result, he is able to charm naive Catherine Morland, and impress her clothes-obsessed chaperone, Mrs Allen, with his knowledge. Hearing that he buys his own cravats and some of his sister's gowns, that he understands the price and quality of muslins well enough to choose 'a prodigious bargain', and that he thinks Catherine's dress 'very pretty', but warns solemnly, 'I do not think it will wash well. I am afraid it will fray', foolish Mrs Allen is 'quite struck by his genius'. Though even Catherine begins to suspect that her admirer may be slyly teasing her chaperone, nevertheless his intimate knowledge of such women's topics as fashion and popular fiction helps to make Henry Tilney one of the most sympathetic male characters in Jane Austen's fiction. He is what twenty-first-century readers could recognize, with pleasure, as a 'new man'.

In Henry's comment, 'My sister has often trusted me in the

choice of a gown', the word 'gown' denotes not a completed garment, but a dress-length of material. Commissioning Cassandra, in 1801, to buy 'gowns for the summer' for their mother and herself, Jane directed 'Buy two brown ones, if you please . . . one longer than the other – it is for a tall woman. Seven yards for my mother; seven and a half yards for me' – adding, 'They must be cambric muslin.' In a shopping-centre such as Bath there was a vast choice of dress-fabrics to browse over, from woollen cloths such as kerseymere or worsted, through the mixes of wool and cotton, or wool and silk, such as bombazine, to fine supple silks and a variety of cottons – from heavy, plain calico and sturdy, striped dimity to jaconet muslins and the flimsiest gauzes. The light muslins were so popular that by 1823 the term 'a bit of muslin' had become slang for a racy, sexually available young woman. Though her ironic little homily in *Northanger Abbey* on 'the frivolous distinction' of fashion reminds Jane Austen's readers 'how little the heart of man . . . is biassed [*sic*] by the texture of their muslins', and points out that most men could not distinguish between 'the spotted, the sprigged, the mull or the jackonet [*sic*]', the author's own sympathies are clearly with eager Catherine Morland, lying awake before a ball, 'debating between her spotted and her tamboured [embroidered] muslin'.

A certain degree of interest in fashion and appearances is shown as entirely proper for a gentlewoman in Jane Austen's fiction. Even the modest, virtuous, and hard-up Fanny Price in *Mansfield Park*, faced with 'the how she should be dressed' for her first ball, is soon 'deep in the interesting subject' with her morally suspect, but impeccably elegant, rival in love, Mary Crawford. The outcome – predictably, to Regency readers – involves white muslin: in this case, Fanny's best gown, given to her as a bridesmaid's dress. Wearing it earlier in the novel, for a small dinner-party, Fanny had feared lest she seem 'too fine', but was assured by the hero, Edmund, 'A woman can never be too fine while she is all in white.'

Though a spectrum of colours could be worn, from dove-grey, pink and yellow to the poppy-red 'coquelicot' (which, Jane noted in 1798), 'is to be all the fashion this winter'), the simple, seductive white gown remained a symbol of elegance throughout her adult life. In *Northanger Abbey*, one of the few pieces of advice which Mrs Allen gives her innocent charge is 'Wear a white gown. Miss Tilney always wears white.' Writing from Bath, in 1801, Jane confided that two new acquaintances were 'so civil, and their gowns look so white and nice . . . that I cannot utterly abhor them'. It was to be expected that her prim, pretty sister Cassandra would own 'a large stock of white morning gowns'.

A taste for 'finery' is always a mark of an inferior character, in Jane Austen's world. The upstart Mrs Elton, in *Emma*, knows enough of well-bred society to pretend to disdain fashion, insisting, 'Nobody can think less of dress in general than I do'; but though she claims to have 'quite a horror of finery', her conversation continually betrays a hankering for pearls and lace, trimmings and ornaments. One speech on her preference for 'simplicity of dress' ends complacently, 'I have some notion of putting such a trimming as this to my white and silver poplin. Do you think it will look well?' The most vulgar of all Jane Austen's female characters, plain, ageing Miss Steele in *Sense and Sensibility*, is embarrassingly concerned with dress: she sports girlish pink ribbons, and a hat with a feather and a bow, in the vain hope of catching a 'beau', and shows an impertinent interest in 'the value and make' of others' attire. 'La! if you have not got your spotted muslin on! – I wonder you was not afraid of its being torn' is her parting shot to Elinor, after a dramatic meeting in Kensington Gardens. Personal remarks – however flattering – are not good manners; and while *nouveau riche* Mrs Elton bestows, and demands, fulsome compliments, the impoverished (but well-bred) old Miss Bates greets Emma's appearance at a ball with 'Must not compliment, I know . . . that would be rude.'

Jane Austen's own highest praise for a female character or acquaintance is to describe her as 'elegant'. The contemporary magazines and journals used a variety of words to express the same combination of good looks and good breeding: the '*ton*' or '*ton*ish' denoted one of the select, polished few who set the tone for the rest of society; a 'first-rater' (borrowed from the naval term for a leading ship of the line) indicated a woman of real style, with a dash of spirit and 'brilliancy'. The most appealing women in Jane Austen's writings, however, invariably possess 'elegance' – as opposed to the 'resolute stilishness' of flashy Isabella Thorpe, or the 'smartness of air' of the two-faced younger Steele sister. Not only heroines, but attractive minor characters, from the heiress Miss Tilney to the former governess Mrs Weston, display this all-important quality; and it is largely the corrupt Miss Crawford's outward 'elegance' which enables her to blind the hero of *Mansfield Park*, Edmund, to her true nature for much of the novel. The ultimate sartorial sin – as Beau Brummell had taught the polite world, from royalty downwards – was vulgar ostentation of any kind; and generations of readers would relish Mrs Elton's discomfiture on finding that at Emma's wedding to Mr Knightley, since the couple had 'no taste for finery or parade', there were 'very little white satin', and 'very few lace veils'.

Following fashion too slavishly was a folly against which magazines sternly warned their readers. What late twentieth-century journalists would dub 'fashion victims', their early nineteenth-century counterparts criticized as 'females [who] disfigure themselves by blindly following the fashions'. An 1807 article in *La Belle Assemblée* reminded readers that 'absurdity kills taste', citing such recent 'disgusting and atrocious' modes as rings set with stones from the Bastille, and earrings shaped like golden guillotines. The innately conservative Jane Austen would not have indulged in such excesses; but she adopted some of the more pleasing trends of the day with enthusiasm – from long sleeves, even for evening wear, in

1814, to lower waists, when they came into vogue in 1809. In 1798, when Nelson's victory at the Battle of the Nile had created a craze for all things Egyptian, she mentioned wearing a 'Mamelouc', or Mameluke, cap (probably turban-shaped), telling Cassandra importantly, 'It is all the fashion.' Public events, from royal celebrations and crises to the Peninsular campaigns, were reflected in such styles as the 'Regency walking-dress', and the 'Vittoria cloak'; in 1799 Jane reported adding 'a black military feather' to a cap, remarking, 'I think it makes me look more like Lady Conyngham now . . . which is all that one lives for now.' As a stout matron, in the 1820s, Lady Conyngham would become the former Regent's much-caricatured mistress; in the late 1790s, however, she was an acknowledged 'first-rater'.

Practicality, as well as elegance, had to be considered in an age when such minor hazards as a cold, or wet feet, could lead to an untreatable 'consumption', and early death. Jane Austen's letters more than once reported the death of a young friend; and in her fiction the risk of catching cold is taken seriously. Jane Bennet's 'violent cold', in *Pride and Prejudice*, causes real alarm to her friends and family; in *Sense and Sensibility* 'the imprudence of sitting in her wet shoes and stockings', coupled with depression and self-neglect, gives Marianne Dashwood a fever which leads to a near-fatal illness. (It is Marianne, ironically, who scorns Colonel Brandon for wearing 'the constitutional safeguard' of a flannel waistcoat – flannel being a loosely woven, somewhat coarse, woollen cloth.) With the flimsy gowns of the period, warm outer clothing was essential, and Jane Austen often mentions such important over-garments as spencers, pelisses and shawls. The spencer – reputedly named after the 2nd Earl Spencer, in the 1790s – was a short, fitted, waist-length jacket, which could be made of silk, velvet or warmer fabrics: 'My kerseymere Spencer is quite the comfort of our Even^g. walks', Jane wrote during a spell of 'cold, disagreeable weather' at Godmersham, in June 1808.

While the spencer was generally long-sleeved, with a high collar, the pelisse – cut more like a long coat or tunic – could be sleeveless and collarless, though it too followed the slender lines of the dress. Over these might be draped a variety of loose shawls and cloaks, from silk or muslin wraps, often home-made (like Jane Austen's own muslin cloak, still pre-served) to luxurious Eastern imports, such as Lady Bertram commissions Fanny Price's sailor brother, in *Mansfield Park*, to bring her from his next tour of duty. 'I wish he may go to the East Indies, that I may have my shawl', she remarks self-centredly. 'I think I will have two shawls.'

Made, originally, from the hair of the Tibetan shawl-goat, and imported from Kashmir (hence the terms 'shawl' and 'cashmere'), the early shawls were usually oblong, and woven with the traditional small pine-cone design. As skilful Scottish and English weavers picked up and adapted the fashion, the prevailing motifs enlarged into distinctive 'Paisley' patterns, and large square shawls became increasingly popular. As well as offering warmth and protection, shawls provided fleeting opportunities for physical contact between men and women: in *Mansfield Park*, Fanny is deprived of the pleasure of a moment's touch from the hero, Edmund, who is taking her shawl from a servant to place round her shoulders, and has to submit instead to the libertine Mr Crawford's 'quicker hand' and 'more prominent attention' in performing the office.

Conforming to the ideals of lightly-shod classical statuary, shoes for indoor and evening wear, in the 1790s, had become insubstantial flat-heeled slippers, which could be made of silk or satin, as well as of fine leather. Such footwear was too del-icate for much outdoor use: when the heroine's sister, in *Emma*, anxious to return home to her children before a snow-fall, insists, 'I should not mind walking . . . I could change my shoes, you know, the moment I got home', her husband retorts derisively, 'You are prettily shod for walking home, I dare say. It will be bad enough for the horses.' For the worst conditions, such as snow or mud, women still had the option of wearing pattens – clog-like overshoes, raised from the ground on a high, hollow, iron ring. One of the street-noises which strike Anne Elliot, arriving in rainy Bath in *Persuasion*, is 'the ceaseless clink of pattens'; in *Northanger Abbey*, on her tour of the Tilneys' great house, Catherine Morland notes that wherever they went, 'some pattened girl stopped to curtsey'. According to Jane Austen's nephew J. E. Austen-Leigh, she and Cassandra, in 'dirty' weather, 'took long walks in pattens'; but in general, by her adult years such coarse footwear had been 'banished from good society'. More elegant, if less weatherproof, were the ankle-length half-boots mentioned in several of Jane Austen's works. As the foppish Lord Osborne observes in her unfinished novel *The Watsons*, 'Nothing sets off a neat ankle more than a half-boot; nankin galoshed with black looks very well.' Nankin, or nankeen, a strong snuff-coloured cotton twill, was named after Nanking in China, where it originated; the galoshing described the lower, leather section around the foot. Half-boots were sturdy enough for light walks; in *Emma*, matchmaking Emma Woodhouse is out walking, in December, with her protégée Harriet and the vicar when she deliberately breaks the lace on her half-boot, so as to leave them together while she seeks 'a bit of ribband or string' as a replacement. Nevertheless, as the heroine of *The Watsons* quellingly tells Lord Osborne, 'Unless they are so stout as to injure their beauty, they are not fit for Country walking.'

Faces, as well as feet, required protection from the weather, and both umbrellas and parasols are mentioned by Jane Austen. During her youth, folding oilcloth umbrellas were available, but were looked on as somewhat feminine accessories; by the early 1800s, however, the French Incroyables and the British dandies had brought them increasingly into use for gentlemen. According to the memoirs of the Regency man-about-town Captain Gronow, the Duke of Wellington was obliged to ban umbrellas from the field of battle during the

Napoleonic Wars, as Guards officers were carrying them to protect their gorgeous, gold-laced uniforms; they were, however, permitted to those on ceremonial duties, in London. In *Persuasion*, completed in 1816, the rugged naval-officer hero Captain Wentworth has no qualms about carrying one: 'I have equipped myself . . . for Bath, you see (pointing out a new umbrella)', he tells Anne Elliot, on meeting her in the city which Jane Austen considered depressingly prone to rain. Though Anne's father, the vain Sir Walter, inveighs against weatherbeaten men who neglect their looks, only women were expected to shield their faces from the sun with parasols. In *Sanditon*, Jane's last, unfinished work, Mrs Parker proposes to buy her daughter 'a little Parasol . . . How Grave she will walk about with it, and fancy herself quite a little Woman'; as for their sons, however, her husband declares robustly, 'I would rather *them* run about in the sunshine than not.'

Jane Austen herself seemed to consider slightly suntanned skin a positive attraction in a woman. Of beautiful Marianne Dashwood, in *Sense and Sensibility*, she comments, 'Her skin was very brown', and her favourite heroine, Elizabeth Bennet in *Pride and Prejudice*, becomes 'rather tanned' through 'travelling in the summer' – which Mr Darcy evidently finds becoming. Whether consciously or not, she may have been influenced by her own colouring, as the rosy cheeks of her early years turned increasingly sallow with illness, so that she cheerfully described herself, in 1816, as 'black and white and every wrong colour'. In general, however, the contemporary fashion was for a fair, unblemished complexion. During the bewigged and whaleboned Georgian era of Jane's childhood, cosmetics had been heavily used, to create a doll-like effect of darkened eyebrows, whitened, powdered skin and rouged cheeks – but such garish artifice, often based on dangerous ingredients such as white lead and mercury, had been discredited amid the new vogue for naturalness and ease of the 1790s. By 1809, the fashion magazines were again recommending a discreet hint of rouge; Ackermann's *Repository*, while warning against unwholesome cosmetics, advocated a touch of the vegetable dye carmine, pressed into a ball and dabbed on with cotton-wool. 'If she would only wear rouge, she would not be afraid of being seen', the appearance-conscious Sir Walter Elliot complains of a middle-aged friend in *Persuasion*; for younger women he urges 'constant use of Gowland' – a popular skin-tonic, advertised in the *Bath Chronicle*. To Gowland's Lotion Sir Walter attributes (with equal inaccuracy) an improvement in coarse young Mrs Clay's 'disfiguring' freckles, and his daughter Anne's return to bloom and beauty, as love re-enters her life. Jane Austen herself, like modest Anne Elliot, would probably have used 'nothing at all' by way of cosmetics and lotions; but she may have liked Steele's Lavender Water as a refreshing scent, since she commissioned Cassandra to buy two bottles of it for a friend, in 1801.

Powdered hair, like painted faces, ceased to be fashionable in the post-Revolution 1790s. In Britain, a tax on hair-powder, imposed in 1795, hastened the decline in its use, particularly among the young and *ton*ish – though older, staider gentlemen continued to wear it until well into the nineteenth century. (In *Pride and Prejudice*, published in 1813, Mr Bennet still wears 'a powdering-gown', to protect his clothes from the starch-based substance, which could be tinted blue, or flaxen, as well as white; as late as 1816, Admiral Croft in *Persuasion* has 'a dab of powder' over his few remaining hairs.) The carefully-dishevelled hairstyles of the swaggering French Incroyables were echoed, in Britain, in the flowing, unpowdered locks of rebels and Romantics such as the poets Southey and Coleridge; by 1799 even Jane Austen's relatively conventional naval officer brother, Charles, had given up powder and opted for a natural-looking short 'crop' – to the evident annoyance of their staid, rich, country-squire brother Edward. 'I thought Edward would not approve of Charles being a crop', Jane wrote to Cassandra. Short hair, brushed forward in a classically-inspired 'Titus' or 'Brutus' cut, became the norm for younger men, however – and some more daring women took up the fashion, including Jane Austen's pretty, headstrong niece Anna, aged 15. 'Anna will not be surprised that the cutting off her hair is very much regretted by several of the party', Jane reported from a family gathering at Godmersham in 1808. Drily, she added, 'I am tolerably reconciled to it by considering that two or three years may restore it again'; but a year later she was still disconcerted by 'that sad cropt head'.

Her own wavy, mid-brown hair – a lock of which is preserved at Chawton – was worn plaited and pinned up at the back, and brushed forward into short, soft curls round her face. Like the poor, but 'elegant', Jane Fairfax in *Emma*, Jane Austen could wash and style her own hair before a ball, but when possible she had it professionally done. Staying at Godmersham in 1805 she shared the services of a visiting hairdresser, Mr Hall, who charged her sister-in-law '5s for every time of dressing her hair' and the same for teaching her lady's maid his techniques, but asked Jane only 2s 6d for a complete cut and style. 'He certainly respects either our Youth or our Poverty', she wrote with amusement to Cassandra. From London, in 1813, she reported, Mr Hall 'curled me out at a great rate. I thought it looked hideous . . . but my companions silenced me by their admiration.' Curls were achieved by wrapping the hair round curl-papers; in one of the few specific references to hairdressing in Jane Austen's novels, she introduces the heroine's friend in *The Watsons*, on the evening of a ball, as 'a genteel looking girl of 22, with her hair in papers'.

The most important reference to hair in her fiction occurs in *Emma*, when lively, good-looking Frank Churchill travels sixteen miles to London, and back again, in a day, purportedly just to have his hair cut. In fact, he has gone to order a piano, to be sent anonymously to his secret fiancée, Jane Fairfax; but while his alibi is believed, he has to bear the stigma of 'foppery and nonsense', for taking so much trouble over his appearance. His indulgent father 'called him a coxcomb' – and to Jane Austen and her readers, as to Beau Brummell and his dandy set, a coxcomb (like a fop) was not a figure to respect. The ill-mannered poseur Robert Ferrars, in *Sense and Sensibility*, is described as 'a great coxcomb', with an affected, neck-twisting bow and a taste for finery which allows him to linger interminably over the choice of a toothpick-case in a jeweller's shop, hovering between 'the ivory, the gold and the pearls', while ladies wait patiently to be served. Ferrars is not 'gentlemanlike' – unlike his unassuming brother Edward, whose 'simple taste' is dwelt on. Just as Jane Austen's heroines are always 'elegant', so her heroes are invariably 'gentleman-like'; haughty Mr Darcy – himself a master of the cutting, Brummell-esque 'put-down' – is deeply chastened by Elizabeth Bennet's rebuke, 'Had you behaved in a more gentlemanlike manner . . .'.

From Darcy – perhaps the ultimate Regency fictional hero – to reticent Edward Ferrars, all the gentlemen in Jane Austen's novels would have dressed in a strikingly uniform style. By day, a coat of dark cloth, double-breasted and high-collared, was worn over a buff waistcoat, with breeches and riding boots, or longer, close-fitting pantaloons and calf-length, tasseled Hessian boots – a costume as becoming to the male figure and appearance as the clinging female dress of the time was to a woman. For evening, men's clothes had acquired a gorgeous severity: in the ball-scenes at Netherfield, Mansfield Park and the Crown Inn at Highbury, Jane Austen's heroes would have led their partners down the set in immaculate tailcoats of black or dark blue cloth, cut high at the waist in front, over light breeches, silk stockings and pumps, or slender, sober, dark trousers, buckled at the foot. Under Brummell's all-pervading influence, a trace of starch had been introduced into the fine linen cravats which the women in Jane Austen's world stitched for their menfolk; in 1813, when *Pride and Prejudice* appeared, Mr Darcy's air of hauteur would have been heightened by the expanse of crisp linen artfully folded and tied beneath his well-bred chin. Though few, Jane Austen's references to men's clothes are highly effective: Mr Bingley's blue coat (the dandy colour); Colonel Brandon's sedate flannel waistcoat; and land-owning Mr Knightley's country leather gaiters – all are mentioned only in passing, yet contribute vividly to the reader's impressions. The glimpse of Henry Tilney, in *Northanger Abbey*, driving his curricle – 'His hat sat so well, and the innumerable capes of his great-coat looked so becomingly important' – is in almost poignant contrast to the sketch of the other 'gentleman-coachman' in the novel, the 'stout' and 'ungraceful' John Thorpe, who 'seemed fearful of being too handsome, unless he wore the dress of a groom'. And in *Emma*, the vignette of Frank Churchill giving custom to local trades-men by buying some gloves at Ford's shop in Highbury, hovering between 'sleek, well-tied parcels' of fashionable 'Men's Beavers' and 'York Tan' shades, shows him as a charm-ing, yet faintly trifling, character, in contrast to the novel's true hero, strong, plain-dealing Mr Knightley.

Shopping, a recurring theme of Jane Austen's letters and novels, is not, in general, shown as a masculine activity. Apart from Frank's propitiatory purchase at Ford's, and Robert Ferrars's foppish deliberations over his choice of a toothpick-case, when her male characters shop it is usually for the benefit of women. Henry Tilney chooses muslins for his sister; Frank Churchill buys a piano at Broadwood's, in London, for Jane Fairfax; Elinor Dashwood's half-brother John visits Gray's, the jeweller's, to order a seal for his spoilt wife Fanny. Jane Austen's brothers, and her fictional gentlemen, might have frequented such fashionable London establishments as Lock, the hatters at No. 6 St James's, or – also still thriving today – the wine-merchants Berry Bros and Rudd, at No. 3, where customers from Beau Brummell to Lord Byron had themselves weighed on the shop's great scales, and the results carefully recorded, 'in half-boots, boots, or boots and great-coats'. But these, like the great tailors of the day such as Weston or Stultz, whose skill at cutting and fitting cloth helped to make British men's clothes internationally admired for generations to come, were evidently of small concern to Jane Austen and her readers, compared with the endless charms of London linen-drapers and Bath milliners. Jane's letters from London were full of accounts of her expeditions to shops such as Grafton House, linen-drapers, in New Bond Street; Newton's (another linen-draper), in Leicester Square; and the silk-mercer's Layton and Shears, at Bedford House in Covent Garden – forerunners of the great department stores of the Victorian era. The details of these shopping-trips often had a timeless ring: in April 1811 she wrote that at Grafton House, 'the whole counter was thronged, and we waited *full* half an hour before we could be attended to'. She was, however, 'very well-satisfied' with her eventual purchases, which included bugle-bead trimming at 2s 4d, and three pairs of silk stockings for less than 12 shillings a pair. Two years later, she reported, 'By going very early we got immediate attendance', adding, 'We must have been 3 qrs of an hour at Grafton House, Edward [their brother] sitting by all the time with wonderful patience.' More convenient was Bedford House, at 21 Henrietta Street, where their brother Henry lived (at No. 10), from 1813. There, in September 1813, Jane found 'Very pretty English poplins at 4/3d; Irish ditto at 6s; *more* pretty, certainly – beautiful'. These excursions provided her with material for fiction, as well as gowns: she brought a seasoned shopper's eye to such glimpses as Harriet Smith, in *Emma*, 'hanging over muslins and changing her mind', or the younger Bennet sisters, in *Pride and Prejudice*, strolling about the market town of Meryton, on the look-out for officers, but always ready to be distracted by 'a very smart bonnet indeed, or a really new muslin in a shop window'. Flirting and shopping, then as now, were key ingredients in a popular 'women's' novel.

Jane Austen's aversion to 'finery and parade' seemed to

extend even to the uniforms of the soldiers so irresistible to Lydia Bennet and her like. The dress of the British army was reaching its most gorgeous phase during the Regency: from the rakish sabretaches and fur-trimmed pelisses of the Hussars and Dragoons, and the scarlet, gold-laced tunics of the line and Militia regiments, to the handsome dark green jackets of Wellington's recently formed Rifles, the 'regimentals' of the period lent an almost theatrical swagger to any officer who wore them. (Even the Prince Regent, who never saw military action but loved dressing-up, appeared to advantage in the waist-nipping, silver-laced tunic of the 10th Hussars, Brummell's old regiment, which he commanded.) Throughout Jane Austen's novels, characters acknowledge the appeal of military dress. 'There is no resisting a Cockade, my dear', Mr Edwards jokes in *The Watsons*; while Mrs Bennet, in *Pride and Prejudice*, remarks, 'I can remember the time when I liked a red coat myself, very well.' Her daughter Lydia's pursuit of officers is central to the novel's plot – and even intelligent Elizabeth Bennet almost has her level head turned by the rakish Wickham, handsomest of all the -shire Militia. For Jane Austen herself, however, Wellington's army evidently held no such allure. ('The first soldier that ever I sighed for', was her trenchant comment on one popular military author, in 1813.) Though her brother Henry held a commission in the Oxfordshire Militia – to the delight of his worldly wife, Eliza de Feuillide – Jane seemed to associate the eye-catching army uniform in general with heartless flirts, such as Captain Tilney of the 12th Light Dragoons, or downright rogues, such as Wickham. Her own preference was for the cocked hat and brass-buttoned blue coat of Nelson's navy; and the moment in *Mansfield Park* when, for the first time, Fanny Price sees her brother William in his naval Lieutenant's uniform – looking 'all the taller, firmer and more graceful for it' – and promptly bursts into tears is clearly written from the heart.

The inspiration for the 'very pretty amber cross' which

William Price brings Fanny from a tour of duty in the Mediterranean was obviously the 'Topaze' crosses which Lieutenant Charles Austen bought for his sisters Jane and Cassandra, in 1801, with some of his naval prize money. 'Of what use is it to take prizes if he lays out the produce in presents to his sisters?' Jane scolded tenderly, adding, 'We shall be unbearably fine.' These topaz crosses – still fashionable today – were typical of the pretty, understated jewellery of the period. Simpler dress-codes, the changing social climate and a burgeoning middle-class market helped to create a demand for affordable, wearable jewellery; and in place of the stately early Georgian designs, glittering with magnificent stones, the early nineteenth century saw a vogue for semi-precious gems such as topaz, garnet and peridot, in decorative, often neo-classical, settings. Branching chandelier earrings gave way to simple drop-shapes; grand parures were replaced by the single row of pearls, or corals. Elinor Dashwood's purpose in visiting Gray's is 'the exchange of a few old-fashioned jewels of her mother'; Frank Churchill, mentioning that his late, rich aunt's jewels are being given to his fiancée, Jane, stresses, 'They are to be new set.' His plans for their remodelling include 'an ornament for the head' – probably meaning one of the Spanish-style combs, or jewelled, plume-shaped 'aigrette' sprays, then in fashion. Hair-ornaments complemented the simple, unpowdered Regency coiffures – just as bracelets and bangles were seen to advantage on the bare arms of the period, and were accordingly much worn. (In *Pride and Prejudice*, Mr Bingley's married sister is 'principally occupied in playing with her bracelets and rings' on a dull evening at Netherfield.)

Such bracelets and rings often featured cameos: these semi-precious, carved stones, so redolent of classical antiquity, were also popular worn singly, as a large brooch at the bosom. The low, bare necklines of the time allowed several ornaments to be worn together; even chaste Fanny Price eventually wears two necklaces with her brother's cross – the ornate chain pressed upon her by Mary Crawford, and the 'perfectly simple and neat' gold chain presented to her by the hero, Edmund, 'in all the niceness of jeweller's packing'. In choosing it, Edmund tells her, 'I consulted the simplicity of your taste'; significantly, while writing this novel, Jane Austen told Cassandra, in May 1813, 'I have bought your Locket . . . it is perfectly plain and neat, set in gold.' This locket cost 18 shillings, more than expected; but with their 'plain and neat' good taste neither Austen sister would have been drawn to the cheap trinkets, in paste or pinchbeck, which were widely available. Such jewellery could even be bought in libraries, while picking up the latest romance by Mrs Radcliffe; in the unfinished *Sanditon*, the heroine goes to buy 'new Parasols, new Gloves and new Brooches . . . at the Library', while in *Pride and Prejudice*, frivolous Lydia Bennet scribbles from Brighton that she has just been to the library, where she saw 'such beautiful ornaments as made her quite wild'.

Cheap or coarse clothes and accessories would not have attracted Jane Austen; her preference was always for quality and 'elegance' in dress. Writing of the purchase of some stockings, in 1800, she remarked to Cassandra, '[I] greatly prefer having only two pair of that quality to three of an inferior sort.' In dress, as in books, she had excellent taste; and at times she seemed to derive an almost equal pleasure from both. 'I have read the *Corsair*, mended my petticoat, & have nothing else to do', she reported in 1814, thus deftly reducing the effect of Lord Byron's latest poetic work to the level of darning clothes; some years earlier, while staying with the Lloyds, she had complained of having 'no variety of books or gowns' to divert her. Modest in her own appearance, she appreciated the nuances of others; and her novels are shot though with hints about character expressed in subtle references to clothes and appearances. No woman writer in English literature is more closely identified with a period of dress than Jane Austen;

and it is a tribute to her art and her powers that, with a minimum of description, she so exquisitely evokes character, and heightens atmosphere, through her passing references to 'the present fashions'.

4

'The Subject of Books'

'While I have *Udolpho* to read, I feel as if nobody could
make me miserable.'

Catherine Morland, in *Northanger Abbey*, 1817

In December 1798 Jane Austen told Cassandra that she had
received 'a very civil note' from a neighbour at Steventon
named Mrs Martin, inviting her to join a new circulating
library: the 'Collection . . . not to Consist only of Novels, but
of every kind of Literature, &c &c'. Though Jane promptly
signed up, she remarked, 'She might have spared this preten-
tion to *our* family, who are great Novel-readers, & not ashamed
of being so.' In literature, as in every other area of life, Jane
Austen had no patience with pretentiousness. She described
herself to the Prince Regent's pompous librarian, in 1815, as
'a Woman who . . . knows only her own mother-tongue, and
has read very little in that', and throughout her career she
championed the cause of popular fiction against the claims of
'enormous great stupid thick quarto volumes'; but she was, in
fact, an avid and erudite reader, whose love of plays and poetry,
travel-books and history – as well as the 'mere Trash' of
sentimental romances and Gothic horror-novels – would be
constantly in evidence, in all that she wrote herself.

As a child growing up at Steventon Rectory, Jane Austen
would have been familiar from an early age with some of the
greatest works in the English language, from the King James
Bible and Book of Common Prayer – in daily use by her

father – to the plays of Shakespeare, and the *Dictionary* of Dr Johnson. Like her own fictional vicar's daughter Catherine Morland, in *Northanger Abbey*, she was probably allowed to browse freely in her father's library of over five hundred volumes; and if at first, like Catherine, she was drawn to those which were 'all story and no reflexion', she also – like the more studious Fanny Price in *Mansfield Park* – had the benefit of a scholarly young relation (in Fanny's case her cousin Edmund Bertram, in Jane's, her eldest brother, James), who would take 'a large share in directing her reading and forming her taste'. The Austens were an academic family: the Revd George Austen was a former Oxford don, as well as a clergyman, and her mother the daughter of a Fellow of All Souls and niece of a Master of Balliol; but with their intellectual interests went a lively sense of fun, and puns and parodies, jokes, charades and word-games were as much a part of Jane Austen's literary education as her 'extensive reading' of the classic poetry and prose of Johnson and Richardson, Cowper and Crabbe.

Young Catherine Morland's spirited little critique, in *Northanger Abbey*, on the tedium of infant schooling – 'poor little children first learning their letters, and then learning to spell' – during which she equates 'to instruct' with 'to torment', might offer hints that Jane Austen did not find her own early lessons particularly agreeable. She retained into adulthood some erratic spellings ('freindship' and 'veiw' among them); and even in her revised, edited, published novels there would be the occasional fault of syntax, such as the dangling clause in Chapter IV of *Mansfield Park*: 'being a warm-hearted, unreserved woman, Mary had not been three hours in the house before she told her what she had planned' – in which 'she' refers not to the visiting Mary Crawford, but to her 'warm-hearted' hostess, Mrs Grant. A pupil as gifted as Jane Austen might well have been bored by Georgian children's books and alphabets, with their charming, but trite, moral and instructive tales and verses. In her own surviving copy of *The History of Goody Two-Shoes* (dating from about 1780, when Jane was about 5, and subsequently given to her niece Anna), several of the woodcut illustrations have been crudely coloured in, by an unknown childish hand; while her French primer *Fables Choisies* – inscribed neatly at the front, 'Miss Jane Austen 5th Decr 1783' – is embellished with pencil notes and underlinings in the text, and some scribbled words and practice-signatures, 'Frank Austen' and 'Jane Austen', at the end. A few years later, the 12-year-old Jane could not resist adding her own comments to the margins of her copy of Oliver Goldsmith's *History of England*: 'Oh! Oh! The Wretches!' she wrote indignantly beside a passage on Cromwell's anti-Stuart activities, and 'I do not like this', in response to an account of the Whig government's suppression of the Scottish Highlanders' wearing of their traditional kilts.

From scribbling in schoolbooks it was a short step for the young Jane Austen to producing her own first literary endeavours. Three manuscript notebooks survive, into which, as an adult, she carefully copied out a selection of her own early writings, dating from about 1787, when she was in her twelfth year, to mid-1793. Labelled, mock-importantly, *Volume The First*, *Volume The Second* and *Volume The Third*, as if they formed a three-volume published work, they contain a treasury of comic juvenile tales, playlets and poetry, and joke-moral essays, as well as hilarious youthful burlesques of popular history and sentimental fiction. The quality varies, but even the most rudimentary contain gems – as in *Frederic and Elfrida*: 'The Door suddenly opened & an aged gentleman with a sallow face & old pink Coat, partly by intention & partly thro' weakness was at the feet of the lovely Charlotte'; or, in *Jack and Alice*, 'Alice had too sincere a respect for Lady Williams & too great a relish for her Claret, not to make every concession in her power.' Though not arranged in chronological order within the volumes, the *Juvenilia* allow the modern reader not merely to enter into the 'fun and liveliness' of life at Steventon, but also to trace the development of Jane Austen's talent and technique as a writer, from the clever child, gleefully identifying and parodying literary silliness, to the maturing young woman, experimenting with narrative, character and dialogue, and already capable of such masterly burlesques as *The History of England* ('By a partial, prejudiced and ignorant Historian') and *Love and Freindship* [*sic*], her immortal skit on the sentimental novels in letter-form which she, her sister Cassandra and their circle so relished.

Completed in November 1791, when she was still only 15, Jane Austen's joke-*History* exposes the shortcomings of popular history in general, and of Oliver Goldsmith's best-selling *History of England*, and its 1774 *Abridgement*, in particular. Slangy, slapdash and biased, Jane's version – illustrated with exquisite, modern-dress portraits of the monarchs by Cassandra – provides a shameless vehicle for the sisters' own professed prejudices, such as antipathy for Elizabeth I ('that pest of Society') and passionate support for Mary, Queen of Scots. Many of its comments anticipate the classic twentieth-century spoof *1066 and All That* – as when she writes of Lady Jane Grey: 'an amiable young woman and famous for reading Greek while other people were hunting', or lists among the loyal supporters of Charles I, 'the King himself, ever stedfast [*sic*] in his own defence'. Yet, like the best parodists, she never loses sight of her originals: thus to Goldsmith's lyrical account of Anne Boleyn – 'Her features were regular, mild and attractive, her stature elegant, though below the middle size, while her wit and vivacity exceeded even her other allurements' – the young Jane Austen ripostes, 'This amiable Woman was entirely innocent of the Crimes with which she was accused, of which her Beauty, her Elegance and her Sprightliness were sufficient proofs.' Contemporary historical debates are duly noted, such as the doubts raised in 1767 by Horace Walpole, as to Richard III's guilt over the 'Princes in the Tower' murders: 'It has also been declared that he did *not* kill his two nephews', Jane records, building to the absurd climax, 'If Perkin Warbeck was really the Duke of York, why might not Lambert Simnel be the Widow of Richard.' She had read (or heard about) the historian John Whitaker's 1787 work *Mary, Queen of Scots Vindicated*, and discussed its theories with her friend Mrs Lefroy and her brother Edward's adoptive mother, Mrs Knight: in Jane's *History* Mary is described as 'this bewitching Princess whose only freind [*sic*] was then the Duke of Norfolk, and whose only ones are now Mr Whitaker, Mrs Lefroy, Mrs Knight and myself'.

The blurring of fact and fiction in historical writing was a topic which clearly interested her. She returned to it in *Northanger Abbey* (first drafted some seven years after her *History of England*, in 1798 or 1799) with a scene in which, discussing books with Henry Tilney and his 'elegant', rational sister, the naive heroine Catherine Morland laments the dullness of 'real solemn history', while remarking, 'Yet I often think it odd that it should be so dull, for a great deal of it must be invention . . . and invention is what delights me in other books.' Tactfully, Miss Tilney demurs, pointing out that despite the customary 'little embellishments', serious history must be based on sound research, and guiding Catherine towards the works of such respected contemporary historians as the eminent Scots Hume and Robertson.

False representations in works of fiction provided still more inviting material for Jane Austen during this early writing-period. Her 15-year-old production *Love and Freindship* ridicules almost every convention and cliché known to the sentimental popular novelist, from absurd characterization and preposterous plot-lines, to melodramatic dialogue and spurious morality. (To the twenty-first-century reader, terms such as 'bodice-ripper', 'Mills and Boon' and 'soap opera' may come to mind, as Jane's irresistible saga of long-lost relations, larceny, fatal road accidents and thwarted love unfolds.) Just as her mature masterpiece *Pride and Prejudice*, some twelve years later, would derive its title from a sentence in Fanny Burney's novel *Cecilia* – the whole 'unfortunate business . . . had been the result of Pride, and Prejudice' – so this apprentice-piece took its title and prefatory motto, 'Deceived in friendship and betrayed in love', from Goethe's 1774 Romantic landmark, *The Sorrows of Young Werther*. Jane Austen's opinion of the great Goethe may be inferred from a comment in Letter 12th of *Love and Freindship* when, on meeting a 'Sensible, well-informed and Agreable [*sic*] man', her heroine responds, 'But as we were convinced he had no soul, that he had never read the Sorrows of Werter, & that his Hair bore not the slightest resemblance to Auburn, we were certain that Janetta could feel no Affection for him, or at least that she ought to feel none.' Certainly Jane Austen's own heroes, from cool, haughty Mr Darcy to plain-dealing Mr Knightley, would have little in common with Goethe's brooding, melancholy Werther; and Edward Ferrars in her first published work, *Sense and Sensibility*, is deliberately presented virtually as an anti-hero, with the dampening words, 'He was not handsome, and his manners required intimacy to make them pleasing.' As the heroine's fervently Romantic-minded younger sister, Marianne Dashwood, laments – misguidedly – 'His eyes want all that spirit, that fire, which at once announce virtue and intelligence.'

The chief target of Jane Austen's early satire was such popular Georgian and Regency fiction as Agnes Maria Bennett's 1789 novel *Agnes de-Courci*, in which the hero, Edward, having inadvertently contracted an incestuous marriage, is discovered dead in a river, still wearing his wedding-clothes, 'embroidered in the first taste, with foil and spangles'. On a similar note, worthy of Miss Bennett's twentieth-century successor Barbara Cartland, Jane's heroes Edward and Augustus are found, in *Love and Freindship*, presenting 'the horrid Spectacle' of 'two gentlemen most elegantly attired but weltering in their blood', after a frightful accident in their 'fashionably high

Phaeton'. Yet the literary allusions scattered throughout the *Juvenilia* also involved some of Jane Austen's best-loved, most respected authors, from Shakespeare and Pope to Fanny Burney. For all her joking at the expense of Goldsmith's *History*, in which only one date, 6 May 1533, appears ('N.B. there will be very few dates in this History', warns the preface to hers), Goldsmith is the historian whom serious-minded Fanny Price, in *Mansfield Park*, chooses to discuss with her sister, and pupil, Susan. The great Georgian playwright and politician Richard Sheridan, whose works the young Austens acted at Steventon, is referred to several times, both overtly – as when his comedy *The Critic* is mentioned as a source of 'many interesting anecdotes' of King James I, in Jane's *History* – and implicitly: the endless fainting-fits in *Love and Freindship* (as in Letter 8th, which ends, 'We fainted Alternately on a Sofa') may owe something to the stage-direction in Act III of *The Critic*, 'They faint alternately in each other's arms.' To be parodied by the young Jane Austen was, in fact, tantamount to a tribute. An entire passage in *Love and Freindship* (Letter 13th) is based on the account of a visit to Glen Sheil by the critic, lexicographer and author whom Jane called 'my dear Dr Johnson', in his 1775 travel book, *A Journey to the Western Isles*. Even the classical satirist Alexander Pope, of whom she wrote fondly in 1813, 'There has been *one* infallible Pope in the world', was not exempt from her teasing: in her 1790s juvenile work *A Collection of Letters*, a gushing female declares, 'Ride where you may, Be Candid where You can', a reworking of Pope's celebrated line, 'Laugh where we must, be candid where we can', in his *Essay on Man* (1733).

Pope's maxim was one which, joking apart, Jane Austen evidently took to heart. The word 'candid', defined in her 'dear Dr Johnson's' *Dictionary* as 'free from malice, not desirous to find fault', would occur often in her writing: it is particularly applicable to Elizabeth Bennet's stance in *Pride and Prejudice*, when she states, 'I dearly love a laugh', but adds seriously, 'I hope I never ridicule what is wise or good', concluding, 'Follies and nonsense, whims and inconsistencies do divert me, I own, and I laugh at them whenever I can.' She might have been speaking in the author's own voice. Unlike many contemporary writers, Jane Austen almost never quotes from the Scriptures in her novels; humble, worthy Miss Bates's cheerful, if inaccurate, remark in *Emma*, 'Our lot is cast in a goodly heritage', is one notable exception. The Revd George Austen's daughter seemingly thought it unnecessary and inappropriate to introduce sacred texts into popular fiction. Yet she was ready to poke fun at pompous sermonizing, in any form. When the tedious clergyman Mr Collins, in *Pride and Prejudice*, on being asked to 'read aloud to the young ladies', chooses not a novel but Fordyce's *Sermons to Young Ladies*, the Bennet sisters are obviously bored, until rescued by the rudeness of Lydia, who interrupts with some gossip about servants. Books of sermons and moral instruction − as opposed to intelligent preaching from the pulpit − are rarely treated with any deference by Jane Austen; and though she was clearly well-acquainted with them, as evinced by her comment to her niece Anna in 1814, 'I am very fond of Sherlock's *Sermons*, prefer them to almost any', she would seem generally to have questioned both the interest and the usefulness of such 'books of a moral stamp'. (Before she had even seen it, she expressed a particular distaste for Hannah More's Evangelical novel of 1809, *Coelebs in Search of a Wife*, finding 'pedantry and affectation' in the title.) In her unfinished juvenile work *Catharine, or The Bower*, the heroine's puritanical aunt, having found her niece innocently tête-à-tête with a young man, laments, 'I bought you Blair's *Sermons*, and *Coelebs in Search of a Wife*, I . . . borrowed a great many good books of my Neighbours for you'; while in *Northanger Abbey*, Catherine Morland's mother seeks to cure her lovelorn daughter's listlessness by lending her *The Mirror*, 'a very clever essay . . . about young girls who have been spoilt for home by great acquaintance'. Mrs Morland's sagacious conclusion, 'I am sure it will do you good', is one which Jane clearly doubts. Cynical Mary Crawford, in *Mansfield Park*, speaks knowingly of Blair's *Sermons*; but they have had no effect on her conscience, or moral character.

What Jane Austen does, emphatically, believe in is the importance of wide reading, for women in particular. When pretentious Miss Bingley, in *Pride and Prejudice*, has listed the attainments she thinks necessary for 'an accomplished woman', Mr Darcy adds seriously, 'To all this she must yet add something more substantial, in the improvement of her mind by extensive reading.' All Jane Austen's heroines, either consciously or intuitively, support this view – from artless Catherine Morland, in *Northanger Abbey*, who, having no 'objection to books at all', finds herself enjoying the poetry of Pope and Gray and the plays of Shakespeare, as well as the 'mere trash' of love-stories and horror-fiction, to studious Fanny Price, whose current reading, in Chapter 16 of *Mansfield Park*, includes two of the author's own favourite works, Dr Johnson's essays from *The Idler* and the poet George Crabbe's 1812 publication, *Tales in Verse*. Witty, intelligent Elizabeth Bennet, in *Pride and Prejudice*, chooses to read a book rather than join in a fashionable card-game ('Do you prefer reading to cards?' enquires a shocked Mr Hurst); in *Emma*, the clever but self-deluding Emma Woodhouse constantly draws up schedules of 'steady reading' for herself and her protégée Harriet, only to abandon them in favour of chatter and amusement – it being 'easier to chat than to study'. Literary taste, in Jane Austen's world, is an invariable guide to character. Coarse, ignorant John Thorpe, in *Northanger Abbey*, roundly condemns all novels (including, implicitly, the great works of Sterne and Smollett, Richardson and Defoe), but singles out for hearty approval Mrs Radcliffe's horror-novels ('some fun and nature in *them*'), and the recent, sensational best-seller *The Monk*, by Matthew Lewis – a sample passage of which runs, 'Heedless of her tears, cries and entreaties, he gradually made himself master of her person, and desisted not from his prey till he had accomplished his crime and the dishonour of Antonia.' (Jane Austen must, presumably, have at least glanced at this sordid saga, to have mentioned it in her own writing.) In complete contrast, the decent, unassuming young farmer Robert Martin, in *Emma*, reads not only the agricultural reports – official papers, published regularly, on such topics as milk yields and crop rotation – but also, appropriately, Oliver Goldsmith's classic rural novel *The Vicar of Wakefield*, and that polite drawing-room staple the *Elegant Extracts*, an anthology of light poetry and prose, with which he entertains his sisters and their guest. It is to his credit that he has never heard of Harriet's schoolgirlish favourites, Mrs Radcliffe's *The Romance of the Forest* and *The Children of the Abbey*, and still more so that he promptly and courteously promises to get hold of them, on her recommendation.

Conversations about books and writers play a central role in Jane Austen's novels, as in her life. Her letters are strewn with comments on her current reading: 'Ought I to be very much pleased with *Marmion?* – as yet I am not'; 'We are reading *Clarentine*, and are surprised to find how foolish it is'; 'We have got *Roseanne* in our Society, and find it much as you describe it; very good and clever, but tedious.' In her juvenile work *Catharine*, or *The Bower*, the heroine, Kitty – 'herself a great reader, tho' perhaps not a very deep one' – on meeting a new friend, Camilla, is 'eager to know that their sentiments as to Books were similar', with disappointing results: Camilla's much-vaunted love of novels turns out to be as shallow and unreliable as her character. Just as Jane herself eagerly discussed Henry Fielding's racy classic *Tom Jones* with her young admirer Tom Lefroy, so 17-year-old Marianne Dashwood, in *Sense and Sensibility*, having established the attractive newcomer Willoughby's social credentials, proceeds rapidly to 'the subject of books', and is overjoyed to find that 'their taste was strikingly alike'. Significantly, her more level-headed sister,

Elinor, comments that she has now learned her lover's opinion on 'almost every matter of importance. You know what he thinks of Cowper and Scott . . . and you have received every assurance of his admiring Pope no more than is proper.' Beneath the somewhat tart teasing, there is a valid point, which Regency readers would have understood: in identifying so passionately with Romantic literature, and rejecting the rational, classical moderation of writers such as Alexander Pope, Marianne is wilfully casting herself in the role of star-crossed heroine, and courting a tragic fate. She constantly indulges her impulses and feelings at the expense of her reason – with the misguided support of her over-emotional mother. 'Common sense, common care, common prudence, were all sunk in Mrs Dashwood's romantic delicacy', the author notes, with concern.

It is a central irony of this novel that the man whom Marianne casts as her idealized 'hero of a favourite story', Willoughby, turns out to be a very different stock character from fiction, the callous seducer, while Colonel Brandon – initially dismissed by Marianne as old and dull – is revealed, as the work progresses, to have all the characteristics of a true Romantic hero. Having been parted from his childhood sweetheart, after an attempted elopement, he has rescued her from a squalid back-street death, raised her illegitimate child by another man, despite society's slurs, and even, in the course of the novel, fought a duel with the licentious Willoughby. (This action was doubly intrepid, since by 1811, when *Sense and Sensibility* was published, duels had long been illegal, though they were still fought on occasion by men of honour, from the Duke of Wellington himself to such eminent politicians as Pitt and Castlereagh.)

Marianne Dashwood's favourite authors, predictably, are the leading Romantic poets James Thomson, William Cowper and Walter Scott; had *Sense and Sensibility* appeared a year later, no doubt Lord Byron, whose verse epic *Childe*

Harold was published in 1812, would have been another of her literary idols. 'I awoke one morning and found myself famous', Byron wrote, with dramatic understatement: in fact, the frenzy of public adulation which surrounded this handsome, aristocratic, young cult-figure was to be unequalled until the twentieth century. Women were said to faint on meeting him; the crowds of sightseers who drove past his lodgings caused carriage congestion all down fashionable St James's. Dubbed 'Mad, bad and dangerous to know' by his tempestuous mistress Lady Caroline Lamb, the poet was himself as much the archetype of the brooding, soulful, Byronic hero as his creations Childe Harold, Don Juan and the Corsair. Jane Austen, naturally, had no intention of succumbing to Byron-mania. 'I have read *The Corsair*, mended my petticoat, & have nothing else to do', she wrote equably to Cassandra in 1814; in *Persuasion*, published two years later, the literary discussion between her heroine Anne Elliot and the bereaved, sensitive young Captain Benwick includes a gentle joke at the expense of many a Byron devotee. Having admired 'the richness of the present age', and singled out for praise Scott and Byron, the conversation progresses from 'whether *Marmion* or *The Lady of the Lake* were to be preferred', to 'how ranked the *Giaour* and *The Bride of Abydos*' – culminating with the ingenuous aside, 'and moreover, how the *Giaour* was to be pronounced'. Few literary exchanges in Jane Austen's fiction are more revealing than this one. Anne – who, like Elinor Dashwood, finds herself counselling others while secretly nursing a broken heart herself – is concerned that young Benwick, by revelling in 'all the tenderest songs of the one poet, and all the impassioned descriptions of hopeless agony of the other', is feeding, and prolonging, his own grief. Her advice is bracing: Benwick should indulge his emotions with less Romantic poetry, and take in 'a larger allowance of prose', from 'the works of our best moralists' and 'collections of the finest letters', to those 'memoirs of characters of worth and suffering' which would 'rouse and fortify the mind'. Wide reading, as ever, is Jane Austen's prescription for moral and intellectual health.

It was not the works of the Romantics themselves, but rather the over-heated reactions of some impressionable readers with which she took issue, in her own novels. (While the bereaved young Captain Benwick is described as having 'a melancholy air, just as he ought to have', so the ardent adolescent Marianne Dashwood 'would have been ashamed to look her family in the face' had she either eaten or slept after parting from her beloved Willoughby.) The title of *Sense and Sensibility* reflects its ironic examination of attitudes to contemporary literature, as well as life. The Swiss-born writer–philosopher Jean-Jacques Rousseau, who not only gave the French Revolution the slogan '*Liberté, Egalité, Fraternité*' but also helped to create the Romantic movement, with its emphasis on nature and mankind's essential innocence, attributed all his acts and impulses to 'Sensibility' – the capacity for feeling. Jane Austen certainly did not lack for feeling; and several leading Romantics, notably Cowper and Scott, were among her favourite poets, as they were Marianne's. But unlike Benwick, Marianne, and the 'downright silly' literary poseur Sir Edward Denham, in her last, unfinished novel *Sanditon*, she did not believe in the indulgence of emotion at the expense of common sense. The nature-poet Cowper, lyrical precursor of Wordsworth, is mentioned frequently and fondly in her letters and works – from Mr Knightley's reference to 'Cowper and his fire at twilight', in *Emma*, to her own comment, when planning the Austen family's garden at their Southampton lodgings, in 1809, 'I could not do without a Syringa, for the sake of Cowper's Line. – We talk also of a Laburnam.' (Both references are to Cowper's *The Task*; the latter, to his lines, 'Laburnam, rich/In streaming gold; syringa, iv'ry pure'.) Nevertheless, Jane's sympathies are with Elinor Dashwood, as she tries to curb 'the excess of her sister's sensibility', pointing out the impracticalities of untamed nature, and remarking, 'It is not everyone ... who has your passion for dead leaves.' Marianne's regeneration is assured, at the end of the novel, when she reflects soberly, 'My own feelings had prepared my sufferings', and announces – inevitably – her intention of embarking on a course of broad, 'serious' reading.

One of the authors about whom Elinor and her like-minded lover, Edward, tease Marianne is William Gilpin, the Cumbrian clergyman whose writings on British scenery, as observed during a series of sketching-tours, did much to promote the late eighteenth- and early nineteenth-century cult of the 'Picturesque' – meaning that formation of landscape and scenic features which would 'look well in a picture'. Here again Jane Austen is making sport with one of her own favourite writers, since, according to her brother Henry's 'Biographical Notice', published with *Persuasion* in 1817, 'at a very early age she was enamoured of Gilpin on the Picturesque'. In her juvenile *History of England* Gilpin is listed among the 'first of Men', next to Delamere, dashing hero of Charlotte Smith's 1788 novel *Emmeline, or The Orphan of the Castle*; while the most rational female in *Love and Freindship* – that brilliant early burlesque on the cult of sensibility – undertakes a tour of Scotland, inspired by Gilpin's *Observations* on the Highlands. The balanced, rational approach to Gilpin's works is illustrated by Henry Tilney and his charming sister in *Northanger Abbey*, when they educate the heroine Catherine Morland in an appreciation of natural beauty through 'the eyes of persons accustomed to drawing' – pointing out the importance of perspective and composition, 'with all the eagerness of real taste'. Marianne Dashwood, by contrast, rhapsodizes with sentimental exaggeration over Gilpin, whom she calls 'him who first defined what picturesque beauty was', until Edward is provoked into responding, 'I like a fine prospect, but not on picturesque principles. I do not like crooked, twisted, blasted trees. I admire them much more if they are tall, straight and flourishing. I am not fond of nettles, or thistles . . . and a troop of tidy, happy villagers please me better than the finest banditti in the world.' This passage must have pleased Jane Austen's brothers James and Henry: in 1789, their Oxford undergraduate magazine *The Loiterer* had censured 'that excess of sentiment and susceptibility which the works of the great Rousseau chiefly introduced', concluding – much as would *Sense and Sensibility*, some twenty years later – that 'restraint and government contribute to happiness'.

Use of language, like taste in reading, is a sure guide to character in Jane Austen's world. Oafish, stupid John Thorpe, in *Northanger Abbey* – a youth of the type known in Regency slang as a 'Yahoo', after the vicious sub-humans in Jonathan Swift's 1726 novel *Gulliver's Travels* – is the only young man who swears in her fiction, with his repeated use of 'Oh! d--n it', in front of ladies. Pretentious Mrs Elton, in *Emma*, affects a fashionable knowledge of Italian, calling her husband 'my *caro sposo*', but betrays her ignorance by varying the phrase, incorrectly, to '*cara sposo*'. (Almost as irksome, the author implies, is her use of the hackneyed term 'my lord and master', which ill-serves the dignity of married women.) The innately vulgar Lucy Steele, in *Sense and Sensibility*, belies her superficial attractions by glaring faults of grammar ('I felt sure you was angry with me'), as does immoral Lydia Bennet in *Pride and Prejudice* ('Mrs Forster and me are *such* friends'). Exaggeration is the hallmark of shallow, insincere characters such as Isabella Thorpe in *Northanger Abbey*, whose speech is larded with verbal excesses, from 'doat', 'frenzy' and 'extasy' [*sic*] to 'beautiful as an angel', 'amazingly shocking', and 'the sweetest girl in the world'. Yet such is Jane Austen's craftsmanship that on occasion a single, subtle word or phrase can convey a wealth of meaning – as when Edmund Bertram, in *Mansfield Park*, exclaims to Fanny Price, 'Hey day!' (her dashing rival Mary Crawford's characteristic expression); or as in the deft scene in

Pride and Prejudice in which shy young Maria Lucas, awed and excited by her first meeting with a real aristocrat, utters a shocked 'La! my dear' to Elizabeth Bennet, in what she clearly trusts is the usage of elegant conversation. There is nothing random about such linguistic details: writing to advise her aspiring novelist niece Anna on the craft of fiction, in 1814, Jane Austen constantly stressed the importance of realistic dialogue. Though she could be critical, as when she wrote, 'The scene with Mrs Mellish ... is prosy & nothing to the purpose', her comments, whenever possible, were encouraging. 'Mr St. J. – & Susan both talk in character & very well', she noted approvingly in September 1814.

Mimicry was evidently one of Jane Austen's talents; according to her brother Henry, reading aloud was another, particularly where her own works were concerned. (Her irritation on hearing *Pride and Prejudice* badly read to the family by her mother, when the first copy arrived at Chawton in 1813, could scarcely be concealed.) From childhood the young Austens were encouraged not only to read aloud, but also to act, recite, and play parlour-games such as riddles and charades – a habit in which they persisted. 'We admire your Charades excessively – but as yet have guessed only the 1st', Jane informed Cassandra in January 1813. The experience of hearing her brothers declaim poetry is surely reflected in *Mansfield Park*, in Tom Bertram's reminiscence, 'I am sure my name was Norval, every evening of my life, through one Christmas holidays', a reference to his schoolboy recitations from the popular eighteenth-century play *Douglas*, by John Home. Among the *Juvenilia* are a number of light-hearted verses, some evidently produced in response to amusing newspaper items, such as a play on 'The Marriage of Mr Gell of Eastbourne to Miss Gill', which begins, 'Of Eastbourne Mr Gell / From being perfectly well, / Became dreadfully ill / For the love of Miss Gill'. Not all the entries in her handwriting were her own inventions, however; among her original verses she copied out a stanza 'On the Universities', which had appeared in the ever-popular anthology, the *Elegant Extracts* – anticipating the scenes in *Emma* in which the heroine and her friend amuse themselves by copying out 'riddles of every sort', and inviting family and friends to contribute examples. ('In this age of literature, such collections on a very grand scale are not uncommon', the author drily notes.) While kindly, semi-senile Mr Woodhouse searches his memory for a verse beginning 'Kitty, a fair but frozen maid', first published in *The Lady's Magazine* in 1762, and written by the celebrated actor–manager David Garrick, author of the patriotic song 'Heart of Oak', the sly, self-seeking clergyman Mr Elton, without telling a direct lie, lets it be thought that his contribution – a charade on the word 'Courtship' – is his own invention. In fact, like his other offering (a play on the word 'Woman'), this appears in a 2-volume anthology of 1761, entitled *A New Collection of Enigmas, Charades, Transpositions &c.* *Emma* is a novel of games and hidden meanings between people, and the theme of word-play vividly underscores the point. Even bluff Mr Weston gallantly produces a conundrum, on 'two letters of the alphabet, that express perfection' – 'M and A', forming 'Emma' – to relieve the embarrassment of Emma's unkind joke at old Miss Bates's expense. Still more effective is the tense scene in which Emma and Frank Churchill tease Jane Fairfax by making words from children's alphabet bricks. The last of these, which the victim sweeps angrily away, 'unexamined', is not divulged to the reader; but Jane Austen told her family that it spelt out 'Pardon'.

Skill in entertaining others by reading aloud is not the automatic sign of an admirable character in Jane Austen's novels. 'How spiritless, how tame was Edward's manner in reading to us last night!' complains Marianne Dashwood in *Sense and Sensibility*, of the honourable, but self-effacing hero, to which her mother justly responds, 'But you *would* give him Cowper', rather than the 'simple and elegant prose' more suited to his tastes. Marianne presumably takes far more pleasure in the readings of Shakespeare's *Hamlet* which they have shared with the reprobate Willoughby; in *Mansfield Park*, even the impeccably virtuous heroine Fanny Price finds herself briefly drawn to her unwanted, unprincipled suitor Henry Crawford on hearing him read from Shakespeare's *Henry VIII* (a play more frequently performed then than now). 'His reading was capital', the author explains; and despite 'shrinking again into herself' once it ends, Fanny is – we infer – attentively following the ensuing discussion, in which Henry Crawford points out, '(He) is part of an Englishman's constitution. His thoughts and beauties are so spread abroad that one touches them everywhere' – with which the hero, Edmund, concurs, adding, 'We all talk Shakespeare, use his similes, and describe with his descriptions.' Jane Austen would no doubt have been amazed to discover that, two hundred years later, her opening phrase from *Pride and Prejudice*, 'It is a truth universally acknowledged . . .' would have become universally known; and that her name would be included not far below Shakespeare's, on any list of the greatest writers in the English language.

William Shakespeare was certainly one of her literary idols; from hearing his works declaimed at home, and exploring them – as does Catherine Morland in *Northanger Abbey* – among the crowded shelves of her father's library, she progressed in later life to seeing them in major productions on the London stage. Though she complained, on a visit to London in 1813, 'I believe the Theatres are thought at a low ebb at present', she was an assiduous play-goer; and in March 1814 she was fortunate enough to be present at one of the most celebrated dramatic performances of all time: Edmund Kean's Shylock, in *The Merchant of Venice*. This was the great actor Kean's first, triumphant season at the Drury Lane Theatre, since its reopening in 1812, re-designed by Benjamin Wyatt, following a major fire. Tickets, naturally, were in high demand: 'so great is the rage for seeing Kean that only a third and fourth row could be got', Jane Austen told her sister Cassandra, in a letter of 13 March 1814. On the night, she found 'the Play heavy', and the Austen party left before the end of the next work, *Illusion*, an Arabian-Nights-style extravaganza, with much 'finery and dancing', but 'little merit'. Nevertheless, Jane reported, 'We were quite satisfied with Kean. I cannot imagine better acting'; and she was eager to share the experience with Cassandra, telling her, 'I shall like to see Kean again excessively . . . it appeared to me as if there were no fault in him anywhere; & in his scene with Tubal there was exquisite acting.' During this London visit she made plans to see the actor Charles Young – Kean's nearest rival – in Shakespeare's *Richard III*, at another newly rebuilt theatre, Covent Garden, on the site of the present Royal Opera House; at Covent Garden she also, on this trip, attended the opera *Artaxerxes* ('very tiresome'), a pantomime, and *The Farmer's Wife*, by Charles Dibdin – 'a Musical thing in 3 acts' – for which her niece Fanny's current admirer, 'Mr J. Plumptre', secured the Austens a box. Despite the range of her theatrical experiences, from major productions of Shakespeare and Sheridan to ephemeral 'sing-song & trumpery' shows, and even an acrobatic display by the 'Indian jugglers' of Pall Mall, who entertained her and Fanny during a morning's shopping, one of her theatrical ambitions remained unfulfilled: she never saw the celebrated actress Sarah Siddons, who retired from the stage in 1812. After a mix-up over tickets in 1811, Jane Austen wrote wistfully 'I have no chance of seeing Mrs Siddons. – I should particularly have liked seeing her in Constance' (in Shakespeare's *King John*), '& could swear at her with little effort for disappointing me.'

Though she remarked of another leading Regency actress, Eliza O'Neill, after seeing her in the Garrick tragedy *Isabella*, 'Acting seldom satisfies me', this performance drew from her the revealing comment, 'She is an elegant creature, however, & hugs Mr Younge [*sic*] delightfully.' Here lay the key to the

1. Jane Austen: the only authenticated, full-face portrait,
by her sister Cassandra, *c.* 1810

2. Steventon Rectory, Hampshire, Jane Austen's childhood home,
by her niece Anna Lefroy

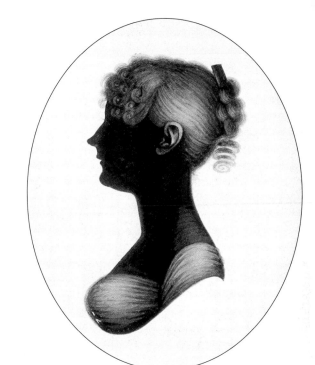

3. Silhouette of Cassandra, Jane's beloved sister, mentor and correspondent, c. 1809

4. Eliza de Feuillide – Jane's cousin, and a frequent visitor to Steventon. Eliza's first husband, a French count, was guillotined; in 1797 she married Jane's brother Henry

5. *Goody Two-Shoes*, one of Jane's first books

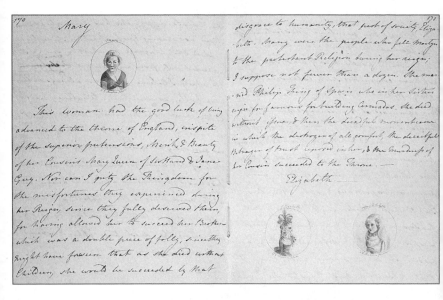

6. The comic *History of England*, by a 'partial, prejudiced and ignorant historian', written when Jane was about 15, and illustrated by Cassandra

7. Detail of a patchwork quilt made by Mrs Austen and her daughters

8. Jane's ivory cup-and-ball game

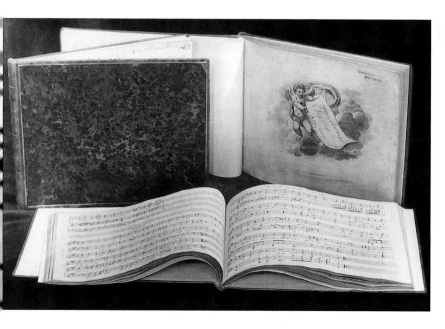

9. Music from Jane's collection

10. Godmersham Park, Kent, inherited by Jane's brother Edward,
from his adoptive parents the Knights. Here, amidst
'Elegance & Ease & Luxury' Cassandra and Jane often stayed

11. Edward Austen-Knight

12. Sydney Gardens, Bath. From 1801-4 the Austens lived at 4 Sydney Place, adjoining these pleasure-gardens

13. Letter from Jane in Bath, 1801, to Cassandra, then staying with the family of her late fiancé, Thomas Fowle

14. 'Our Chawton Home', where Jane Austen lived from 1809 until her death, with her mother, sister and friend Martha Lloyd. Sadly, Jane did not live to see Martha become the second wife of her brother Frank, who rose to be Admiral Sir Francis Austen

15. Jane's friend Martha Lloyd photographed in old age

16. 'The present fashions': morning dress and full dress for June 1807,
from the magazine *La Belle Assemblée*

17. George ('Beau') Brummell – the ultimate dandy,
and arbiter of modes and manners

18. 'A fashionable party' in Paris, 1807.
The gentleman's haircut has recently been in vogue again

19. The topaz cross bought in 1801 for Jane by her brother Charles, with naval prize money. It was the inspiration for Fanny Price's 'very pretty amber cross' in *Mansfield Park*

20. A pattern for 'new and fashionable embroidery' such as Jane and her heroines might have worked, from *La Belle Assemblée*

New pattern for Needlework, designed and printed for La Belle Assemblée N.º 15 April 1. 1807.

21. Jane's own portable writing-desk

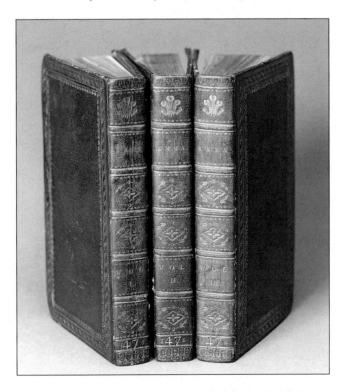

22. The 3-volume set of *Emma* specially bound for the
Prince Regent, to whom the novel was dedicated

23. A page of cancelled text from Jane Austen's first draft of *Persuasion*,
revised in 1816

Dᵣ. Miss Austen

1815

Dec. 19 2 Emma to Hans Place p. Jⁿ Ec.
  1 " Prince Regent
  memd Binding in Morocco 24/-
  1 " Countess of Morley Bᵒ
  1 " Revᵈ J.S. Clarke
  1 " Jas Leigh Perrot Esq
  2 " Mrs Austen
  1 " Captain Austen
  1 " Revᵈ Jⁿ Austen
  1 " H.F. Austen Esq
  1 " Miss Knight
  1 " Miss Sharpe
Apr 2 Entering in Stationers Hall as below
Jne 4ᵗ " British Museum
Jne 21 19 Copies to Stationers Hall
    for Libraries

24. An entry in John Murray's ledger, listing those to whom presentation copies of *Emma* should be sent – from the Prince Regent himself, to Anne Sharp, the Godmersham governess whom Jane had befriended

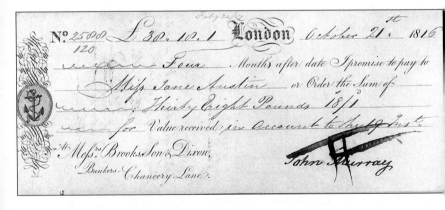

25. A Regency royalty cheque: a payment of £38 18s 1d from John Murray to Jane Austen, 1816

objections of virtuous Fanny Price and Edmund Bertram to the proposal of amateur theatricals, in *Mansfield Park*: acting (as opposed to reading aloud or reciting) was likely to involve active physical contact, in public, between the sexes – acceptable for professional actresses, with their presumed lack of 'delicacy of feeling', but most improper for a gentleman's daughter, with a reputation, and marriage prospects, to consider. The Austen family themselves evidently had no qualms about putting on plays in the dining-room, or the barn, at Steventon, but these were kept within the circle of family and close friends, and mounted under the supervision of Jane's clergyman father. In *Mansfield Park*, however, the stern, conventional Sir Thomas Bertram is absent from home; several unmarried, non-family members are to take part; above all, the play eventually selected, *Lovers' Vows* (adapted from a German original by Mrs Inchbald) is a risqué work, involving daring scenes, speeches and caresses (of which Henry Crawford and Maria Bertram evidently take full advantage). As a shocked Fanny Price discovers, on reading the text, the two leading female roles of Agatha and Amelia were 'unfit to be expressed by any woman of modesty'.

Morality in literature was of great importance to Jane Austen. She was not a prude: in her *Juvenilia* she was happy to write of drunkenness, thieving, seduction and fraud; and in her adult works, published during her lifetime, she dealt freely with such subjects as bastardy, pre-marital sex and adultery. But the moral structure of her mature fiction is clear: wrong-doing (such as Maria Bertram's liaison with Henry Crawford) is inevitably punished, and virtue (such as the resolute courage of Elinor Dashwood) is rewarded. She certainly disliked any impropriety in others' writings; according to her brother Henry, in his preface to the first, posthumous edition of *Persuasion* (1817), she 'recoiled from anything gross', and in 1807 she had returned Mme de Genlis's popular novel *Alphonsine* to the lending-library, declaring, 'We were disgusted in twenty pages, as, independent of a bad translation, it has indelicacies which disgrace a pen hitherto so pure.' An educationalist, as well as a fiction writer, Mme de Genlis was not out of Jane Austen's favour for long; in *Emma*, published in 1815, the heroine fondly compares her own relationship with her governess, Miss Taylor, with that of the admirable Baronne d'Almane and Comtesse d'Ostalis, 'in Madame de Genlis' *Adelaide and Theodore*'. Her favourite novel, Samuel Richardson's *Sir Charles Grandison* (published in 1753), dealt with the shocking subject of attempted rape; but here any risk of salaciousness was outweighed by the high moral tone of the treatment. Though a relatively little-read work today, overshadowed by Richardson's more famous masterpieces *Pamela* and *Clarissa*, *Grandison* was immensely popular in its time; the author, a prim, middle-aged bookseller, evidently touched a chord with eighteenth-century female readers, with his favoured theme of feminine virtue repelling masculine lust. Though 'every circumstance' of *Grandison* 'was familiar to her', and she knew its characters, from priggish Sir Charles to the beleaguered heroine, Harriet Byron, 'as if they had been living friends', Jane Austen could not resist poking fun even at this 'great master': an existing manuscript in her handwriting, entitled *Sir Charles Grandison*, or *The Happy Man*, shows how she reduced the elaborate 7-volume novel-in-letters to a lively 5-act play, focusing chiefly on the attempted rape scenes – and intended, partly in burlesque, partly in homage, for her family's entertainment. Some thirteen years later, Richardson's novel was still to the forefront of her thoughts: on a trip to London, in September 1813, she informed Cassandra that she had ordered a new cap, with 'a little white flower perking out of the left ear, like Harriet Byron's feather'.

One of the clearest statements of Jane Austen's attitude to morality in literature is voiced by Charlotte Heywood, heroine of her last, unfinished novel *Sanditon*. Described as a 'sober-minded young Lady, sufficiently well-read in Novels to supply her Imagination with amusement, but not at all unreasonably influenced by them', sensible Charlotte clashes on 'the subject of books' with the handsome, but foolish, young Sir Edward Denham, who has read widely, but with a 'perversity of judgement' which leads him to derive 'false principles', as well as 'hard words and involved sentences', from 'our most approved writers'. While professing to despise popular novels – 'the mere Trash of the common Circulating Library' – Sir Edward, it turns out, is titillated by Richardson (and secretly contemplates trying a similar violent seduction himself). On the subject of poetry he is equally ill-judging: despite his fulsome praise of Walter Scott, he proceeds to dismiss him as '*tame*', and gives the preference to another Scottish Romantic, the earthy, sensual, vigorous Robert Burns. At this, Charlotte demurs: though, she says, she has read some of Burns's works with pleasure (presumably such classic verses as 'Oh, my love's like a red, red rose'), she adds coolly, 'I am not poetic enough to separate a Man's Poetry entirely from his Character', explaining that 'poor Burns's known Irregularities' make her doubt 'the *Truth* of his Feelings as a Lover' – and as a poet. Truthfulness in writing is always inseparable from Jane Austen's art, and ideas; and here, at the end of her career, she makes the fact explicit.

Compared with the immortal comic portraits of her earlier works – pompous Mr Collins and pushy Mrs Elton, mean John Dashwood and garrulous Miss Bates – Sir Edward Denham is a broad, overdrawn character; had she lived to complete the novel, no doubt Jane Austen would have 'lop't and crop't' so successfully as to produce a more realistic creation. Yet with Sir Edward's sneering castigation of light, enjoyable, fiction as 'mere Trash' her literary career comes full circle. It was in *Northanger Abbey* – her first-completed, though last-published, work – that she wrote her famous defence of the popular novel, protesting at the denigratory phrase 'Only a novel' to describe those works in which, as she put it, are displayed 'the most thorough knowledge of human nature', and 'the liveliest effusions of wit and humour' in 'the best-chosen language'. It is a brilliantly witty, perceptive and timely homily; and one which would reverberate through the history of popular culture.

The specific novels which Jane Austen names in this passage – 'It is only *Cecilia*, or *Camilla*, or *Belinda*' – are, admittedly, by two major writers: Fanny Burney and Maria Edgeworth. Fanny Burney was, in her own time, admired and endorsed by Dr Johnson himself, to the point where some believed that he had actually written her works; Maria Edgeworth was later to be cited as a source of inspiration by the Russian novelist Turgenev, who particularly admired her treatment of the peasantry. She was also a particular favourite of Jane Austen's: 'I have made up my mind to like no Novels really, but Miss Edgeworth's, Yours & my own', she wrote jauntily to her niece Anna in 1814. Yet the intelligent, well-read hero of *Northanger Abbey*, Henry Tilney, puts up a spirited defence of even the lighter sort of novels, stating, 'The person, be it lady or gentleman, who has not pleasure in a good novel must be intolerably stupid', and referring to his own enthusiasm for the works of Mrs Radcliffe – mistress of the Gothic horror-novel genre so popular at the time. The trend had begun with the publication of Horace Walpole's Gothic fantasy *The Castle of Otranto*, in 1764, some ten years before Jane Austen's birth. A bizarre narrative (which Walpole claimed had come to him in a dream, and been written in a few weeks), *Otranto* and its exoticism found further expression in Walpole's designs for his remarkable mock-medieval house, Strawberry Hill; and a vogue was set in architecture, as well as literature. Another rich eccentric, William Beckford (a distant connection of the Austens), took up the torch, producing, in 1781, *Vathek*, an Arabian-Nights-style confection of caliphs, magic and legendary treasure, which became one of Byron's favourite books. By the time Jane Austen's Catherine Morland was exploring the delights of reading (between 1798 and 1817), the genre was well established, with all its conventions of foreign (preferably Italian) locations, ruined abbeys and castles, spectral apparitions, long-lost heirs, sliding panels and secret passages – and, of course, merciless, blackguardly villains, much given to carrying off vulnerable, virtuous heroines. Leading the field was Mrs Radcliffe's *The Mysteries of Udolpho* (1794) which, Henry Tilney tells Catherine solemnly, 'I could not lay down; I remember finishing it in two days, my hair standing on end the whole time.'

Udolpho had its rivals, and successors: when appealed to by Catherine for more such 'horrid' reading, Isabella produces a list of titles, from *The Italian* (Mrs Radcliffe's 1797 follow-up), to *The Castle of Wolfenbach*, *Clermont*, *Mysterious Warnings*, *The Necromancer of the Black Forest*, *The Midnight Bell*, *The Orphan of the Rhine*, and *Horrid Mysteries*. It is small wonder that when she encounters the Tilneys' house, so evocatively named Northanger Abbey, the impressionable Catherine fully expects to find secret documents in the old chest in her bedroom (which turn out to be laundry bills), and entertains the awful belief that her host, General Tilney – who walks about with 'the air and attitude of a Montoni', villain of *Udolpho* – has either murdered his wife, or is keeping her locked up in a hidden room. One of Jane Austen's sternest critics, Charlotte Brontë, would indeed incorporate the device of a secret, incarcerated wife into her best-known work, *Jane Eyre*; but in *Northanger Abbey*, published thirty years earlier, the idea is kindly, but realistically, laughed away by the hero, with the tender words, 'Consult your own understanding, your own sense of the probable, your own observation of what is passing around you.' In the course of this novel, Catherine, like all Jane Austen's heroines, is educated in 'understanding and sense' – to become, like Emma Woodhouse at the end of *Emma*, 'more rational' and 'more acquainted with herself'.

One who would presumably not have enjoyed *Udolpho* and

its ilk is Fanny Price, in *Mansfield Park*, who acknowledges that she is 'graver than other people'. When her cousin Edmund examines her current reading, he notes that it ranges from 'a great book' of contemporary travel-writing, Lord Macartney's *Journal of his Embassy to China*, edited by Sir John Barrow, and published in 1807, to *The Idler*, containing moral essays by Dr Johnson, and the poet George Crabbe's sensitive, reflective *Tales in Verse*, which appeared in 1812. Apart from the absence of novels, Fanny's literary taste has much in common with Jane Austen's: the history, biography and poetry which Fanny 'so delighted in' includes not only the works of Crabbe (whom Jane pretended, as an ardent fan, to harbour thoughts of marrying, despite never having met him), but also those of her other favourites, Cowper and Scott, which Fanny can quote by heart. When tutoring her sister, Fanny refers to Goldsmith's *History of England*, which Jane both parodied and respected. What is noticeable, to many a modern reader, is the omission, among all Jane Austen's references to 'books of a serious stamp', of many works now regarded as milestones of late eighteenth- and early nineteenth-century writing, and thought. Neither Fanny, the closest to a blue-stocking of any Jane Austen heroine, nor the author herself, in either her letters or her fiction, makes any mention of Edmund Burke's *Reflections on the French Revolution*, published in 1790; of Thomas Paine's *Essay on the Rights of Man* (1791); or Adam Smith's far-reaching economic treatise of 1776, *An Inquiry into the Nature and Causes of the Wealth of Nations*. Even in the realm of poetry Jane Austen's tastes did not always accord with those of later generations: she made no reference to the visionary William Blake, nor to Shelley, Keats or Coleridge; while Wordsworth – who might seem, to today's readers, to loom over the Romantic period – is named only in passing, when the fatuous Sir Edward Denham in *Sanditon* comments that he has 'the true soul' of poetry, listing him between the now-obscure figures of Montgomery and Campbell. In history, she revealed no interest in one of the greatest works in the English language, Edward Gibbon's *Decline and Fall of the Roman Empire*, completed in 1788 – though she wrote in 1800 that she was reading aloud the seven sections of Robert Henry's *History of Great Britain*, informing an expected house-guest, Martha Lloyd, 'Friday's lot, Commerce, Coin & Shipping, You will find the least entertaining; but the next Even^g:'s portion' (on Manners) 'will make amends'.

Yet she was anything but the ill-read, ignorant female she so modestly claimed to be in her correspondence with the Regent's librarian, James Stanier Clarke. Typically, she told Cassandra in 1813, 'We are quite run over with books.' Despite the relatively high cost of books – 15 shillings for a 3-volume novel in paper covers, which would then need binding, at the owner's expense, was not unusual – she evidently acquired as many of her favourites as she could afford. Though she sold some (including her copy of Dodsley's *Poems*, which fetched 10 shillings), at the time of the Austens' move from Steventon, other works which survive bearing her signature range from Goldsmith's *Animated Nature* to Hayley's *Poems and Plays*. She certainly possessed one of the first copies of Fanny Burney's third novel, *Camilla* (1796), since the name 'Miss J. Austen' is listed among those who subscribed to pay for its publication – ensuring, in advance, a profit for the author. Much of her and her family's reading was, however, supplied by lending-libraries. Here the passing shopper might call in to see the latest publications displayed, browse through the array of trinkets, costume jewellery and 'beautiful ornaments', such as made the unliterary Lydia Bennet 'quite wild' in *Pride and Prejudice*, and select a volume to borrow, at a cost of about 2*d* per day. According to Anna Austen, on one visit to a library with her aunt Jane, in 1811, she picked up a new novel, but remarked that with such a title, it could not be worth reading, and left it. Since the title in question was *Sense and Sensibility*, 'By A Lady', Jane Austen must have been highly amused.

There were also the private circulating libraries, such as that set up by the Austens' neighbour Mrs Martin in 1798; it was from one such local 'Society' that Jane was lent, in 1813, an unusual work for her: *An Essay on the Military Policy and Institutions of the British Empire*, by Capt. Pasley of the Engineers. Since it was written by a military, rather than naval, officer, and was highly critical of Britain's foreign policy and the conduct of the war against Napoleon, it was (she told Cassandra) 'a book which I protested against at first', but found to be 'delightfully written' and entertaining. Typically, she claimed to be 'in love with the author', calling him 'the first soldier I ever sighed for', and explaining, 'he does write with extraordinary force and spirit'. Another library book which, to her surprise, she enjoyed was the poet Robert Southey's *Letters from England by Don Manuel Alvarez Espriella* (1807), which purported to be an account of travels through England by a high-born, Catholic Spaniard. Harshly condemnatory of the conditions of the poor, and the eccentricities and excesses of the ruling classes, *Espriella's Letters* (which Jane read aloud by candlelight) led her to the conclusion, 'The Man describes well, but is horribly anti-English. He deserves to be the foreigner he assumes.' Fact or fiction, any work which truthfully illustrated human nature and manners would always interest her far more than those 'enormous great stupid thick quarto volumes' such as even her dear friends the Bigg sisters liked to keep on display in the breakfast-parlour at Manydown. Jane Austen never ceased to poke fun at those who read to impress others, slighting the popular novel, and claiming to prefer such stuff as old bound volumes of Joseph Addison's *The Spectator*, founded in 1711 – the contents of which, she wrote in *Northanger Abbey*, generally involved 'Improbable circumstances, unnatural characters, and topics of conversation, which no longer concern anyone living'.

Though she could be a scathing critic herself, Jane Austen was always (like virtually all authors) avid to know what others thought of her own works. After the publication of *Mansfield Park* and *Emma*, she drew up detailed lists of the 'Opinions' of her friends, family and other readers: these ranged from 'My Mother . . . Thought Fanny insipid'; 'Mrs Bramstone – Thought Lady Bertram like herself', and 'Mrs Lefroy – liked it, but thought it a mere Novel', to (of *Emma*) 'Mr K(nightley) liked by every body', and 'Mrs Digweed . . . if she had not known the Author, could hardly have got through it'. Any snippet of praise delighted her: 'I have more of such sweet flattery from Miss Sharp!', she told Cassandra in 1813, as the popularity of *Pride and Prejudice* grew, adding, 'I am read and admired in Ireland too. – There is a Mrs Fletcher, the wife of a Judge . . . who is all curiosity to know about me – what I am like & so forth.' She also, like other writers in every era, lived with constant self-doubt. She was relieved when her brother Henry, given the first chapters of *Mansfield Park* to read, judged them 'interesting' – a term of far higher praise then than now – and gave 'great praise to the drawing of the characters'; but, she wrote worriedly, 'I am afraid he has gone through the most entertaining part.' To the Countess of Morley, who wrote praising *Emma* on its publication in 1815, Jane wrote gratefully of her 'present state of doubt' as to the novel's reception, adding that she was encouraged 'to believe . . . that I have not yet – as almost every Writer of Fancy does sooner or later – overwritten myself'. Many a novelist would sympathize with her comment on learning, in 1814, that the poet Walter Scott had published his first work of prose fiction, *Waverley*: 'Walter Scott has no business to write novels, especially good ones. It is not fair. He has Fame and Profit enough as a Poet, and should not be taking the bread out of other people's mouths.'

Her joking conclusion, 'I do not like him', would surely have been altered had she known that he would become one of her earliest, and most celebrated, admirers. Her first novels, *Sense and Sensibility* and *Pride and Prejudice*, received few reviews – two for the former; three for the latter; and these were coolly encouraging: the *Critical Review* called *Sense and Sensibility* 'a genteel, well-written novel'; the *British Critic* approved its 'pleasing and entertaining narrative'. When *Emma* appeared, however, in 1815, its publisher, John Murray, approached no less a figure than Scott himself, with the request, 'Have you any fancy to dash off an article on *Emma*?' Though he added, dampeningly, 'It wants incident and romance, does it not?', the result was a long, and commendatory, review in the influential *Quarterly Review*, owned by John Murray himself, and edited by William Gifford, whose approving reader's report on *Emma* had first brought Jane Austen to this leading publishing firm. Scott's critique went so far as to compare the novel's merits to those of 'the Flemish school of painting'; as he put it, 'The subjects are not often elegant, and certainly never grand; but they are finished up to nature, and with a precision which delights the reader.' Jane Austen's letter to Mr Murray, after seeing the *Quarterly Review*, seemed somewhat cool: 'The Authoress of *Emma* has no reason, I think, to complain of her treatment in it', she wrote, but expressed disappointment that 'so clever a Man as the Reveiwer [*sic*]' should have overlooked *Mansfield Park*.

Good reviews, as she well knew, might help to increase a novel's sales: and as she wrote to Fanny Knight in 1814, 'Tho' I like praise as well as anybody, I like what Edward calls *Pewter* too.' The desire to make money from her writing – the only profession, apart from the unthinkably downtrodden role of a governess, open to her – was much in her thoughts, underlying all her aspirations for her writing career. At a time when sensational, ephemeral novels such as Lady Caroline Lamb's *roman-à-clef Glenarvon* could run through three reprints in a year, and some women writers died rich, Jane Austen earned less than £650 during the course of her writing career. 'I wish', says the youngest Dashwood girl, Margaret, in *Sense and Sensibility*, 'that somebody would give us all a large fortune a-piece!' It is one of the ironies of British literary history that

Jane Austen never lived to see the fortune which her works would earn.

Had she done so, there can be little doubt that, as Edward fondly responds to Margaret's remark, 'in such an event', it would have been 'a happy day for book-sellers'.

5

'Of Lovers and Husbands'

'Anything is to be preferred or endured
rather than marrying without Affection.'
Jane Austen, letter to her niece Fanny, 1814

In the autumn of 1814 Jane Austen had new cause to be grateful to the creaking door into the front parlour at Chawton, which gave her warning when anyone was approaching. In addition to the manuscript of *Emma*, on which she had been secretly at work since January, she had also, that September, to conceal a highly personal (and revealing) correspondence with her favourite niece, Fanny Knight. Eldest of the eleven children of Jane's brother Edward, who had been adopted in boyhood by the rich Knights of Godmersham Park, Fanny had been a lovable girl of 15 when, in 1808, her mother died in childbirth. At the end of 1814, now aged 21, and in the throes of her first serious love-affair, Fanny turned for counsel to her aunt Jane. It was a fortunate decision – both for herself, and for literary posterity. 'Indeed you must not let anything depend on my opinion', Jane warned with alarm; but as Fanny recognized, in matters of love and courtship she was lucky to have as her confidante the author of *Pride and Prejudice*.

Jane Austen's own experience of love was, almost certainly, limited. As an attractive young woman, in the 1790s, she had evidently been something of a flirt, dancing and bantering with a series of young men, without seriously losing her heart to any. In 1796, aged just 20, she wrote gaily of handing over one suitor to her friend Mary Lloyd, 'and not only him, but all my other admirers into the bargain ... even the kiss which C. Powlett wanted to give me'. The letter went on lightly, 'I mean to confine myself in future to Mr Tom Lefroy, for whom I do not care sixpence.' Beneath the jokes, it was clear that she and Tom Lefroy were attracted to one another. She called him 'a very gentlemanlike, good-looking, pleasant young man', discussed Fielding's bawdy novel *Tom Jones* with him, and reported with satisfaction that he was 'excessively teased' about his feelings for her. In later years, having risen to be Lord Chief Justice of Ireland, Thomas Lefroy told a relation that he had been in love with Jane Austen, adding, 'but it was a boy's love'. There was an element of 'boy's love', too, in her next relationship – with a clever, lively clergyman, Samuel Blackall. In 1798, Jane mentioned seeing a letter which hinted strongly that he had entertained thoughts of marrying her; though flattered, she did not return his feelings, concluding resolutely, 'Our indifference will soon be mutual.' Yet she was not entirely indifferent to Mr Blackall: on hearing of his marriage, in 1813, to a Miss Lewis, she mused, 'I should very much like to know what sort of a Woman she is. He was a piece of Perfection, noisy Perfection himself which I always recollect with regard.' Typically, she proceeded to invent a character for the unknown Miss Lewis – imagining her 'of a silent turn and rather ignorant, but naturally intelligent ... fond of cold veal pies, green tea in the afternoon, & a green window blind at night'.

Cassandra's ruthlessly loyal editing of her sister's correspondence, after her death, resulted in the loss of many passages (and presumably whole letters) relating to Jane Austen's emotional life. Yet second-hand evidence, from reliable quarters, suggests that she had at least one serious love-affair, with the mysterious gentleman whom she met on holiday with her parents, in the early 1800s. According to the *Memoir of Jane*

Austen by her nephew J. E. Austen-Leigh, at a fashionable seaside resort she met a man 'whose charm of person, mind and manners was such that Cassandra thought him worthy to possess and likely to win her sister's love'. This person declared his intentions of seeing her again, and Cassandra 'felt no doubt as to his motives'. Tragically, before the hoped-for reunion, the Austens received word that he had died suddenly. 'I believe that, if Jane ever loved, it was this unnamed gentleman', her nephew concluded. There were parallels with Cassandra's situation: in 1795 she had become engaged to a childhood friend, who had died while serving as an army chaplain in the West Indies, before the marriage could take place. Years later, while counselling her niece Fanny, Jane Austen was to write pithily of thwarted love, 'It is no creed of mine, as you must be well aware, that such sort of Disappointments kill anybody.' It may be that Fanny was 'well aware' of her aunt Jane's 'Disappointments'; she must surely have known of her aunt Cassandra's.

Jane herself caused disappointment to her last known ad-mirer, the eligible young Harris Bigg-Wither, brother of her great friends the Bigg sisters. Again, the precise facts are uncertain; but according to Austen family tradition, about a year after her tragic holiday romance, Jane went to stay at Manydown, the Bigg family's delightful estate near Steventon. While there she received a formal proposal of marriage from the son and heir, Harris – which she accepted. After a sleep-less night, however, she apparently rose early, told him she could not marry him, and left the house forthwith. Though six years her junior, and not handsome, Harris Bigg-Wither was an excellent match: a respectable young man, with a good inheritance. Yet unlike her cynically practical character Charlotte Lucas, in *Pride and Prejudice*, Jane Austen was not prepared to marry for the 'pure and disinterested desire of an establishment', however bleak the alternatives might be. As she insisted to her niece Fanny, in 1814, with uncharacteristic vehemence, 'Anything is to be preferred or endured rather than marrying without Affection.'

Jane Austen was almost 27 years old when she declined young Harris's offer; tellingly, Charlotte Lucas is 'about twenty-seven' when she shocks her friend Elizabeth Bennet by sacrificing 'every better feeling', and accepting the risible clergyman Mr Collins. 'A woman of seven-and-twenty', says 17-year-old Marianne Dashwood in *Sense and Sensibility*, 'can never hope to feel or inspire affection again'; while in *Persuasion*, snobbish, socially ambitious Elizabeth Elliot, 'being nine-and-twenty', feels with trepidation 'her approach to the years of danger'. There was no great onus on a gentlewoman to marry early in Regency England: the average age of first marriage for middle- and upper-class females had risen, at the end of the eighteenth century, to about 22; and as late as 1817, when Fanny Knight was already 23 years old, Jane urged her to wait for 'the next 2 or 3 years' before choosing a husband. Nevertheless, marriage remained the eventual goal of most women. Old maids were figures of fun: they fulfilled (in the words of the Victorian economist John Stuart Mill) 'no use or function or office' in society, and were always liable to pity or laughter. 'It is very bad to grow old, & be poor, & be laughed at', sighs the heroine's older sister in *The Watsons* – while the unfortunate Charlotte Lucas's younger brothers welcome her acceptance of the unworthy Mr Collins, since it relieves them of 'their apprehensions of Charlotte's dying an old maid'. Good-hearted Emma Woodhouse, heroine of *Emma*, would surely not have made her (regretted) gibe at Miss Bates for talking too much, if that garrulous, but well-intentioned, spinster had had a husband to give her consequence.

Though Jane gently reminded her niece, 'Single women have a dreadful propensity for being poor', Fanny Knight, as an heiress, was unlikely ever to face poverty; but for many women of the period financial hardship was a constant, haunting threat, as Jane herself was painfully aware. 'Young ladies that have no money are very much to be pitied!' exclaims Lady Denham baldly in *Sanditon*. Jane Austen herself descended from being the eligible daughter of a respected clergyman, who kept his carriage, to the position of ladylike spinster, dependent upon a brother's generosity for a home. Writing in 1808 of a family friend, Miss Murden, who had just been found lodgings above a chemist's shop (much like Miss Bates and her mother in *Emma*), she reflected, 'At her age . . . one may be as friendless oneself, and in similar circumstances quite as captious.' Behind the quest for a happy, 'companionate' marriage, based on mutual respect and 'Affection', which is the joyous central theme of all her novels, lies the darker debate – whether for a woman any marriage is preferable to none. Charlotte Lucas – initially described in *Pride and Prejudice* as a 'sensible, intelligent woman' – is in no doubt: matrimony, 'however uncertain of giving happiness', must be her 'pleasantest preserve from want'. The author clearly disagreed. Her most high-minded heroine, Fanny Price, under pressure to marry the rich, agreeable but immoral Henry Crawford in *Mansfield Park*, reflects on 'how wretched and how unpardonable, how hopeless and how wicked it was, to marry without affection'; and in 1814, the year in which this novel appeared, Jane urgently warned the heroine's namesake, her niece Fanny, 'Nothing can be compared to the misery of being bound *without* Love, bound to one, & preferring another.' More than once she suggests in her fiction that without the threat of poverty many women might opt to remain independent. 'I could do very well single for my own part', remarks the heroine's sister in *The Watsons*; 'A little Company, & a pleasant Ball now & then, would be enough for me.' And in *Emma*, the 'handsome, clever and rich' Emma Woodhouse claims to have 'very little intention of ever marrying'. As she explains to her awed protégée, Harriet, 'It is poverty only which makes celibacy contemptible.' To such startling notions Harriet can only respond in wonder, 'Dear me! – It is so odd to hear a woman talk so!'

Intrepid women who defied convention were not uncommon in late eighteenth- and early nineteenth-century society, but they moved in very different circles from Jane Austen's. Lady Hester Stanhope, who acted as political hostess for her uncle, the Prime Minister William Pitt the Younger, at No. 10 Downing Street, threw up an honoured place in British public life to travel and live among the Bedouin tribes. Doughty, eccentric Lady Holland – a divorced adulteress – established a glittering salon at Holland House, to the west of London, where she drew together (and domineered over) leading figures of the day, from politicians to poets. Among the aristocracy, many women enjoyed the same sexual freedom as their husbands. The Whig beauty Georgiana, Duchess of Devonshire, lived in a celebrated *ménage-à-trois* with her husband and his mistress, Elizabeth Foster. The children of Lady Oxford (whose married name was Harley) were so widely believed to have different fathers that they were nicknamed 'The Harleian Miscellany', after the famous British literary collection accrued by the family, and donated to the nation. Lady Caroline Lamb flaunted her adulterous affair with Lord Byron, even parading with him in public dressed as a pageboy – yet still retained the devotion of her highly respectable husband, the future Victorian Prime Minister, Lord Melbourne. Intellectual females might be mocked for their 'damn brains' (Horace Walpole famously dubbed the feminist writer Mary Wollstonecraft 'a Hyena in petticoats'), but they were not ostracized merely for taking lovers. In Jane Austen's world, however – the middle-class, respectable world of the squirearchy, gentry and clergy – a different morality prevailed. When Fanny Price's married cousin Maria commits adultery with Henry Crawford, in *Mansfield Park*, she faces social ruin, and is banished to the country with odious Mrs Norris for companion. The disgrace of Lydia Bennet's elopement, and cohabitation, with Mr Wickham, in *Pride and Prejudice*, is just about remedied by their patched-up marriage;

but for Colonel Brandon's fallen sister-in-law in *Sense and Sensibility*, there is no such salvation, and her Hogarthian progress ends in a bastard child and a pauper's spunging-house deathbed. The sententious Bennet sister, Mary, is truthful, if tactless, when she moralizes in *Pride and Prejudice* 'that loss of virtue in a female is irretrievable – that one false step involves her in endless ruin'.

For Jane Austen herself, as for her fictional heroines, loss of virtue was an unthinkable prospect. She showed a far from prudish interest in others' sexual adventures: 'Ld. Lucan has taken a Mistress', she wrote casually in 1807, as 'a matter of Joy . . . to the Actors'; in 1801 she had reported with satisfaction, 'I have a good eye at an Adultress', having identified the subject of a current scandal at a party in Bath. 'She was highly-rouged', she noted, 'and looked rather quietly & contentedly silly than anything else.' Her own physical experience with the opposite sex was, however, almost certainly slight. Apart from the kiss which Charles Powlett, a Hampshire neighbour, had apparently wanted to give her, there was an incident in 1801 when she found herself alone in a drawing-room with a no-torious local lecher: 'nothing could prevail upon me to move two steps from the door, on the lock of which I kept one hand constantly fixed', she assured Cassandra, with mock theatricality. But even with a man whose attentions she welcomed, modesty, and the need to preserve her reputation, would have ruled out almost any intimacy. Men and women – even the hero and heroine – rarely touch in Jane Austen's novels; and they do not kiss. The newly engaged Mr Bingley and Jane Bennet, in *Pride and Prejudice*, reveal their situation by merely standing close to one another, tête-à-tête, 'as if engaged in earnest conversation', when interrupted by Elizabeth; she herself, for all her wit and confidence, cannot look Mr Darcy in the face while he is declaring his love for her at the end of the book, let alone touch him. Though Fanny Price, secretly in love since childhood with her cousin Edmund in *Mansfield*

Park, finds herself thrillingly 'pressed to his heart' at a climactic moment, this is the embrace of a brother, not a lover. For most of Jane Austen's men and women, physical contact is confined to eloquent handclasps. 'A hand taken and pressed' was to have accompanied Captain Wentworth's passionate speech to Anne Elliot, in the cancelled chapter in *Persuasion*; in *Emma*, a horrified Emma Woodhouse finds 'her hand seized' by the presumptuous vicar, Mr Elton, during his unwelcome proposal – a counterpoint to the moment when the hero, Mr Knightley, takes her hand, is 'on the point of carrying to his lips', then, tantalizingly, releases it, unkissed. The most powerful of these exchanges occurs early in *Mansfield Park*, when Henry Crawford and Maria Bertram are interrupted rehearsing a scene in their amateur theatricals: Henry, who is holding Maria's hand against his heart, does not relinquish it when the acting stops – to Maria, 'an earnest of the most serious determination'; to the reader, a strong hint of sexual misconduct to come.

Couples who defy society's strict codes of introduction and courtship can never prosper, in Jane Austen's novels. Willoughby's first meeting with Marianne Dashwood, in *Sense and Sensibility*, is excitingly unconventional: she has injured herself out walking; he, 'perceiving that her modesty declined what her situation rendered necessary', sweeps her up in his arms and carries her home. 'Marianne's preserver', the youngest Dashwood girl excitedly calls Willoughby; but he will turn out to be her sister's near-destroyer. Jane Austen never underestimates the force of sexual desire. In each of her novels at least one sympathetic character is temporarily misled by superficial erotic attraction – from Emma Woodhouse's brief, self-induced fancy for charming Frank Churchill, and Anne Elliot's fleeting interest in her eligible cousin William Walter Elliot, to high-minded Edmund Bertram's fascination with the unprincipled Mary Crawford. Even witty, cynical Elizabeth Bennet is initially drawn in by the handsome rake

Wickham. Charlotte Brontë's dismissive 1850s comment on Jane Austen, 'The passions are perfectly unknown to her; she rejects even a speaking acquaintance with that stormy Sisterhood', is facile and unjust: no 'insensible woman' (as Charlotte Brontë slightingly called her Regency predecessor) could have portrayed Marianne Dashwood, as she 'almost screamed', in the agony of betrayed love, 'Misery such as mine has no pride.' The key to Jane Austen's treatment of 'the Passions' can be found in the opening chapter of that great novel, when she says of her heroine, Elinor, 'Her feelings were strong, but she knew how to govern them.' The tempering of profound sensibility with sound good sense – the balancing of the Romantic with the rational – remained, as her advice to her lovelorn niece Fanny would demonstrate, her formula for ultimate feminine happiness and fulfilment.

Beneath the social constraints, the strength of women's sexuality is never in question. Jane Austen's female characters are expected to feel 'modest loathings' at the very thought of adultery; when ultra-virtuous Fanny Price, in *Mansfield Park*, learns that her cousin Maria has fled the matrimonial home to live with philandering Henry Crawford, she spends a sleepless night, and passes from 'feelings of sickness to shudderings of horror'. Yet with every mention of the 'crime' of adultery, or the lesser 'folly' of elopement and pre-marital sex, Jane Austen takes care to portray the woman as an eager, equal participant. Lydia Bennet and Wickham are 'a couple who were only brought together because their passions were stronger than their virtue'. Of his sister's liaison with Henry Crawford, Edmund Bertram states icily, 'With whom lay the greater seduction, I pretended not to say.' And when Willoughby tells Elinor Dashwood the shameful details of his seduction of Colonel Brandon's young ward, he mentions 'the violence of her passions', and urges Elinor not to assume that 'because she was injured she was irreproachable; and that because I was a libertine, she must be a saint'. There is a Regency robustness to such passages which is entirely at odds with Victorian prudery; and for all the absence of any explicit sex-scenes, the erotic interplay between Jane Austen's heroes and heroines is never less than powerful. The moment in *Pride and Prejudice* when Darcy calls on Elizabeth just as she has learned of Lydia's elopement is all the more dramatic because he may not touch her: while she, looking 'miserably ill', has 'burst into tears as she alluded to it', he, burning with sympathy and love, can only 'observe her in compassionate silence'. Had he taken her in his arms, and covered her with kisses, the atmosphere of that critical scene could not have been more thrillingly charged.

The term 'Feminist', which entered the English language some eighty years after Jane Austen's death, was not one which she would have claimed for herself. Unlike such contemporary 'Female Philosophers' as Mary Wollstonecraft, whose best-known work, *A Vindication of the Rights of Woman*, appeared in 1792, when Jane was 16, the author of *Pride and Prejudice* did not seek to unpick the stitches which bound society. With her enquiring mind, and wide literary tastes, she may well have read Mary Wollstonecraft's writings: it was fashionable to do so, even among such society figures as Lady Palmerston, mother of the future Victorian Prime Minister, who gaily warned her husband, 'I have been reading the *Rights of Woman*, so you must in future expect me to be very tenacious of my rights and privileges.' No such subversive talk – even in fun – is uttered by Jane Austen, or any of her characters. The reader of *Pride and Prejudice* is not expected to question Mr Bennet's advice to his beloved, clever daughter Lizzy, 'I know that you could be neither happy nor respectable unless you truly esteemed your husband; unless you looked up to him as a superior.' In *Persuasion*, Anne Elliot, separated in youth from Captain Wentworth by obeying Lady Russell, 'who deprecated the connexion', says, when blissfully reunited with him, 'I was right in submitting to her ... if I mistake not, a strong sense of duty is no bad part of a woman's portion'.

In this novel, the hero seems to speak for the author when, summing up his ideal woman, he says she must have 'a strong mind, with sweetness of manner'. There is no place for what Mary Wollstonecraft called 'the truant heart' in Jane Austen's fiction. She does not openly challenge the dependent female role within marriage: her message, rather, is that it is both a woman's right, and her duty, to choose wisely and responsibly whom to marry – and failing a compatible, 'companionate' partner, to stay resolutely single (as the financially independent Emma Woodhouse initially proposes to do). As her heroine Elinor Dashwood reflects, in *Sense and Sensibility*, 'the worst and most irremediable of all evils' is 'a connection, for life, with an unprincipled man'.

In fact, despite the well-worn accusation expressed by Charlotte Brontë, that 'she ruffles her reader by nothing vehement, disturbs him by nothing profound', Jane Austen is often fiercely angry on behalf of her sex. In her unfinished juvenile work *Catharine, or The Bower* – written, strikingly, soon after the publication of Wollstonecraft's *Rights of Woman* – she condemns the practice of shipping impoverished gentlewomen out to India to find husbands, a custom which she had encountered at first hand, through the experiences of her own father's sister. Sent out to India 'for her maintenance', Philadelphia Austen had duly married an elderly surgeon, Tysoe Hancock, from whom she eventually became estranged, after bearing a daughter, Eliza (perhaps by the celebrated Governor-General, Warren Hastings). 'Do you call it lucky, for a Girl of Genius and Feeling to be sent in quest of a husband to Bengal?' the heroine of *Catharine* asks trenchantly, adding, 'To a Girl of any Delicacy, the voyage in itself, since the object of it is so universally known, is a punishment.' Though the adroit 16-year-old author also proffers the opposing view – 'She is not the first Girl who has gone to the East Indies for a Husband, and I declare I should think it very good fun if I were as poor' – this is voiced by an unsympathetic character, the shallow and ignorant Camilla, a forerunner of empty-headed Isabella Thorpe in *Northanger Abbey*. Such women would be a constant target for Jane Austen's ironic censure. Like Mary Wollstonecraft, she was shocked by the deficiencies of female education and opportunities; and in her fiction she sought to expose the system by which women were brought up to value good looks and worthless 'accomplishments' above solid principles and an informed, 'improved' mind.

Jane Austen's harshest comment on the suppression of women's potential in a society run by, and for, men appears in *Northanger Abbey*. To the 'larger and more trifling part of' the male sex, the author notes acerbically, 'imbecility in females is a great enhancement of their personal charms'. Generously, she concedes, 'there is a portion of them too reasonable, and too well-informed themselves, to desire anything more in woman than ignorance'; but the charge remains, and reverberates. Again and again Jane Austen returns to the question of women's education – from cool asides in her letters, such as 'Her hair is done up with an elegance to do credit to any education', to the ironic examination of feminine accomplishments and learning which recurs throughout her novels. 'A woman must have a thorough knowledge of music, singing, drawing, dancing and the modern languages', besides 'a certain something in her air and manner of walking, the tone of her voice, her address and expressions', Miss Bingley declares in *Pride and Prejudice*, seeking to impress Mr Darcy – to which Elizabeth Bennet replies calmly, 'I never saw such a woman. I never saw such capacity, and taste, and application . . . united.' The affectation of accomplishments, with a view to ensnaring a husband, is a device with which Jane Austen, like Mr Darcy himself, has no patience. Lizzy Bennet's plain, dull sister Mary embarrasses her family by showing off tunelessly at the piano and uttering would-be intellectual platitudes; pushy Mrs Elton, in *Emma*, tries to conceal her social inadequacies beneath a veneer of music, Italian phrases and ostentatious

'elegance'. Honest ignorance is preferable to all such pretensions: as the authoritative hero of *Emma*, Mr Knightley,
pronounces, 'An unpretending, single-minded, artless girl',
such as naive Harriet Smith, is 'infinitely to be preferred by
any man of sense and taste to such a woman as Mrs Elton'.
What counts for more than any accomplishments is 'principle,
active principle'. At the beginning of *Mansfield Park*, gentle
little Fanny Price is snubbed by her grand cousins for being
'so very ignorant', while their own smattering of learning
ranges from drawing and geography to 'a great deal of the
Heathen Mythology, and all the Metals, semi-Metals, Planets
and distinguished philosophers'; by the end of that novel,
however, their father can only lament that 'with all the cost
and care of an anxious and expensive education', his daughters have grown up selfish and immoral, 'without their
understanding their first duties'.

The best upbringing for a girl, Jane Austen concludes, is that
which will equip her to be a worthy partner and companion
for a husband of 'sense and taste' such as Mr Knightley and Mr
Darcy. She does not dwell on the injustice whereby even such
a witless hobbledehoy as John Thorpe, in *Northanger Abbey*,
could be a student at Oxford University, while no woman,
however intelligent or dedicated, could expect to receive any
formal education after 'coming out' of the schoolroom, into
adult society and the marriage-market, at the age of 17 or 18.
Anne Elliot, in *Persuasion*, gently points out men's 'advantage'
in 'telling their own story', saying, 'Education has been theirs
in so much higher a degree; the pen has been in their hands.'
Yet, though she mentions the inequality of opportunities
between the sexes, remarking, 'We live at home, quiet,
confined . . . You have always a profession, pursuits, business
of some sort or other, to take you back into the world', this
state of affairs is, ultimately, treated as natural and inevitable,
rather than as a wrong to be righted. Regency readers might,
nevertheless, have appreciated the sly joke which Jane Austen

drops into her description of an ideal girls' school, in *Emma*. Not a grandiose 'seminary', or 'establishment', where 'young ladies for enormous pay might be screwed out of health and into vanity', this is described as 'a real, honest, old-fashioned Boarding-school', where girls might be sent to 'scramble themselves into a little education, without any danger of coming back prodigies'. The proprietress is called Mrs Goddard – and Dr Goddard was the name of the head-master (from 1793 to 1809) of Winchester College, the ancient and illustrious boys' public school attended by Jane's beloved nephews.

Though Jane Austen's heroines are all intelligent, and – to varying degrees – interested in improving their minds by reading, none is a blue-stocking. Similarly (in a device employed by generations of 'women's' novelists), none is a devastating beauty. Two of them, Elinor in *Sense and Sensibility* and Elizabeth in *Pride and Prejudice*, are described from the outset as being outshone in looks by a more strikingly attractive sister (as Jane herself evidently was by Cassandra). The average female reader – then or now – can identify with young Catherine Morland, gratified to be called 'almost pretty today', or with fading Anne Elliot's pleasure at finding herself the object of a handsome stranger's interested glances. They all, in differing degrees, gain in good looks, as well as self-knowledge, as the novel develops. Fanny Price is judged to have 'the sort of beauty that grows on one'; Lizzy Bennet, initially slighted by Mr Darcy as 'tolerable, but not handsome enough to tempt *me*', is later acknowledged by him to be 'one of the handsomest women of my acquaintance'. The heroine of *Emma* is agreed to be 'handsome' from the outset – but even she briefly fears losing Mr Knightley to her protégée Harriet, who, though generally Emma's inferior, is undeniably 'a very pretty girl', in the most seductive fair-haired, blue-eyed, doll-like mode. Jane Austen, who was insecure enough about her own looks to record the occasional compliments she received, had no illusions about the role of beauty in a woman's marriage prospects. Plain Charlotte Lucas in *Pride and Prejudice* marries the tedious Mr Collins because she will get no better offer; in *Sense and Sensibility*, acerbic Mr Palmer is aware that 'Through some unaccountable bias in favour of beauty, he was the husband of a very silly woman'; however, the author notes sagely, 'This kind of blunder was too common for any sensible man to be lastingly hurt by it.'

Ultimately, in Jane Austen's world, the question for women is not whether, but whom, to marry. In 1798 she wrote affectionately of one younger friend, 'She goes on now as young ladies of seventeen ought to do, admired and admiring'; in 1817, shortly before her death, she assured her niece Fanny, 'Depend upon it, the right Man will come at last.' The creator of the romantic meddler Emma Woodhouse was not above match-making herself: 'I have got a Husband for each of the Miss Maitlands', she announced on one occasion; on another, she told Cassandra that a governess of their acquaintance, Miss Sharp, 'writes highly' of her employer, Sir William, confiding, 'I do so want him to marry her.' The passage ends, 'Oh Sir Wm! Sir Wm! How I will love you, if you will love Miss Sharp.' Unlike the fictional Emma, however, Jane Austen did not interfere in others' lives; and unlike vulgar, good-natured Mrs Jennings, in *Sense and Sensibility*, 'who was always anxious to get a good husband for every pretty girl', she did not think that conversation with young women should consist chiefly of jokes and teasing on 'the subject of lovers and husbands'. Privately, she might speculate to Cassandra, 'Young Wyndham . . . is such a nice, gentlemanlike, unaffected sort of young Man, that I think he may do for Fanny', but in public she strongly disapproved of such personal remarks. Only the ill-bred and second-rate in her novels risk embarrassing others with allusions to love-letters, 'beaux', or (worst of all), pregnancy. Mrs Jennings's well-meant 'raillery' causes real pain to the jilted Marianne; in *Emma*, Mrs Elton's arch hints on the subject of

Jane Fairfax's secret engagement show up her inferior breeding, rather than her superior knowledge. Lord Byron might
write scathingly of love as 'Woman's whole existence', but in
Jane Austen's works women are expected to have an identity
independent of their relationships; and while silly girls such
as Isabella Thorpe and Lydia Bennet can think and talk of
little but young men and flirtation, intelligent females enjoy
'rational discourse' on such subjects as poetry and landscape.
When they do speak of love, they use dignified language – 'he
admires her' and 'she esteems him', rather than the 'head over
ears in love' of an ignorant Isabella. 'I have no doubt of her
being extremely attached to him' is Mrs Weston's delicate
assessment of Jane Fairfax's passionate, clandestine love, in a
private exchange with her intimate friend Emma; even sisters
as close as Jane and Elizabeth Bennet talk restrainedly to one
another of their feelings for the men they long to marry.

Particularly offensive to Jane Austen was any suggestion that
women should be grateful for men's attentions – 'as if', she
wrote indignantly in 1807, 'it cd. be only ask and have'.
Marianne Dashwood's angry protests to Sir John Dashwood
that 'setting one's cap at a man' and 'making a conquest' are 'the
most odious' of expressions are met by him with jovial incom-
prehension – just as Elizabeth Bennet's attempts to refuse Mr
Collins's proposal of marriage are received, at first, with bland
disbelief. The repellent Mr Collins is no more able than the
gorgeously eligible Mr Darcy, later in the same novel, to
imagine that a woman with Elizabeth's limited social prospects
might choose to turn his offer down. Yet she does so; and
without hesitating. Her sister Jane – echoing the author's own
words to her niece Fanny – begs: 'Oh Lizzy! Do anything rather
than marry without affection'; but such a warning is unnecessary. Elizabeth Bennet, like all characters with 'principle and
integrity' in Jane Austen's fiction, would never marry for
worldly motives. Only when she has begun to know Mr Darcy
better, and sees his true nature reflected in the management of

his great estate, Pemberley, does she feel 'something like regret', and reflect, 'Of this place I might have been mistress!' No bullying or cajoling can persuade Fanny Price, in *Mansfield Park*, to accept the rake Henry Crawford's suit, which would transform her Cinderella existence into one of wealth and privilege; in the unfinished work *The Watsons*, the hard-pressed heroine was, apparently, to have refused an offer from rich young Lord Osborne, of Osborne Castle, in favour of his former tutor, Mr Howard. At a time when, unable to improve her lot in life through work, a gentlewoman could only increase her wealth and status through marriage, the social pressure to accept almost any 'advantageous' offer could be intense; but though heartless and mercenary marriages abound in Jane Austen's novels, they are universally condemned by the author and her heroines.

'The woman who marries him cannot have a proper way of thinking', Elizabeth Bennet says scornfully of her former friend Charlotte Lucas's 'prudential' match with the despised Mr Collins. What constitutes 'a proper way of thinking' is, however, defined differently by others. 'It is every young woman's duty to accept such a very unexceptionable offer as this' is 'almost the only rule of conduct' which Fanny Price ever receives from her indolent aunt Lady Bertram, in *Mansfield Park*; in *Persuasion*, a heartbroken Anne Elliot is separated in youth from the man she loves by her mentor, Lady Russell, on the grounds that he is 'without alliance or fortune'. Materialistic attitudes to marriage are the source of some of Jane Austen's most sparkling comedy – from the immortal opening to *Pride and Prejudice*, 'It is a truth universally acknowledged, that a single man in possession of a good fortune, must be in want of a wife' – to the portrait of John Dashwood, in *Sense and Sensibility*, earnestly calculating how rich a husband each of his sisters may aspire to, on the basis of their relative claims to beauty. But such attitudes also inspire some of Jane Austen's darkest and most heartfelt writing – most notably in *Mansfield Park*, in which the blithe cynicism of Mary Crawford's creed ('Matrimony was her object, provided she could marry well') contrasts painfully with Fanny Price's moral conflict, as she finds herself torn between refusing the unprincipled Henry Crawford's suit, as her conscience and wishes dictate, and observing her duty to her uncle and benefactor Sir Thomas Bertram, who thinks her 'selfish and ungrateful' for 'throwing away . . . such an opportunity of being settled in life'. Behind Sir Thomas's reproaches lies, implicitly, an unpalatable truth: until she marries, Fanny will remain his financial responsibility. More explicitly, Mrs Bennet's selfish upbraiding of Lizzy, in *Pride and Prejudice*, for refusing Mr Collins, strikes a rare note of reason when she cries, 'Who is to maintain you when your father is dead – I shall not be able to keep you.' Many women of Jane Austen's generation must have faced such emotional pressure – whether as open coercion (such as the heroine of her youthful, unpublished work *Lady Susan* endures from her cruel mother), or, more insidiously, as the sort of well-meant manoeuvring to which even the hero of *Mansfield Park*, Edmund, misguidedly subjects Fanny, on Mr Crawford's behalf. (Having reassured her, 'You did not love him . . . nothing could have justified your accepting him', he ends by urging, 'Let him succeed at last, Fanny . . . prove yourself grateful and tender-hearted.') Under comparable pressure from a trusted mentor, Anne Elliot, in *Persuasion*, succumbs – as Fanny would surely have done, Jane Austen tells her readers. It takes a woman of Lizzy Bennet's independence of spirit to declare fearlessly – when pressed by Lady Catherine de Bourgh to give up Mr Darcy – 'I am only resolved to act in that manner which will, in my own opinion, constitute my happiness.'

Any attempt, however well-meant, at meddling in others' emotional lives is abhorrent to Jane Austen – from Emma Woodhouse's schemes to have Harriet Smith, in *Emma*, marry above her station, to Darcy's efforts to prevent Mr Bingley, in *Pride and Prejudice*, from marrying below his. Parents who seek their children's happiness in marriage, rather than their advancement, such as the unpretentious Mr and Mrs Musgrove in *Persuasion*, and the Revd Richard and Mrs Morland in *Northanger Abbey*, are warmly commended – unlike Sir Walter Elliot and General Tilney in the same novels, whose snobbish and mercenary marital ambitions for their offspring help to place them among Jane Austen's most unsympathetic characters. Throughout the correspondence in which, between 1814 and 1817, she secretly counselled her niece Fanny on her love-affairs, 'Aunt Jane' was anxious to stress her impartiality. 'You frighten me out of my wits by your reference' (to her judgement), she wrote in November 1814, adding firmly, 'Your own feelings, and none but your own should determine such an important point.' Scrupulously, she examined the merits and faults of each suitor, from John Plumptre ('Poor dear Mr. J.P.!') with his 'uncommonly amiable mind, strict principles, just notions', but unfortunate 'deficiencies of Manner', to the evidently 'more animated Character' 'Mr. J.W.', James Wildman, of whom Jane admitted cautiously, in February 1817, 'I have rather taken a fancy to him than not.' Her deliberations focused on each young man's character, qualities and feelings towards Fanny; in only a few passing references – to Mr Plumptre as 'the eldest son of a Man of Fortune', or to Mr Wildman's family seat ('I like Chilham Castle for you') – did she take into account their material prospects. While insisting that she could offer no 'Opinion or Counsel ... worth having', on one point Jane Austen was adamant: what her fictional counterpart, the Bennet sisters' wise and delightful aunt Mrs Gardiner, sums up in *Pride and Prejudice* as 'a real, strong attachment' was the only honourable basis for marriage. She might have been pleased when, in 1820 – in a curious echo of Marianne Dashwood's acceptance of Colonel Brandon in *Sense and Sensibility* – the 26-year-old Fanny married a family connection, Sir Edward Knatchbull, a widowed Baronet aged almost 40. She would surely have been saddened, however, had she known that, years later, this 'inimitable, irresistible niece', who had once set so much store by her judgement, would look back on her authoress aunt with stiff Victorian snobbery, describing her as 'not so *refined* as she ought to have been for her *talent*', through having been 'brought up in the most complete ignorance of the world and its ways'.

Certainly the world and its ways are treated, throughout Jane Austen's fiction, as generally inimical to happy, respectable marriage. Sexual wrongdoing and worldly, property-based marriages are constantly linked in her writing, for both sexes. Dissolute men who corrupt innocent girls, such as Willoughby in *Sense and Sensibility* and Wickham in *Pride and Prejudice*, seek to restore their fortunes by pursuing heiresses; women who make marriages of convenience, from Maria Bertram in *Mansfield Park* to Colonel Brandon's unfortunate sister-in-law, 'married against her inclination' in *Sense and Sensibility*, become easy prey for rakish seducers. 'To marry for money I think the wickedest thing in the world', the most naive of Jane Austen's heroines, Catherine Morland, hotly declares in *Northanger Abbey* – while the most worldly-wise of her female characters, Mary Crawford, in *Mansfield Park*, states matter-of-factly, 'It is everybody's duty to do as well for themselves as they can.' Both she and her brother Henry are well aware of society's ideals of marriage. 'I think too well of Miss Bertram to suppose she would ever give her hand without her heart', Henry says mockingly of Maria Bertram's loveless engagement to rich Mr Rushworth; but throughout the novel Mary expresses (and Henry, ultimately, illustrates) the fashionable, cynical approach to matrimony. 'There is not one in a hundred of either sex who is not taken in when they marry', Mary observes coolly. She is amused, and even proud, that her brother is 'the most horrible flirt', whom scheming women seek to 'reason, coax or trick ... into marrying'; and even while encouraging his courtship of the admirable Fanny, she assumes that, once they are wed, Henry's love will inevitably cease. It is, naturally, Mary Crawford who makes the only improper joke in the whole of Jane Austen's fiction. Referring to her life in London with her disreputable uncle, Admiral Crawford, she mentions being acquainted with 'a circle of admirals' – and adds, 'Of *Rears*, and *Vices*, I saw enough. Now, do not be suspecting me of a pun, I intreat.' The allusion is not – as some twenty-first-century commentators have assumed – to sodomy: in a light romantic novel aimed largely at young, innocent, female readers, Jane Austen would never have hinted at an act then considered so vilely perverted as to be a capital crime. (In 1807, she had written of the popular novelist Mme de Genlis's latest work, *Alphonsine*, 'We were disgusted in twenty pages ... it has indelicacies which disgrace a pen hitherto so pure.') Mary's naughty innuendo clearly concerns flagellation: utterly unfit for a lady's conversation, but legal; widely popular, not only with old roués and young bucks, but even among such eminent figures as the future Prime Minister Lord Melbourne; and familiar enough to any citizen who ever glanced in a print-shop window at the satirical cartoons of Gillray or Rowlandson, in which birches and buttocks made frequent appearances.

Perhaps the broadest witticism which Jane Austen ever permitted herself in her correspondence was contained in one of her last surviving letters, dated February 20 1817. Noting the birth of an eighteenth child to a friend, Mrs Deedes, she concluded briskly, '& then I would recommend to her & Mr D. the simple regimen of separate rooms'. Fond as she was of children, she appears to have found pregnancy distinctly unappealing. Certainly, childbirth was a dangerous event, for women of all classes: in 1817, the year of Jane Austen's death, the heir to the throne herself, the Regent's daughter Princess Charlotte of Wales, was to die giving birth to a stillborn son. In 1798, while her brother James's wife Mary was expecting her first child, Jane had written to Cassandra, 'Mrs Coulthard and Anne, late of Manydown, are both dead, and both died in childbed. We have not regaled Mary with this news.' Though Mary Austen was safely delivered of a boy (Jane Austen's future biographer, J. E. Austen-Leigh), two of her other sisters-in-law – Edward's first wife, Elizabeth, and Charles's first wife, Fanny – would die from childbirth complications. It was the burden of pregnancy, rather than the risk, however, which Jane seemed to find disquieting. 'That Mrs Deedes is to have another Child I suppose I may lament', she wrote in 1807; and of another friend, Mrs Tilson, in 1808, 'poor Woman! How can she be honestly breeding again?' Almost every reference to pregnancy in her letters was couched in the same pitying tone, from 'Poor little F. looked heavy', and 'Little Embryo is troublesome I suppose', to 'Anna has not a chance of escape ... Poor Animal, she will be worn out before she is thirty.' Her niece Anna's rapid pregnancies were probably in her thoughts (though she referred to another fecund friend) when, counselling her niece Fanny against marrying in haste, she added hearteningly, 'And then, by not beginning the business of Mothering quite so early in life, you will be young in Constitution, spirits, figure & countenance, while Mrs Wm Hammond is growing old by confinements and nursing.'

This somewhat aloof attitude towards 'confinements and nursing' did not extend to Jane Austen's treatment of children, either in life or in literature. 'She seemed to love you, and you loved her in return', her brother James's younger daughter, Caroline, wrote long after, recalling an aunt of infinite patience and playfulness, who amused her and her little cousins with stories, 'chiefly of Fairyland', in which all the fairies had individual characters, provided them with dressing-up clothes from her own wardrobe, and charmed them with such fancies as an imaginary conversation between the little girls, 'supposing we were all grown up, the day after a ball'. With 'great sweetness of manner', as her letters demonstrate, 'Aunt Jane' treated the young with respect as well as affection, entering with tender interest into their concerns, and providing jokes, sympathy or advice as their changing ages and situations required. When her beautiful sister-in-law Elizabeth, Edward Knight's wife, died suddenly and tragically in childbirth, in 1808, it was Jane who took charge of the two elder boys, Edward and George, while her sister Cassandra – who had gone to Godmersham for the confinement – stayed on there to care for the widower, his daughter Fanny, and the smaller children. To 14-year-old Edward and 12-year-old George, both now Winchester College schoolboys, Jane showed a wonderfully compassionate blend of sense and sensibility, encouraging them to shed tears if they wished, without feeling unmanly, and then cheering them up with every amusement she could devise, from the indoor games of spillikins, cards and conundrums to the open-air pleasures of walks and rowing. 'While I write now', she reported on 24 October, George was busy bombarding paper ships with horse-chestnuts, while Edward – in true Austen fashion – was immersed in a book, *The Lake of Killarney*, by Anna Maria Porter, 'twisting himself about in our of our great chairs' as he read.

The image of the boy fidgeting contentedly in a vast Georgian chair was typical of Jane Austen's delicate observations of children. Other characteristic vignettes in her letters included the mention of a 'little visitor', Catherine Foote, in 1807, who, as Jane wrote, was 'talking away at my side & examining the Treasures of my Writing-desk drawer', and a tender glimpse of her brother Charles's daughter Cassy, aged 5, arriving at a Godmersham family house-party in 1813 looking 'tired & bewildered' amid the high-ceilinged grandeur of her surroundings; then, as the visit progressed, getting on 'pretty well with her cousins' but, Jane reported, 'not quite happy among them: they are too many and too boisterous for her'. Such observations would naturally re-emerge in her fiction, resulting in such images as the little Gardiners in *Pride and*

Prejudice, welcoming their parents' return from holiday with a 'joyful surprise that ... displayed itself over their whole bodies, in a variety of capers and frisks'; or the deft cameo of Emma Woodhouse, in *Emma*, entertaining her small niece, 'a nice little girl about eight months old, who was ... very happy to be danced about in her aunt's arms'. What ensues in that scene is still more telling: the novel's hero, Mr Knightley, strides into the room, and 'with the unceremoniousness of perfect amity', scoops up the gurgling baby from Emma's arms and proceeds to dandle her himself. It is central to Jane Austen's enduring appeal as a novelist that her, and her contemporary readers', image of an ideal man accorded so well with that of many women in the twenty-first century: tall, handsome, self-assured Mr Knightley is as much at ease holding a baby as he is discussing crops with a tenant farmer, or points of law with his barrister brother. Sensitivity is an indispensable quality in a Jane Austen hero; and while this can be displayed in any number of ways, from Henry Tilney choosing gowns for his sister, in *Northanger Abbey*, to Mr Knightley courteously asking Harriet Smith to dance with him when she has been rejected as a partner by Mr Elton, it is never better displayed than in these gentlemen's dealings with children. One of the most powerful instances occurs in *Persuasion*, when put-upon Anne Elliot – still in love with her former suitor, the now-disdainful Captain Wentworth – is being tormented by her younger nephew, 'a stout, forward child, of two years old', who has climbed on her back; suddenly she is aware that 'someone was taking him from her, though he had bent down her head so much, that his little sturdy hands were unfastened from around her neck, and he was resolutely borne away, before she knew that Captain Wentworth had done it'. It is an almost painfully naturalistic, and effective, passage.

There was nothing sentimental in Jane Austen's attitudes to children. Those in her novels are almost always unruly and self-willed – and they can be downright unpleasant. The naughtiness of Anne Elliot's small nephew is minor compared with the 'impertinent encroachments and mischievous tricks' of the spoilt Middleton children of Barton Park, in *Sense and Sensibility*. After a visit during which the guests have had 'their sashes untied, their hair pulled about their ears, their work-bags searched and their knives and scissars [*sic*] stolen away', followed by a frightful scene of screaming and kicking, Elinor Dashwood says with feeling, 'I confess that while I am at Barton Park, I never think of tame and quiet children with any abhorrence.' The remark is a measure of the young Middletons' unpleasantness, since 'tame and quiet' children in general have little place in Jane Austen's world. Her own merry childhood, with its games, jokes, laughter and play-acting, seems to have remained her model of happy domesticity; and far from being 'seen and not heard', as would be expected of their Victorian successors, the children in her fiction are a boisterous bunch – from the shouting, door-slamming, squabbling young Prices, in *Mansfield Park*, to the jolly cricket- and baseball-playing Morlands in *Northanger Abbey*, who preferred 'running about the country' to 'books, or at least books of information'. A 'young Lucas', accompanying his older sisters on a visit to the Bennets in *Pride and Prejudice*, boldly wrangles with his hostess, Mrs Bennet, over how much wine he would drink, if he were 'as rich as Mr Darcy'; in *The Watsons*, the hero's charming 10-year-old nephew not only attends a public ball, but has the confidence to invite an eligible, grown-up lady to dance with him. 'What is become of all the Shyness in the World?', Jane wrote to Cassandra in 1807, describing the visit from little Catherine Foote; fondly, she added, 'She is a nice, natural, open-hearted, affectionate girl, with all the ready civility which one sees in the best Children in the present day.'

Where 'ready civility' and good behaviour were lacking in the young, Jane Austen clearly believed that the parents were to blame. Lady Middleton's selfish vanity allows her to assume that her offspring's antics are as delightful to others as to herself; Mrs Price's brood are wild and mannerless because she is 'a partial, ill-judging parent, a dawdle, a slattern who neither taught nor restrained her children'. Discipline is conspicuously absent from Jane Austen's fictional families. There are no grim punishments, as in the works of her Victorian successors such as Charlotte Brontë and Charles Dickens; instead, 'caresses' and treats are frequent. Most fathers in her novels are indulgent, from gentle Mr Woodhouse, in *Emma*, to detached, permissive Mr Bennet, in *Pride and Prejudice*; even the would-be stern paterfamilias Sir Thomas Bertram, in *Mansfield Park*, is cheerfully defied by his grown-up heir and daughters once he is absent from home. What is required, in bringing children up well, is proper 'management'; without it, the grandmother of Anne Elliot's troublesome nephews complains, in *Persuasion*, 'one is obliged to be checking [them] every moment, "don't do this, and don't do that"', or keeping them 'in tolerable order' with 'more cake than is good for them'. She admires Anne's 'method' – remarking, 'They are quite different creatures with you!' Anne's way with her nephews, combining affection and firmness, is similar to that of Mr Knightley, in *Emma*, with his, as he makes them take turns at their favourite sport of being thrown up in the air. This is the exemplary approach to bringing up children spelt out in *Pride and Prejudice* when Jane Bennet, left in temporary charge of her little Gardiner cousins, cares for them 'with steady sense and sweetness of temper', by fondly 'teaching them, playing with them, and loving them'.

Dearly as she loved her own nieces and nephews, Jane Austen could be critical of them – and of their parents. In 1813, after a visit from her brother Charles and his family, she wrote that his elder daughter, Cassy, was 'very much improved . . . but Method has been wanting'; loyally, she added, 'She will really be a very pleasing Child, if only they will exert themselves a little.' Her niece Anna, James Austen's daughter by his first marriage, was a constant source of both pleasure and concern; whether cropping her hair fashionably short, contracting an unsuitable, short-lived engagement to a neighbour's son, or plaguing her authoress aunt for advice on her own attempts at writing a novel, she was, Jane commented wryly in 1811, 'quite an Anna with variations'. Marriage, and the births of the first two of her seven children, seemed to bring about a more settled, steady variation; but in her first great-niece Jane found new cause for concern. 'Jemima has a very irritable bad Temper', she wrote to Fanny Knight, in March 1817. 'I hope as Anna is so early sensible of it's [sic] defects, that she will give Jemima's disposition the early & steady attention it must require.' With Fanny Knight herself, Jane had no such anxieties. While staying at Godmersham in the summer of 1808 she had described the engaging 15-year-old as 'almost another sister', confessing to Cassandra, 'I could not have supposed that a niece would ever have been so much to me.' Over the years she clearly came to look on Fanny not merely as niece, or even sister, but rather as the daughter she never had: in February 1817, just five months before her death, Jane told the 'pretty Dear' dotingly, 'You are inimitable, irresistible. You are the delight of my Life ... It is very, very gratifying to me to know you so intimately.' Anxious though she was to help with Fanny's romantic dilemmas, she could not resist exclaiming, 'Oh! What a loss it will be when you are married. You are too agreable [sic] as a Neice [sic]. I shall hate you when your delicious play of Mind is all settled down into conjugal and maternal affections.' After such an uncharacteristic burst of feeling, she added, more guardedly, 'And yet I do wish you to marry, very much, because I know you will never be happy till you are.'

If Fanny was privately acknowledged as her favourite, Jane Austen nevertheless tried to show affection impartially to all her nieces and nephews, of whom there were twenty-four at the time of her death. With the little ones she was playful and whimsical ('My sweet little George! I am delighted to hear that he has such an inventive genius as to face-making', she wrote of Fanny Knight's second brother, in 1799); towards their elder brothers and sisters she showed a humorous respect which was no less agreeable. After her nephew (and future biographer) Edward left school in 1816 she wrote to him with chaffing camaraderie, 'I give you joy of having left Winchester. Now you may own, how miserable you were there; now, it will gradually all come out – your Crimes & your Miseries – how often you went up by the Mail to London & threw away Fifty Guineas at a Tavern, & how often you were on the point of hanging yourself.' To Edward's 13-year-old sister Caroline, when their half-sister Anna had her first child, she joked 'Now that you are become an Aunt, you are a person of some consequence & must excite great Interest whatever you do.' The letter – signed to her 'dear Sister-Aunt' – concluded solemnly, 'I have always maintained the importance of Aunts as much as possible, & I am sure of your doing the same now.'

As her hopes of marriage and motherhood receded, the roles of sister and aunt became of increasing importance to Jane Austen. She continued to joke about finding a husband: meeting a Mr Lushington, during a Godmersham house-party in October 1813, she mused, 'I am rather in love with him. – I dare say he is ambitious & Insincere'; a month later she wrote flippantly, 'Perhaps I may marry young Mr D'Arblay', as though the success of *Pride and Prejudice* might make her an eligible wife for the great Fanny Burney's 19-year-old son. In the same year, on hearing that the wife of her favourite poet, George Crabbe (whom she had never met), had died, she had told Cassandra, 'I will comfort *him* as well as I can, but I do not undertake to be good to her children. She had better not leave any.' The obvious parallel between producing books and producing children was one which seemed to amuse her: she referred to it herself, several times. 'I can no more forget it, than a mother can forget her sucking child', she wrote in 1811, while preparing *Sense and Sensibility* for publication; when the first copy of *Pride and Prejudice* arrived at Chawton, in January 1813, she reported 'I have got my own darling child from London'; and in 1815, following the birth of Anna's first baby, Jemima, she sent the young mother an early copy of *Emma*, with the message, 'As I wish very much to see *your* Jemima, I am sure you will like to see *my* Emma.' There was something both sisterly and motherly in her attitude towards her heroines: while Elinor Dashwood was 'my Elinor', and Anne Elliot described as 'almost too good for me', she wrote lovingly of Elizabeth Bennet, 'I must confess that I think her as delightful a creature as ever appeared in print.'

Sisterhood between women was a matter of considerable importance to Jane Austen. No emotional attachment in her life was ever more strong than her bond with Cassandra; and some of the most intense relationships depicted in her fiction are those between the elder Dashwood and Bennet sisters. 'Almost another sister' was her highest praise for a woman – applied both to her niece Fanny Knight and her dear friend Martha Lloyd; and even when there was no actual tie of blood or friendship, she felt an instinctive loyalty and duty towards her own sex. When the wronged, but troublesome, Princess of Wales published a letter of complaint against her husband the Prince Regent, in February 1813, Jane wrote to Cassandra, 'Poor woman, I shall support her as long as I can, because she *is* a Woman, and because I hate her Husband'; in her novels, women are expected to show a similar sense of kinship. 'How could you behave so unfairly by your sister?' Elinor Dashwood exclaims, appalled, on learning that Miss Steele has listened at the door while her sister was closeted with her betrothed; in *Mansfield Park*, Mary Crawford's pursuit of her brother's interests at the expense of Fanny Price's feelings earn her, not approval for being 'complaisant as a sister', but censure, for being 'careless as a woman and a friend'.

It was as a woman and friend, as well as loyal aunt, that Jane devoted so much attention to counselling Fanny Knight on her love-affairs. 'I really am impatient', she assured her niece in 1814, 'to be writing something on so very interesting a subject.' Readers past and present have had cause to be grateful that, while remaining single herself, Jane Austen should have written with such extraordinary skill and perception, wit and tenderness, on 'so very interesting a subject' as love and marriage.

6

'The Beauty of the Place'

'It is a charming house, I assure you . . .
and with modern furniture it would be
delightful.'

    Marianne Dashwood, in *Sense and Sensibility*, 1811

Jane Austen had the good fortune to live, and write, during one of the greatest periods of British architecture and design. When she was born, in 1775, the cabinet-makers Chippendale and Hepplewhite had thriving furniture workshops in London, and the Adam brothers were transforming noblemen's houses into masterpiece of airy elegance and grace; by the time of her death, in 1817, John Nash was at work on the idyllic stuccoed villas of Regent's Park, and the terms 'interior decoration' and 'landscape gardening' had entered the English language. She mentions only one architect, Bonomi, and one garden designer, Repton, by name in her works, and rarely describes any location in detail, yet no novelist in English literature is more closely associated with the visual style of an era. 'Very great was my pleasure in going over the house and grounds', she wrote to Cassandra in 1805, after visiting one of their adopted brother Edward's family properties; and this pleasure in 'going over' the houses and grounds, gardens and scenery of her Georgian and Regency world was one which Jane Austen would share with generations of her readers.

Ironically, the creator of such famous houses as Mr Darcy's

Pemberley and the Bertrams' Mansfield Park never had a real home of her own. Unlike her mother's kinswoman Mary Leigh, whose bachelor brother left her the 'fine old large house' Stoneleigh Abbey, in Warwickshire, on his death, Jane Austen was not born to inherit property; and unlike all her fictional heroines, from rich Emma Woodhouse to poor-relation Fanny Price, she was not destined to marry, and thus acquire an 'establishment' to decorate, furnish and manage as she pleased. Yet, though she disapproves, in *Pride and Prejudice*, of the plain, ageing Charlotte Lucas marrying a detestable man, Mr Collins, 'from the pure and disinterested desire of an establishment', she is highly aware of the charms of becoming mistress of a Regency household. Self-effacing Anne Elliot, in *Persuasion*, having lost both her childhood home and her hopes of marriage, may dream of hardy shipboard life, and love in a seaside cottage, but most of Jane Austen's females aspire to a handsome, modern house, well-situated, with new furniture, fashionable wallpaper, and the latest amenities of a Rumford stove and Wedgwood china.

The house in which she grew up and wrote her earliest works was neither modern nor elegant. Steventon Rectory was a mellow, rambling, Hampshire parsonage, about five miles from Basingstoke; though it had a symmetrical façade, with a dining-room and sitting-room on either side of a central hall, it bore little resemblance to the graceful, neo-classical buildings then springing up around the country, which were popularized by the spread of 'pattern books' containing detailed plans and designs by leading architects, for the middle-class public to copy. In place of modish decorative details, such as the painted ceilings and ornate plasterwork shown in *The Works in Architecture of Robert and James Adam Esquires*, published in 1773, the interiors at Steventon had simple, white-washed ceiling-beams, and no cornices; the furniture was presumably country-made, and considered of little value, since (according to Austen family tradition), it arrived piled on a farm-cart, with the doughty Mrs Austen perched on a feather mattress on top. Like many of their contemporaries, the Austens made 'improvements' to their property – adding a bow-window to the Rector's study, and creating a 'sweep', or curving carriage-drive, in front of the house. (Elinor Dashwood, in *Sense and Sensibility*, would similarly 'invent a sweep' when planning the renovations to her future married home, Delaford Rectory.) But though a respectable house in its day, and 'commodious' enough to accommodate well-to-do boarding pupils, as well as the Rector's own six healthy children, by the 1820s Steventon had become too antiquated for nineteenth-century needs, and was demolished. To Jane Austen, however, this childhood home, which she left with regret in 1801 at the age of 25, would remain the epitome of cheerful domesticity; and it would seem to have provided the model for the Morlands' vicarage household in *Northanger Abbey*. The 'chief beauty of the place', according to her nephew and biographer J. E. Austen-Leigh, who spent his own childhood there, was the abundance of sprawling, bushy hedgerows lining the local pathways. 'If you could discover whether Northamptonshire is a country of hedgerows I should be glad', she wrote to Cassandra in 1813, while at work on *Mansfield Park*. In the event, *Persuasion*, too, would feature a hedgerow, in a crucial scene of accidental eavesdropping.

Both by birth and by inclination, Jane Austen was a staunch countrywoman. 'God made the country and man made the town', wrote one of her favourite poets, William Cowper; and unlike the aristocracy of pre-Revolutionary France, for whom banishment from Court and town was a penance, the British upper classes, in general, relished rural life. 'English verdure, English culture, English comfort', runs a famous passage in *Emma*, reflecting on 'a sweet view' over Mr Knightley's well-ordered estate. All Jane Austen's heroines are countrywomen, deeply imbued with country ways and values, and half-suspicious of the supposed moral and physical ills of the cities. 'Here I am once more in this Scene of Dissipation & vice, and I begin already to find my Morals corrupted', she wrote merrily to Cassandra, while visiting London in 1796. Gazing up at the starlit sky over Northamptonshire, in *Mansfield Park*, Fanny Price muses, 'On such a night as this, I feel as if there could be neither wickedness nor sorrow in the world', adding earnestly, 'There certainly would be less of both if the sublimity of Nature were more attended to.' And – like the author herself – Anne Elliot in *Persuasion* is desolate at having to leave her family home in the heart of the countryside for the 'white glare' and dubious pleasures of Bath, which she did not think 'agreed with her'. To later generations, this west-country watering-place, with its classically planned squares and crescents built of honey-gold stone, would be regarded as one of the triumphs of eighteenth-century civilization: but to Jane Austen it was a place of 'vapour, shadow, smoke and confusion' where, as a reluctant resident from 1801 to 1806, she would pass the most unhappy (and uncreative) period of her life.

Bath's popularity was founded on the warm mineral waters which welled up through the limestone rock to temperatures of some 120°F. The Romans – who had called the city Aquae Sulis Minerva, combining the name of the local Celtic deity, Sulis, with that of their own goddess of wisdom, Minerva – had created an ingenious system of baths and steamrooms where the public might benefit from their healing powers; some 1,600 years later, early Georgian businessmen and architects saw the potential of the now-ramshackle (and increasingly disreputable) spa as a centre for health-conscious, fashionable society. In 1704, an astute, agreeable gamester named Richard Nash was appointed official Master of Ceremonies by the Bath Corporation; 'Beau Nash', as he became known, proceeded to transform the city's social life – forbidding duelling and boorish conduct, imposing strict dress codes, and establishing a carefully regulated round of public promenades and assemblies. A new Pump Room was built, where the polite world could meet to take the all-important medicinal waters, and civic improvements from good street-lighting to broad, even pavements were introduced; but it was not until the late 1720s that a then little-known architect named John Wood embarked on what he boldly termed 'the improvement of the city by building'. Like Rome, Bath was set among hills; and the austere, symmetrical principles of Roman classical architecture provided Wood with his inspiration for the city's Georgian renaissance.

By the time Jane Austen first visited Bath, in the 1790s, the city was already past its heyday. The aristocracy had begun to move on to rival spas, such as Cheltenham and Tunbridge Wells, and the seaside resort of Brighton, where the Prince Regent was building a holiday home; and sedate, rich couples such as Jane Austen's aunt and uncle, the Leigh-Perrots, who rented a house in the Paragon, were increasingly setting the tone for Bath society. On a summer holiday in 1799, with her mother, her brother Edward, his wife and their two eldest children, Jane lodged at No. 13 Queen Square: 'We are exceedingly pleased with the house', she reported, commenting on the 'nice-sized rooms', the view from the drawing-room window and the 'little black kitten' who played about on the stairs. Laid out by John Wood as though the north side of the square formed the façade of one great pillared and porticoed mansion, this location was originally one of the best addresses in Bath; but by 1816, when Jane Austen was writing *Persuasion*, times, and fashions, had changed: 'We must be in a good situation', declares one of the Musgrove sisters; 'None of your Queen Squares for us.' The two novels which were partly set in Bath reflect the difference in her experiences there. For a still-youthful holiday visitor in the late 1790s, when *Northanger Abbey* was conceived, the bustle and amusements of the city still held a certain appeal; as a year-round resident, approaching 'the years of danger', lodging with her retired father and self-centred mother, Jane would find Bath, in the early 1800s, far less agreeable, as the mood of *Persuasion* suggests.

Ingenuous young Catherine Morland in *Northanger Abbey* is delighted with the 'variety of amusements' which the city affords. 'Every morning now brought its regular duties', the author writes; 'shops were to be visited, some new part of the town to be looked at; and the Pump Room to be attended'. In the Pump Room near the Abbey, invalids such as Jane Austen's father and Catherine Morland's 'gouty' host Mr Allen could drink their prescribed glasses of mineral water, pumped up from the thermal springs of the King's Bath, while those in search of pleasure, rather than health, paraded about the elegant room to the sound of 'a good band of musick', and inspected the visitors' book, where new arrivals inscribed their names and addresses. (It is from the all-important 'Book' that Catherine Morland is able to find out where the Tilneys are lodging, in Milsom Street.) The early 'rendez-vous' at the Pump Room took place between seven and ten in the morning, according to the *Bath Guide* (a visitors' handbook published, and updated, regularly); after which it was customary to take walks about the city, admiring the buildings and the views, to drive out into the surrounding countryside, to ride, pay calls on friends, or shop for food and fashions.

Jane Austen shared many of these experiences with Catherine Morland. She met her acquaintances strolling in the beautiful curve of the Royal Crescent, built by John Wood the Elder's namesake son and successor; watched a friend, Miss Chamberlayne, 'look hot on horseback' in the riding-school, and was driven out — like Catherine in Henry Tilney's curricle — for an 'airing' in the 'very bewitching Phaeton & Four' of a family friend, Mr Evelyn. She shopped indefatigably for the luxury goods for which Bath was renowned, from fashionable hats and modish fabrics to delicious local produce, such as fish from the River Severn, west-country cheeses and 'Bath bunns', as she jokingly spelt the famous teacakes invented by a local pastry-seller, Sally Lunn. (Like the plain digestive biscuits known as 'Bath Olivers', after their creator, the physician Dr Oliver, these are still popular today.) 'Tho' we had plenty of room in our Trunks when we came, We shall have many more things to take back', she reported happily to Cassandra from her Queen Square sojourn in 1799. Their brother Edward seemed to gain little benefit to his health from drinking the waters during this visit, but he evidently enjoyed such daytime activities as walks, visits, and 'going out to taste a cheese'. The evenings brought a round of predictable pleasures, neatly summed up in Catherine Morland's first, formal exchange with Henry Tilney: asked what she has done so far in Bath, she lists the standard proceedings. On Monday, she attended the Upper Rooms (the newer, more fashionable Assembly Rooms, completed in 1774, as the city spread up the hill); on Tuesday, she visited the theatre (the old Theatre Royal in Orchard Street, where Jane Austen saw several performances before its closure in 1805); and on Wednesday attended a concert (presumably in the octagonal room adjoining the Upper Assembly Rooms, which served both as a tearoom for the crowds on Assembly nights and as the venue for musical recitals, such as that which Anne Elliot hears in *Persuasion*). Occasionally there would be a break in the routine engagements: 'There is to be a grand gala on Tuesday evening in Sydney Gardens', Jane told Cassandra in June 1799, 'a concert with illuminations and fireworks'. Wryly, as a determined non-music-lover, she added, 'Even the Concert will have more than its usual charm for me, as the gardens are large enough for me to get pretty well beyond the reach of its sound.'

Jane Austen's longing for open air and green spaces was poignantly apparent during her residence in Bath. As a visitor in 1799 she had mentioned, gratefully, the view of poplar trees from their Queen Square lodgings, and she relished the opportunities for walks and drives into the nearby countryside.

When living, against her will, in the city in the early years of the century, she would seem to have shared Anne Elliot's gloom at the crowds and noise of the place – the 'heavy rumble of carts and drays, the bawling of newsmen, muffin-men and milkmen, and the ceaseless chink of pattens'; and she deplored the tedious snobberies of the Bath social round. 'A good address' was of increasing importance, as the focus of Bath's evening entertainment shifted from public assemblies to private parties. While the Viscountess Dalrymple, in *Persuasion*, lodges in elegant Laura Place, Anne – anticipating 'an imprisonment of many months' – finds herself residing in style in 'a very good house in Camden-Place' (now Camden Crescent), looking down, appropriately, from a lofty rise over the lower echelons of the city. The Musgrove sisters, having rejected the heavy, unmodish, Georgian symmetry of Queen Square, are comfortably accommodated at the White Hart Hotel; unpretentious Admiral Croft and his jolly wife are situated in Gay Street; while at the lowest end of the respectable scale, the heroine's sick, impoverished, former schoolfriend Mrs Smith, seeking better health, not better society, is poorly situated in Westgate Buildings, conveniently close to the hot bath. 'And who is Miss Anne Elliot to be visiting in Westgate Buildings?' enquires Anne's father, Sir Walter, with a sneer.

Escaping from the 'imprisonment' of Bath into the lush surrounding country was clearly important to Jane Austen as well as to her heroines. Driving out with the delightful Tilneys, impressionable Catherine Morland, who is already deeply struck by one artistic movement of the day, the Gothic novel, is introduced to another – the fashionable cult of the Picturesque. A favourite with Jane Austen, who refers to his ideas frequently in her novels, the country clergyman and amateur artist William Gilpin introduced to the British public, in the 1770s, a new way of looking at scenery, focusing on 'that kind of beauty which would look good in a picture' – by which he meant (among other notions) that rough nettles and thistles could make a flourishing foreground, far vistas should be shown through a becoming haze, and objects such as trees, or cattle, should be depicted in irregular groups of three or five, never in a banal four. With the Tilneys, Catherine visits Beechen Cliff, the hill above Bath, 'whose beautiful verdure and hanging coppice render it so striking an object' when viewed from the city. Having had the precepts of the Picturesque, as laid down by Gilpin, explained by her companions, Catherine becomes so ardent a convert that she ends up by dismissing the whole peerless vista of Bath as 'unworthy to make part of a landscape'. Here, Jane Austen is not only creating individual character, but also gently satirizing a public which, in pursuit of fashionable taste, would sweep away natural beauty and outstanding architecture, to satisfy artificial notions of aesthetics. In *Sense and Sensibility*, rational Edward and romantic Marianne illustrate two different approaches to looking at scenery, when he – while evidently familiar with Picturesque principles – gently mocks them (and her), saying, 'I shall call hills steep, which ought to be bold . . . and distant objects out of sight, which ought only to be indistinct through the soft medium of a hazy atmosphere.' His conclusion, 'A troop of tidy, happy villagers please me better than the finest banditti in the world', brings in a teasing shot at the conventions of the Gothic novel. Shocked, Marianne decides sorrowfully that her sister's suitor has no taste; whereas, in fact, in professing a determined preference for that which 'unites beauty with utility', Edward is expressing an abiding principle of good taste which transcends centuries and artistic movements.

According to her brother Henry, Jane's own favourite reading, from 'a very early age', included 'Gilpin on the Picturesque'; and all three of the novels begun at Steventon make some reference to his ideas. Even level-headed Lizzy Bennet, in *Pride and Prejudice*, refusing to join Mr Darcy and the Bingley sisters in a stroll, teasingly tells them, 'You are charmingly group'd, and . . . The picturesque would be spoilt

by admitting a fourth.' When offered a trip to the Lake District
– the subject of Gilpin's second book, published in 1789, and
a source of poetic inspiration to Wordsworth and the 'Lake
poets' – she exclaims, joyously, 'What are men to rocks and
mountains?' Yet readers can be in no doubt that Jane Austen
herself endorses Edward Ferrars's 'innate propriety and simplicity of taste', and shares his preference for scenery which
'unites beauty with utility'. The scene in *Emma* in which the
heroine admires the 'sweet view' over Mr Knightley's Donwell
Abbey estate, dominated – from this perspective – by Abbey-
Mill Farm, 'with all its appendages of prosperity and beauty,
its rich pastures, spreading flocks, orchard in blossom and
light column of smoke ascending', conjures up the tranquil,
pastoral atmosphere of a painting by Constable, Jane's near-
contemporary. Fanny Price in *Mansfield Park*, watching the
passing scenery from a carriage window, becomes immersed
in 'observing the appearance of the country, the bearings of
the roads, the difference of soil, the state of the harvest, the cottages, the cattle, the children' – a pleasure which is decidedly
not shared with her companion and rival in love, townish,
*ton*ish Mary Crawford, whose interest in 'nature, inanimate
nature' is almost non-existent. Since Miss Crawford intends
always to buy, rather than grow, her plants and provisions, her
lack of concern for the land is predictable; but it contrasts ill
with Fanny Price's 'delicacy of taste, of mind, of feeling',
which leads her to appreciate the stars in the night sky, the
beauty of evergreens, the Turner-esque sea 'dashing against
the ramparts' at Portsmouth, and all the fruitful splendours of
the natural world. All Jane Austen's heroines care – in varying
degrees – for the English landscape: and all, once in charge of
a household, will take an intelligent interest in its husbandry.
The saving grace of Charlotte Lucas's grimly respectable
marriage, in *Pride and Prejudice*, is that it enables her to find
fulfilment in 'her home and her housekeeping, her parish and
her poultry'; her dreadful husband's one redeeming quality is

that he enjoys digging in his garden – though this, too, under Jane Austen's ironic scrutiny, might be interpreted as a determination to improve his lot, in every sense.

Anne Elliot in *Persuasion* brings in a rare political reference when, strolling through the countryside, she counters her private poetical musings on 'the sweet scenes of autumn' by noting the surrounding 'large enclosures', full of 'ploughs at work'. Between 1750 and 1812 the English population almost doubled; the privations of the Napoleonic Wars, limiting imports, and the growing movement of the rural poor away from the villages to the cities, as the Industrial Revolution gathered pace, all added to the pressures on Britain's agricultural productivity. The process of enclosing common land, which Anne Elliot notes with apparent acceptance, disempowered those small-holders who had previously worked little individual strips of land, but enormously increased the nation's farming efficiency, and by the year 1800 most of the countryside had been 'enclosed' into the broad, hedge-bordered patchwork of fields to be seen today. The Agricultural Revolution, like the Industrial Revolution, was stimulated, in the century of Jane Austen's birth, by major mechanical innovations, from Jethro Tull's seed-drill of 1701, which enabled seed to be sowed in rows by a horse-drawn contraption, rather than scattered by hand, to such inventions as the threshing-machine, and the chaff-cutter, which assisted the production of cattle-fodder. As the century progressed, crop rotation was introduced; stock-breeding became a serious, and scientific, business, its results celebrated in the vogue for paintings of prize animals; while the 'agricultural reports' of the newly formed Board of Agriculture were avidly studied by interested parties, from landowners to tenant-farmers such as Harriet's admirer Robert Martin, in *Emma*, who is deeply involved with the land and its ways. In that novel, Emma's future husband Mr Knightley, wise and benevolent squire of Highbury, draws a firm distinction between rustic idyll and rural reality when he counsels Mrs Elton not to pursue the pleasures of nature by holding a picnic in his grounds, after her strawberry-picking excursion, but by returning to the comfort of the house, as befitting civilized society people. As he puts it, drily, 'The nature and the simplicity of gentlemen and ladies, with their servants, and furniture, I think is best observed by meals within doors.'

Living in an age when Greek and Roman, Chinese and Egyptian, Fantasy-Gothick and pseudo-peasant influences collided to shape the prevailing decorative mode, Jane Austen was clearly intrigued by the relationship between fancy and reality in housing styles. In 1815, as *Emma* was about to be published, she had the extraordinary experience of receiving a private, guided tour – at the Prince Regent's personal invitation – round one of the most remarkable architectural achievements of the age: Carlton House, his London palace, where, at vast expense, he indulged his taste for all the decorative fads and fashions of the time, from French carpets, ormolu desks, Oriental lighting and japanned cabinets, to clocks, bronzes, automata – even a table made for the enemy Napoleon, inlaid with cameo portraits of history's great commanders. From this fairy-tale visit – of which, sadly, she left no account – Jane Austen returned home to the modest surroundings of her mother's 'Chawton home'. Had he known that his guest lived in a house small enough to be designated a cottage, the style-conscious Prince might well have exclaimed, like foppish Robert Ferrars in *Sense and Sensibility*, 'I am excessively fond of a cottage: there is always so much comfort, so much elegance about them.' The darker reality of life in a Regency cottage is hinted at in *Mansfield Park* when Maria Bertram, showing off the glories of her future home, Sotherton Court, notes while passing through the adjoining village, 'Those cottages are really a disgrace.' Mr Rushworth is clearly a neglectful landlord; but to many of Maria's fashionable contemporaries, the lifestyle of the cottage suggested not poverty, damp and deprivation, but a Rousseau-esque fantasy, combining characterful charm with elegance and comfort on a small scale. The Prince Regent's mother, Queen Charlotte, had a *cottage orné* in the grounds of Kew Palace, to which she and her daughters would repair for simple picnics served by liveried footmen; and among the aristocracy and monied middle-classes cottage-building became a craze – encouraged by a series of publications such as James Smith's *Remarks on Rural Scenery* (1797), which included hazy engravings of dilapidated cottages, and James Malton's influential *British Cottage Architecture*, (1798), containing detailed designs for constructions in the vernacular, Picturesque style. 'I advise everybody who is going to build, to build a cottage', concludes the fatuous Robert Ferrars, in *Sense and Sensibility*; while Catherine Morland in *Northanger Abbey*, artlessly admiring 'a sweet little cottage' seen from Woodston parsonage, 'among the trees', is assured by her style-conscious future father-in-law, General Tilney, 'You approve it as an object . . . The cottage remains.' Almost inadvertently, Catherine is demonstrating her newly acquired grasp of the principles of 'the Picturesque'.

General Tilney, like so many Georgian and Regency landowners, is a modernizer, avid to make 'improvements' to his properties, from demolishing, restoring or building a cottage, for the sake of a pleasing view, or remodelling a room by adding on a bow-window, to carrying out extensive alterations to an ancestral home and its grounds – as Mr Rushworth proposes to do in *Mansfield Park*. Tastes had changed radically during the eighteenth century, as Baroque opulence gave way to classical elegance, and structured, formal garden design to freer, more seemingly natural scenery and surroundings. With the re-publication in England, in 1716, of the works of the Italian Renaissance architect Andrea Palladio – who took much of his inspiration from the first-century Roman, Vitruvius – an interest in 'Palladianism' was rekindled in Britain; and as the century progressed, great public buildings and private mansions alike reflected Palladio's version of Roman classicism, with columns, porticos and pilasters expressing harmony, symmetry and a respect for the classical architectural orders. Out of doors, Lancelot Brown – nicknamed 'Capability' for his ability to see the 'capabilities' of a place – brought a new spirit to the gardens and grounds of great estates: excavating lakes, planting groups of trees, and creating smooth, flowing expanses of restful green lawn. By 1775, when Jane Austen was born, however, a certain monotony had begun to set in, in these styles; and the fashionable were increasingly turning for inspiration to the brilliant Scottish design-team of the Adam brothers. By-passing Palladio, Robert and James Adam looked back directly to original Greek and Roman sources; and the result was a lighter, fresher decorative style, which focused on exquisite plasterwork and interior painting, with a plethora of ovals, curves and niches, set off by subtle colour-schemes in soft greens, smoky blues, dusty reds and warm yellows.

The charm of neo-classicism in domestic design was complemented, as Jane grew up, by the new vogue for 'landscape gardening' – a term which the great Humphrey Repton was said to have introduced into the national vocabulary. Working closely with the scale and layout of the patron's house, Repton created pleasing vistas in which, in place of Brown's interminable sweeps of grass and water, the eye was drawn to agreeable features such as shrubbery walks, flower-beds and sheltered nooks, with rustic benches. Rather than the outdoor world coming directly up to the house and stopping abruptly, as before, Repton advocated the idea that an 'enfilade', or series of linked rooms, indoors, should lead through to a light conservatory, and then out to a paved, perhaps balustraded terrace, which in turn would give way to sculpted lawns and imaginative scenery. Laid out for public perusal in his works such as *Fragments on the Theory and Practice of Landscape Gardening*, and its still more wordily titled predecessor, generally abbreviated to *Observations* (1803), Repton's ideas found a special niche in the 'Red Books' which he prepared for individual clients, in which he showed the possibilities of their grand houses and grounds, both before and after his treatment. 'Your best friend . . . would be Mr Repton, I imagine', says Maria Bertram in *Mansfield Park*, to her future husband, the rich, dull-witted Mr Rushworth, when he talks of 'improving' his ancestral seat, Sotherton Court. 'His terms are five guineas a day', Mr Rushworth muses; but, he decides, 'I think I had better have him at once.' Among his listeners, only the sensitive heroine, Fanny, demurs: hearing that (in accordance with Repton's dictates) Mr Rushworth may cut down an ancient avenue of trees leading up to his house, she protests, 'What a pity!' and wistfully quotes the Romantic poet Cowper: 'Ye fallen avenues,/ Once more I mourn your fate unmerited.' Cowper – a prime favourite with Marianne Dashwood in *Sense and Sensibility* and Jane Austen herself, as well as with Fanny – was an ardent opponent of the destruction of natural beauty in the name of modern taste; and despite her eye for 'elegance' in her surroundings, as in all else, Jane Austen evidently concurred. Her most famous fictional house, Mr Darcy's country seat Pemberley in *Pride and Prejudice*, delights Elizabeth Bennet at first sight: though splendid, it has been 'improved' with admirable restraint and discretion. The stream has been enlarged, in the Capability Brown style, 'without any artificial appearance', and its banks are 'neither formal nor falsely adorned'; Elizabeth had 'never seen a place', she concludes, 'where natural beauty had been so little counteracted by an awkward taste'.

The original working title for *Pride and Prejudice* was *First Impressions*; and in her first impressions of Pemberley Lizzy Bennet demonstrates how far she has come from her early

misjudgements of the rival merits of the charming (but villainous) Mr Wickham, and the haughty (but noble) Mr Darcy.
As she takes the guided tour of Pemberley, everything about
the place confirms the innate excellence of its 'proprietor'.
The rooms (like their owner) are 'lofty and handsome', their
decoration and furniture 'neither gaudy nor uselessly fine',
with 'less of splendor [*sic*], and more real elegance' than their
counterparts at Rosings, the home of Darcy's snobbish, ignorant aunt Lady Catherine de Bourgh, where even a single
chimneypiece (according to her acolyte Mr Collins) has cost
£800. With exquisite precision, Jane Austen uses her fictional houses to express the character of the 'proprietor'. Mr
Rushworth's Sotherton, like himself, is 'heavy, but respectable-
looking'; dutiful Fanny Price, with her feeling for history,
may appreciate its mid-Georgian decor, 'in the taste of fifty
years back, with shining floors, solid mahogany, rich damask,
marble, gilding and carving', but to beautiful, self-willed Maria
Bertram it becomes, indeed, 'a dismal old prison'. The sym-
bolism of her pre-marital tour of the house and grounds is
inescapable. Having viewed the high iron gates and the 'ha-ha'
– a favourite Capability Brown feature, of a steep drop at
the end of the lawn, intended to keep deer and cattle from the
house – she exclaims (quoting Laurence Sterne), 'I cannot get
out, as the starling said'; to which Henry Crawford, her future
seducer, replies meaningfully, 'You might with little difficulty
pass round the edge of the gate here, with my assistance.' In
Emma, the superficial, jumped-up vicar Mr Elton lives in a 'not
very good house', with 'no advantage of situation', but which
has been 'very much smartened up by the present proprietor'.
And Fanny Price's own cool, virginal, unadorned private
spaces, the 'white attic' and the East Room, underscore her
personality, just as her parents' noisy, messy, ill-lit and ill-
managed household at Portsmouth does theirs.

Jane Austen's own preference in architectural and domestic
style was clearly for the balanced, dignified understatement

of handsome Georgian houses such as her brother Edward's inherited country seat, Godmersham Park, in Kent. 'To sit in idleness over a good fire in a well-proportioned room is a luxurious sensation', she wrote to Cassandra from Steventon, after a visit to another such house, neighbouring Ashe Park, in 1800; in her last, unfinished novel, *Sanditon*, the heroine refers approvingly to 'the usual sitting-room, well-proportioned and well-furnished'. At Godmersham, built around 1732, on the site of an Elizabethan precursor, the 'improvements' made in the 1780s by Edward's adoptive father included bow-windows thrown out on to the garden façade and two new wings, linked to the main house by low pavilions; but the graceful proportions remained. The avenue of tall limes and oaks where Jane and the family liked to 'saunter', was left intact, despite the edicts of Mr Repton, and fashion; and the little classical temple to the north-west of the house, where Jane was said to have sought privacy on fine days to work on her novels, still stands. Her letters make no reference to writing out-of-doors; but while at Godmersham during her visit of 1813, she might have taken the opportunity, when alone in the large and comfortable library (another late eighteenth-century 'improvement'), to catch up with writing, or revising, *Mansfield Park*. Years later her niece Marianne would claim that 'Aunt Jane' would often put down her sewing when they were in the library, 'burst out laughing', then run to a table where pens and paper were lying, and 'write down something', before returning, tranquilly, to her needlework. Whether or not she could actually write in such a way, when in company, Jane certainly spent a good deal of time at Godmersham 'alone in the Library, Mistress of all I survey', as she wrote to Cassandra in September 1813, quoting her beloved Cowper. During this visit she may well have been making preliminary notes – in her head or on paper – for *Emma*, on which she began work in earnest in January 1814. Among her letters from that 1813 visit there are several references which might strike a chord with *Emma*'s readers – among them, the mention of a Mrs and Miss Milles, a local mother and daughter whose combined characteristics of Christian cheerfulness and inconsequential talkativeness would seem to prefigure kindly, chatty Miss Bates. There are hints, too, of Mrs Elton in the doctor's wife Mrs Britton, 'an ungenteel woman with self-satisfied and would-be elegant manners', who, Jane wrote, 'amuses me very much with her affected refinement and elegance'. Yet, like almost all great novelists, Jane Austen was adamant that none of her fictional characters was based on any real person. The same would surely apply to her depictions of houses. Godmersham, like Mr Darcy's Pemberley, is a grand, early Georgian house with a stream in front, not overly affected by the vagaries of fashionable taste; yet Godmersham is not Pemberley, not is it specifically a model for *Mansfield Park*, whatever features they may have in common. The infuriatingly opinionated Mrs Elton helps (inadvertently) to make an important point in *Emma* when, looking round the heroine's delightful country house, Hartfield, she remarks with 'easy conceit' on its resemblance to her sister's much-vaunted house, Maple Grove, near Bristol – exclaiming, among other banal comments, 'how very like the staircase was: placed exactly in the same part of the house!' Since any staircase in a late eighteenth-century country mansion was likely to occupy a central position on the ground floor – for reasons of practicality if not of taste – Mrs Elton is here exposing her limited acquaintance with the grand houses of the day, rather than proving any special resemblance. Jane Austen herself knew that, in referring to a character's home as 'a handsome, modern-built house, well-situated', she would evoke for her contemporaries an immediate image of the standard, symmetrical, porticoed, early nineteenth-century manor houses so familiar to readers in her own day, and still (to many people) the ideal of an English country house.

Among the 'improvements within' made by her brother

Edward at Godmersham was the redecoration of some of the upstairs rooms, with delightful results. The layout of the bedrooms is today almost impossible to establish: but Jane Austen's letters mention a spacious 'yellow room', a 'white room', a 'hall chamber' (presumably directly above the grand black-and-white flagged entrance hall), and a charming-sounding 'chintz room' which she admired during her 1813 visit. Chintz, a strong, cotton fabric, originally imported from India, reached a height of popularity during the early years of the Regency: practical and washable, often printed with lively designs of leaves and flowers, it was used in royal residences as well as more modest households, and would have been a particularly appealing fabric for use in a fashionable young lady's bedroom. There may well have been a profusion of fresh chintz in the 'very pretty sitting-room' at Pemberley, which, Elizabeth notes with pleasure, Mr Darcy has had newly 'fitted up with greater elegance and lightness' than the other, more stately, apartments, as a surprise for his young sister. (Here again, the sympathy of a Jane Austen hero towards women's feelings is highlighted: in his understanding of the female need for 'a room of one's own', in Virginia Woolf's famous phrase, Mr Darcy is once again what twenty-first-century jargon would term 'a new man'.)

In her descriptions of houses, as of dress and physical appearance, in her fiction, Jane Austen is always deliberately sparing, so that the reader may fill in her or his own ideal images. Certain key words and themes do, however, stand out; and in decorative matters, 'lightness' and 'elegance' are all-important. The opulence of early Georgian interiors had long come to seem stuffy and *démodé* by 1811, when the Regency began, and her first published novel, *Sense and Sensibility*, appeared; looking round splendid Sotherton Court, in *Mansfield Park*, even the conservative, traditionalist Edmund Bertram concedes that it wants 'a modern dress', to offset the William-Kent-style heaviness of polished mahogany and stiff, rich damask. (Both materials had lost ground in furnishing fashion – dark mahogany, imported from the West Indies, to the lighter woods such as satinwood and walnut; lavish damask silks and satins to the crisp freshness of practical cottons.) The more relaxed new mood pervaded the arrangement of furniture: chairs ceased to be placed against the walls, but were moved, more conveniently, into the room, where an air of clutter was replacing the formality of the past. The fashionable Musgrove sisters in *Persuasion* illustrate the growing trend in interior styling: unlike their unambitious parents, who hark back to the era of the bluff, rustic squirearchy, content with traditional life in 'substantial and unmodernised' country manors, the Misses Musgrove are determinedly updating their surroundings – introducing 'the proper air of confusion', with a new piano-forte, a harp, flower-stands and little tables 'in every direction'. As Anne Elliot reflects, with rueful amusement, the velvet-clad ancestors in the portraits on the walls seem to be 'staring in astonishment' at 'such an overthrow of order and neatness'. Nearby in the village, the eye-catching modern cottage where her sister and brother-in-law (the squire's heir) live is, similarly, a symbol of dubious social (and decorative) progress. Updated from an unpretentious vicarage, the 'cottage' at Uppercross has all the proper Regency cottage features, with its 'viranda, French windows, and other prettinesses'; but as the novel progresses, the ephemeral nature of such values becomes apparent. The 'once elegant' furniture is 'growing shabby', after the onslaughts of 'four summers and two children'; and when seen through a rainstorm, the cottage presents a thoroughly dismal prospect, its fine new 'viranda black, comfortless and dripping'. The Musgrove parents may be dull and staid, but there is a cool irony in the author's comment that their family, like their properties, was in a 'state of alteration, perhaps of improvement'.

Despite her innate conservatism, and Cowper-esque reservations about the effects of 'the improver's hand', Jane Austen was by no means opposed to all innovations, indoors or out. 'Our Improvements have advanced very well', she wrote from Steventon in 1800, commenting on some changes to the layout of the garden; and in a subsequent letter she reported happily on the arrival of several new tables at the Rectory, 'which give general contentment'. One of them was of typically ingenious early nineteenth-century design, since, when not needed for large dinner-parties, it could be taken apart, and the two ends slotted together to form a smaller version, while the centre section looked 'exceedingly well' standing alone against a wall, below a large mirror. Another was a 'Pembroke' table – a popular design, with a square centre and two hinged flaps, with a lockable drawer beneath. 'My mother has great delight in keeping her money & papers locked up', Jane recorded. In *Emma*, old Mr Woodhouse has for forty years had his meals 'crowded' on to 'a small-sized Pembroke'; it is a sign of the changing times that Emma has persuaded him to replace this with 'a large modern circular table', presumably with a single, central pedestal beneath, which would allow a large group to sit round at their spacious ease.

In comparison with the stiff-backed decorum imposed (and reflected) by earlier Georgian design, comfort was, increasingly, a factor in Regency interiors. Women in softly flowing dresses, as depicted in the ravishing prints of Adam Buck, could lounge gracefully in the curving Regency chairs with their sabre legs and arching backs: and reclining on an ottoman, or a chaise-longue, à la Madame Recamier in David's famous portrait, became socially acceptable. The sofa (also spelt sopha) was a prominent item in Regency households: Lady Bertram, pug-dog snoring beside her, is constantly lolling on one in *Mansfield Park* – while fashionable, aloof Mr Hurst, in *Pride and Prejudice*, stretches out and goes to sleep on one of Mr Bingley's sofas during a dull evening at Netherfield. When weak and in pain during her last illness Jane Austen lay, when downstairs, on an arrangement of two or three chairs pushed together, rather than deprive her mother of the relaxation of the sofa.

While a family of the Woodhouses' wealth and social position might have ordered their new furniture from a leading London maker, such as the firm of Gillows, the Austens would have been likely to employ local craftsmen to make theirs, reproducing, skilfully, the detailed designs shown in the pattern-books produced by some of the greatest cabinet-makers of the day. Many of the parlour chairs and dining-tables, chiffoniers and bureaux so sought-after today as examples of Chippendale, Hepplewhite and Sheraton designs were not made by the masters themselves, but by others working from their books. There was a vast range of such publications, ranging from the furniture bible, Thomas Chippendale senior's *Gentleman and Cabinet Maker's Director*, of 1754, to Sheraton's *Cabinet-Maker and Upholsterer's Drawing-Book*, which reached its 3rd edition in 1802, having originally appeared in instalments in the early 1790s. With handsome, relatively affordable furniture readily available, when the Austens left Steventon for Bath in 1801 Jane reported that the trouble and 'risk' of transporting their own pieces – even 'the side-board, or a pembroke table, or some other' – would probably be greater than the cost of replacing them, 'at a place where everything may be purchased'. Though the Revd George Austen's principal furniture was originally listed for sale at an estimate of some £200, in the event Jane was disappointed to receive 'only Eleven Guineas for the Tables'; 8 guineas for her piano was, however, 'about what I really expected to get'. Wisely, in her opinion, her parents opted to take their own beds with them from Steventon – but she looked forward to replacing the family's chests-of-drawers with new ones, 'of a much more commodious form, made of deal, & painted to look very neat'. Even young Catherine Morland, in *Northanger Abbey*, makes a purchase of furniture while in Bath. 'Her own new writing-desk' – which is almost left behind in the Tilneys' hurry to depart – would not have been a free-standing desk on legs, in the modern sense, but a neat, portable object, something like a large jewellery-casket, which would open to provide a leather-covered slope, with space for inkwells, and a handy drawer beneath, but which would close into a box, for travel. Jane Austen's own writing-desk, of early nineteenth-century design, has survived: made of mahogany, inlaid with brass, its lower drawer still containing a pair of spectacles reputed to have been hers, it is one of the most evocative objects in literary history. Reporting on a visit from a friend's child, in 1807, she wrote fondly to Cassandra, 'She is now talking away at my side, & examining the Treasures of my Writing-Desk drawer.' It is tempting to imagine that, among the usual pencils and sealing-wax, these 'Treasures' might have included the little pair of folding-spectacles.

The similarities between decorating fashions in Jane Austen's day and our own are often striking. Paint-effects, such as marbling and wood-grain, on every surface from cheap 'deal' (or, today, pine) furniture to walls, were much in vogue, as were fitted carpets, rush matting (used by the Prince of Wales himself at Carlton House), and ready-made, Adam-style plaster mouldings. Practicality, and the growing pace of life, demanded adaptable furniture, such as desks with prop-up surfaces for displaying architects' drawings, maps, or prints; library steps which would convert into handy seats; beds, tables and cutlery-canteens which were easy to pack and transport for officers on campaign, or travellers making business voyages to the East Indies, and beyond. As today, the public were avid for publications of all kinds on the subject of design. Pattern-books – whether detailing fashions in furniture, or full-scale plans from which to build houses – were best-sellers; and illustrated periodicals, anticipating the glossy decorating magazines of the twenty-first century, made their mark. Ackermann's *Repository of Arts, Literature, Commerce, Manufactures, Fashions and Politics*, from 1809 onwards, showed, in

26. The influential feminist writer Mary Wollstonecraft, 1802

GOVERNESS or ENGLISH TEACHER.—A young Lady, of respectable connections and amiable disposition, is desirous of procuring one of these situations, in which salary not so much as comfort is her object; as Governess to young Ladies under 12 years of age, she would engage to teach in English, French, geography, music, &c. Address, post paid, E. C. 94, Strand.

27. The 'governess trade': advertisement from *The Times*, 1815

28. The Pump Room, Bath

29. Carlton House, London. Jane would have seen this façade when she visited the Prince Regent's residence in 1815

30. Fashionable transport: the Prince Regent's 'spider phaeton', 1790

31. The Prince Regent as Prince of Wales,
in the uniform of the 10th Light Dragoons

32. Pavilion and greenhouse for a gothic mansion, by Humphrey Repton,
1802. Mr Rushworth in *Mansfield Park* plans to employ Mr Repton,
when 'improving' his house

33. Count Rumford, inventor of the practical Rumford stove. In *Northanger Abbey*, the fireplace is 'contracted to a Rumford'

34. The showroom of Wedgwood and Byerley, London,
where Jane Austen bought china

35. Saucer, possibly 'of Staffordshire make', as favoured by General Tilney in *Northanger Abbey*. The transfer print is by Adam Buck

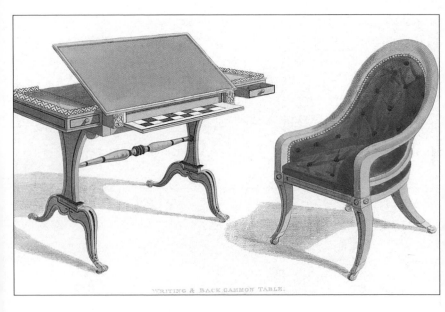

WRITING & BACK GAMMON TABLE.

36. From the fashion and interiors magazine, Ackermann's *Repository*, the latest writing-cum-games table and sabre-legged chair, 1807

37. Fanny Austen-Knight, Jane's adored niece, by her sister Cassandra, 1805

38. 'The Bottomless Pitt': the brilliant, ascetic, Tory Prime Minister,
William Pitt the Younger, by Gillray, 1792

39. Britain's arch-enemy, for much of Jane's adult life: the
Emperor Napoleon at his Coronation in 1804, by David

40. The trial of Warren Hastings, in Westminster Hall. Hastings, a friend of the Austens, was impeached for misconduct as Governor-General of India, but exonerated. Jane sent him an early copy of *Pride and Prejudice*, which he admired

41. Anti-slavery medallion, with the slogan, 'Am I not a man, and a brother?' produced by Josiah Wedgwood

42. Oxfordshire Militia uniform, as worn by Jane's brother Henry

43. Patriotic enamel box, in support of Nelson's navy, in which Jane's brothers Frank and Charles served

In Memory of
JANE AUSTEN,
youngest daughter of the late
Rev.d GEORGE AUSTEN,
formerly Rector of Steventon in this County
she departed this Life on the 18th of July 1817,
aged 41. after a long illness supported with
the patience and the hopes of a Christian,

The benevolence of her heart,
the sweetness of her temper, and
the extraordinary endowments of her mind
obtained the regard of all who knew her, and
the warmest love of her intimate connections.

Their grief is in proportion to their affection
they know their loss to be irreparable,
but in their deepest affliction they are consoled
by a firm though humble hope that her charity
devotion, faith and purity, have rendered
her soul acceptable in the sight of her
REDEEMER.

44. The tombstone of Jane Austen, in Winchester Cathedral.
It praises her Christian virtues, but makes no mention of her novels

enticing coloured plates, the latest developments in every aspect of interior style, from chair designs to curtain arrangements and bed-hangings. The unpretentious Austens, living modestly at Chawton, might not have been overly influenced by such publications: but as in matters of dress, Jane liked to keep abreast of the nuances of current taste, and both her letters and her novels demonstrate her awareness of what was (or was not) in fashion. Harriet Smith's passing reference to Mr Elton's yellow curtains, in *Emma*, is subtly significant: in 1814, when the novel was being written, yellow was a somewhat daring and striking colour for household furnishings, and its use at the vicarage hints at the showy presumption of this newcomer. By contrast, when speculating, in a letter of 1813, as to the character of her former admirer Mr Blackall's bride, Jane decided that she would be fond of 'green tea . . . and a green window-blind at night' – the latter being a standard, and commonplace, feature of contemporary bedrooms.

There was nothing unusual in gentlemen of all ranks, from Mr Darcy to Mr Elton, taking a close interest in the redecoration and refurbishment of their properties. The very term 'interior decoration' was introduced into the language by a man, the rich connoisseur and patron of the arts Thomas Hope, whose work *Household Furniture and Interior Decoration*, published in 1807, inspired a new direction in British domestic style – with an emphasis on clean, elegant, pared-down lines and an abundance of Egyptian themes and motifs, reflecting the public interest in Egypt aroused by Nelson's victory at the Battle of the Nile. It was another rich, artistic gentleman, Horace Walpole (son of the Prime Minister Robert Walpole), who had helped to create the Gothic movement in British culture – both in literature, with the publication of his fantasy novel *The Castle of Otranto*, in 1764, and in architectural style, with the building of his extravagant folly-castle, Strawberry Hill, which he converted from a Twickenham coach-house in the 1760s. By the time Jane Austen first presented *Northanger Abbey* to a publisher, in 1803, Walpole had been dead for six years: but his influence in both creative fields lived on. *The Mysteries of Udolpho*, by Walpole's best-selling successor Mrs Radcliffe, is Catherine Morland's favourite, spine-chilling reading – and her joy at the prospect of visiting a real, ancient abbey, replete (in her imagination) with all the trappings of secret passages and incarcerated wives, is central to the novel's burlesque plot. To Catherine's mingled relief and disappointment, her host, General Tilney, is another wealthy man who takes a keen interest in improving and decorating his properties, and Northanger Abbey turns out to be as up-to-date a family house as Regency taste and technology could afford. The furniture in the drawing-room displays 'all the profusion and elegance of modern taste'; the windows, though preserving the pointed Gothic arches which suit both the Abbey's origins and the popular mode, have large, light, new glass panes; and the fireplace, instead of flaunting a vast chimney-piece in the William Kent style, ornamented with 'the ample width and ponderous carving of former times', is 'contracted to a Rumford'. With this form of small, ingenious, practical grate, invented in the 1790s by an American named Benjamin Thompson, Count Rumford, the maximum of heat and minimum of smoke would be emitted – thus adding greatly to the comfort of a room.

Catherine's experiences at Northanger provide something of a checklist of well-to-do early nineteenth-century decor, as she is shown all round the house and grounds. In her bedroom, in place of gloomy tapestry and velvet, she finds that 'the walls were papered, the floor was carpeted'. Some of the furniture is 'not of the latest fashion', having been relegated from the rooms below – just as the Austens, on receiving their new Pembroke table in 1800, banished its predecessor to 'the best bed-room' at Steventon. But despite the presence of an antique cedarwood chest, and a sinister-looking tall cabinet, 'japanned' (or lacquered) in black and yellow, the room is far from 'uncheerful'. The wallpaper – an innovation of the 1790s – would have been light and pretty, perhaps featuring a hand-blocked design of leaf, sprig or small geometric motifs; the carpet might have been fitted wall-to-wall, possibly with practical cloth 'druggets' laid over areas liable to hard wear. Downstairs there are ornaments of 'the prettiest English china' over the fireplace – and the 'breakfast-set' is also English, of Staffordshire make, which, out of proper patriotic sentiment, General Tilney favours over exquisite Continental artefacts such as Dresden or Sèvres. With anxious pride, he assures Catherine that this was 'quite an old set', being two years old, adding that manufacturing methods were 'much improved since then'. This china might have been produced by any of several leading Staffordshire factories; but the General's pride in his own 'simple and neat' taste might suggest New Hall, or Wedgwood. The latter firm, set up in 1754 by Josiah Wedgwood, a man of conscience as well as genius, became one of the great industrial success stories of the age; though the founder died in 1795, output remained prolific, and by the time Jane Austen's novels appeared, superb Wedgwood urns and vases, in finest earthenware, were an established status symbol for the mantelpieces of the ultra-rich, while the less exclusive coffee-pots and cameos, teabowls and scent-bottles could be seen in almost every genteel house-hold. While staying in London in 1813, Jane Austen visited the Wedgwood shop and showroom by St James's Square, where, she reported, 'My Br. & Fanny chose a Dinner Set,' adding, 'The pattern is a small Lozenge in purple, between Lines of narrow Gold; & it is to have the crest.'

Fascinated though Catherine Morland is by the potential of Northanger Abbey indoors, she has 'scarcely any curiosity about the grounds'. General Tilney's pride in his 'pinery' (for growing fashionable pineapples), and his 'succession-houses' (greenhouses of carefully regulated, different temperatures, for encouraging the growth of vulnerable plants) makes little impression on her as yet uncultivated mind. A 'gloomy' grove of 'old Scotch firs' holds more promise; but she tires of the shrubberies – 'always so smooth and so dry'. In fact, the dryness of a shrubbery, being planted around gravel paths where ladies might walk in comfort even after rain, was one reason for the appeal of such a garden feature; Jane Austen was delighted with the shrubbery at Chawton, insisted on planting shrubs at the family's Southampton lodgings, and sets several major scenes in her novels – including, notably, Mr Knightley's proposal to Emma – in shrubberies. Yet she was always able to separate her own tastes and traits from those which fitted her characters. Growing flowers was an aspect of garden design which held overtones of Repton, and 'improvements'; thus, while loving colourful flowers herself she frequently ascribes this interest to unworthy fictional women. Selfish Mrs John Dashwood, in *Sense and Sensibility*, is having such wild, picturesque beauties of nature as an old walnut tree and clumps of rambling thorns cleared, to make way for her new flower-beds; idle Lady Bertram sends Fanny Price out to pick roses, in *Mansfield Park*, in the midday heat; hard-hearted Elizabeth Elliot, in *Persuasion*, is mistress of a flower-garden at Kellynch Hall. Jane Austen herself wrote tenderly of a variety of flowers, from Sweet William, auricula, mignonette and blowsy peonies to scented lilacs – yet there is a refreshing honesty to her observation of an unaffected young woman when she has Catherine Morland admit, frankly, 'I am naturally indifferent about flowers.' On a more hopeful note, however, Catherine adds that, under Miss Tilney's tutelage, she has 'lately learned to love a hyacinth'.

Jane's letters from London underline her constant need for the beauties of nature. 'The garden is quite a love', she wrote fondly from her brother Henry's new house in Hans Place, in August 1814; and while in town she took the opportunity to walk in Kensington Gardens, with evident pleasure.

'Everything was fresh & beautiful', she reported after one such outing, in 1811; in *Sense and Sensibility*, published in that same year, Elinor Dashwood encounters the unpleasant Miss Steele during an otherwise agreeable stroll in this fashionable royal park adjoining Kensington Palace. Though she pretended to regard London as a hot-house of vice, joked about its corrupting influence, and referred to it as a region of 'Wit, Elegance, fashion, Elephants & Kangaroons [*sic*]', as though the capital were as distant and exotic a place as India or Australia, London, with its population of almost 1,000,000 citizens, its newly gas-lit main streets and rudimentary public sewage-system, did not seem to depress Jane's spirits, unlike Bath. She enjoyed driving about town, visiting shops and theatres, and calling on friends and acquaintances; and she seemed charmed by Henry's successive houses – first in Sloane Street, on the outskirts, then in Henrietta Street, in bustling Covent Garden, and finally back in Chelsea, at No. 23 Hans Place. With her usual precise eye for society's nuances, she registered the hierarchy of different addresses, which emerges clearly in her novels: the Bennet girls' uncle, as a tradesman, is sneered at by the Bingley sisters for living in the City, Gracechurch Street, 'within view of his own warehouses' – whereas elegant, ostentatiously well-bred and wealthy characters such as the John Dashwoods, the Bingleys and the Rushworths live in the exclusive environs of the West End – at addresses such as Berkeley Street, Conduit Street and Harley Street. Dining with her half-brother in Harley Street, Elinor Dashwood notes jadedly, 'Everything bespoke the Mistress's inclination for show, and the Master's ability to support it'; and in her description of a large party at this house, Jane Austen sums up, with eloquent understatement, the worst aspects of a snobbish London social gathering, from the insufferable heat to the stifling crush of pretentious people. (Even a party given by her beloved brother and his wife Eliza, in 1811, seemed not much to her liking, as her account of the 'lordly company' of some sixty-six people crammed into a terraced house bedecked with a borrowed mantel-mirror, hired musicians and expensive floral arrangements suggests.) Yet, as she wrote after visiting two of London's best-known cultural sights, the Liverpool Museum, and the British Gallery, during that same visit, 'I had some amusement at each, tho' my preference for Men & Women, always inclines me to attend more to the company than the sight'; and London offered every opportunity for the study of men and women.

What Jane Austen does not record, from these town trips, is any sense of the architectural beauty of the place. This was the age of the great developers – Henry Holland, Thomas Cubitt, and, above all, John Nash. Nothing in her letters suggests the charm of the pretty new stuccoed terraces with their glassed, iron-fretted fanlights, the grandeur of elegant squares such as 'airy' Brunswick Square, near the Inns of Court, where Emma Woodhouse's sister and her lawyer-husband live in *Emma*, or handsome, harmonious St James's Square, where, during a party in 1815, the news of the victory at Waterloo would be given to the Prince Regent – and which Jane must have seen when buying china at Wedgwood's. She does not refer to the enticing shop-fronts of Bond Street, where Nelson had lodged, and where Mr Elton takes Harriet Smith's portrait to be framed; and if she was aware of John Nash's exquisite hand at work during her visit to Carlton House, no record of the fact survives. At a time when Nash was reaching the peak of his career, laying out the picture-book terraces and villas of Regent's Park, and planning – as the Regent's favourite architect – the grandiose redevelopment of central London, it is fittingly ironic that the only architect to be named in Jane Austen's fiction is the now-obscure Joseph Bonomi, whose designs for a grand house Robert Ferrars claims to have thrown on the fire, insisting that his noble friend should, instead, build a cottage.

That lavish cottage might well have been commissioned

from Nash. It would have had little in common with the Austens' own simple Chawton, with its small rooms, uneven floors and cramped passageways – but would no doubt have had all the charm, comfort and Regency modernity of such fanciful cottages as those at Blaise Hamlet, near Bristol, built by Nash and his mentor Repton, in 1812. Nearby is Blaise Castle, the 1760s folly which artless Catherine Morland longs to visit in *Northanger Abbey*, earnestly believing it to be an ancient ruin – 'the oldest in the kingdom', she is told. To read the novels of Jane Austen is to enter a world where the classical house, in all its order and reason, meets the zest, playfulness and spirit of the Regency villa and cottage.

7

'The Distinction of Rank'

'She knew not how such an offence as hers might be classed by the laws of worldly politeness.'

Jane Austen, *Northanger Abbey*, 1817

'When Mr Portman is first brought in, he would not be introduced as the *the Honourable*. *That* distinction is never mentioned at such times', Jane Austen instructed her niece Anna, in a letter of August 10, 1814. The lively, headstrong daughter of Jane's eldest brother, James, Anna had considerable talent as an artist; but in the summer of 1814 she was trying her hand at another creative endeavour: writing a novel. Naturally, she turned to her 'authoress' aunt at Chawton for help and advice – and was rewarded with a series of letters which would provide not only her, but history, with extraordinary insights into Jane Austen, both as a writer and as a woman. Though she was then at work on her fourth novel, *Emma*, as well as tending her mother and overseeing their day-to-day lives, Anna's aunt responded to every instalment of *Enthusiasm*, or *Which Is the Heroine?*, with unflagging attention, offering, by turns, praise, suggestions, and tactfully worded criticism. Above all, in this unique course of literary tutorials, Jane Austen stressed the need for scrupulous accuracy, in characterization, dialogue – and, in particular, social detail. She calculated journey times ('They must be *two* days going from Dawlish to Bath,'), corrected speech ('Bless my Heart' would be 'too familiar and inelegant' an expression for

'Sir T.M.'), and explained the proper form for introductions. ('As Lady H. is Cecilia's superior, it wd. not be correct to talk of *her* being introduced.') Her own superb craftsmanship shone through every comment. 'Let the Portmans go to Ireland', she directed, in response to one query, 'but as you know nothing of the Manners there, you had better not go with them. You will be in danger of giving false representations.' In Jane Austen's own fiction, there are no 'false representations' where 'Manners' are concerned.

While Anna, like many novice authors, peopled her work with unconvincing aristocrats, her aunt – always a social realist – confined hers to circles where she was 'quite at home'. ('Stick to Bath and the Foresters', she advised Anna; 'There you will be quite at home.') Whether the setting is Bath or London, the Dashwoods' cottage or Mr Darcy's mansion, Jane Austen's fiction unfolds, invariably, from the perspective of a woman of her own social class – that of the respectable, unpretentious gentry and squirearchy, officers and clergy. 'I am a gentleman's daughter' is Elizabeth Bennet's haughty response to Lady Catherine de Bourgh's arrogance, in *Pride and Prejudice*. What constitutes 'a gentleman' is never defined by Jane Austen; yet it is a recurring theme in her fiction, and in *Pride and Prejudice* in particular. Lizzy's uncle Mr Gardiner lives by trade, rather than by owning land or pursuing a profession such as the church or law, but his appearance and quiet good manners entitle him to be accepted as a gentleman – whereas the Bennet girls' other uncle, Mr Phillips, who is stout, florid and greedy, is all too clearly not 'gentlemanlike'. It is as 'a gentleman's daughter' that Jane Austen unerringly writes. ('Miss A.'s works', one early reader of *Mansfield Park* noted with pleasure, 'are so evidently written by a Gentlewoman.') To the ludicrous proposal from the Prince Regent's librarian, in 1816, that, to flatter the new royal bridegroom Prince Leopold of Saxe-Cobourg, her next novel should be 'an historical romance', based on the 'august House of Cobourg', she replied with barely concealed mirth, 'I could no more write a romance than an epic poem'; and after reminding him of 'such pictures of domestic life in country villages as I deal in', concluded gently, but decisively, 'No, I must keep to my own style and go on in my own way.' The letter echoed her earlier advice to Anna; '3 or 4 Families in a Country Village is the very thing to work on'. According to her nephew's *Memoir*, it was her policy 'Not to meddle with matters which she did not thoroughly understand', and she had no more wish to write of bygone royal courts than of the servants' hall, the quarterdeck, or the gunroom in her own day. She never even published a scene which might risk 'false representations' by showing servants alone together, or gentlemen talking out of earshot of a lady. Charlotte Brontë, thirty years later, would object to the 'Chinese fidelity' of her art: but to Jane Austen enthusiasts, past and present, this was central to her appeal. Among the 'Opinions' of her contemporary readers which she copied out after the publication of *Mansfield Park* and *Emma*, one acquaintance, Lady Gordon, was listed as remarking, 'You fancy yourself one of the family', while another, Mrs Pole, wrote, 'Everything is natural . . . told in a manner which clearly evinces the writer to *belong* to the Society whose Manners she so ably delineates.'

Underlying all Jane Austen's novels is a code of 'Manners' and conduct which would have been wholly familiar to her Regency readers. Particular importance was attached to 'the distinction of rank', and matters of precedence, at all levels of society – and even between sisters. In any family with more than one daughter, the first-born would be addressed, by her equals and servants alike, as 'Miss ——', with her surname only, while younger sisters were 'Miss' followed by the Christian name: thus in *Pride and Prejudice* Jane is 'Miss Bennet' and her sisters 'Miss Elizabeth Bennet', 'Miss Mary Bennet', and so on. Only in situations where the elder was absent, or unknown to the speaker, would Lizzy have been called 'Miss Bennet' – a style which would not rightfully be hers until her senior married, and took on her husband's name. The same system applied to men, which is why the hero of *Emma*, as an elder son, and heir, is 'Mr Knightley', while his younger brother is 'Mr John Knightley'.

Marriage conferred an immediate rise in social status on all women, whatever their position in life. Silly, disgraced Lydia Bennet, on marrying her seducer Wickham, reminds Jane exultantly at the family dinner-table, 'I take your place now, and you must go lower, because I am a married woman.' Still more irksome are the claims of the newly-wed Mrs Elton, in *Emma*; through her position as a recent bride (though not her birth), she assumes the role of guest of honour at the Westons' ball – helping to greet the guests, and expecting to lead off the dancing. For Emma Woodhouse, who had 'considered the ball as peculiarly for her', it is, gallingly, 'almost enough to make her think of marrying'. Among servants, likewise, marriage increased a woman's status – with the result that a senior domestic such as a cook or housekeeper would be addressed as 'Mrs' as a mark of respect, whether actually married or not. The housekeepers at Sotherton, in *Mansfield Park*, and Pemberley, in *Pride and Prejudice*, are thus 'good old Mrs Whitaker', and 'respectable-looking' Mrs Reynolds: while Lady Bertram's personal maid, in the former novel, is 'Mrs Chapman' to the deferential heroine, Fanny Price.

While lesser servants were generally known by their Christian names alone – Jane Austen's letters mention, among others, an Eliza, a Hannah, a James, and 'the two Betsies' – in the world of their employers the use of first names was rare, outside the family. It is a sign of dashing intimacy between Isabella Thorpe and Catherine Morland, in *Northanger Abbey*, that 'having passed so rapidly through every gradation of increasing tenderness', they call one another by their Christian names so soon after first meeting. With the more genuinely 'elegant' (and sincerely affectionate) Eleanor Tilney, the hero's sister, Catherine Morland retains the formal 'Miss Morland' and 'Miss Tilney' mode of address for most of the novel – even while staying as the Tilneys' house-guest at Northanger. Just as the Austen sisters called their best friends, Alethea Bigg and Martha Lloyd, 'Alethea' and 'Martha', so Lizzy Bennet, in *Pride and Prejudice*, is on first-name terms with her confidante Charlotte Lucas; but these are the familiarities of long-standing friendship and mutual respect. For all his 'indifference to a confusion of rank', and 'lively spirits', Frank Churchill, in *Emma*, is incensed (as is the well-bred Emma herself), when his secret fiancée Jane Fairfax is addressed as 'Jane' by vulgar Mrs Elton – 'with all the insolence of imaginary superiority', Frank later writes angrily. As he points out, 'I have not yet indulged myself in calling her by that name'. For Emma, with all the advantages of wealth and breeding, to call her illegitimate, ignorant, schoolgirl protégée 'Harriet' is a charming mark of favour; for the upstart Mrs Elton to seek to patronize the elegant officer's daughter Miss Fairfax by using her Christian name is inappropriate, and impertinent.

Between men and women forms of address were still more formal; even, in many cases, for married couples. Elizabeth Bennet's parents still call one another 'Mr Bennet' and 'Mrs Bennet' after more than two decades of married life, just as the grander Bertrams, in *Mansfield Park*, unfailingly use one another's titles, 'Sir Thomas', and 'Lady Bertram'. Some younger members of Regency society were beginning, in Jane Austen's day, to do away with such stiff formality; it was even reported in the newspapers that Princess Charlotte called Prince Leopold 'my love', while he addressed her simply as 'Charlotte', despite her superior rank as heir to the throne. Among Jane Austen's young married characters the trend is much in evidence: pettish, country-dwelling Mary Musgrove, in *Persuasion*, and aloof London lawyer Mr John Knightley, in *Emma*, alike, call their spouses by their Christian names; and after Mr Darcy's engagement to Lizzy Bennet, he addresses her, for the first time, as 'Elizabeth'. The 'elegant' heroine of *Emma*, however, has reservations about the practice. To the fond request from her fiancé, 'Cannot you call me George now?' she replies 'Impossible! I can never call you anything but Mr Knightley.' Underlying this teasing exchange is their shared contempt for the vulgarisms of Mrs Elton, who, though her husband addresses her as 'Augusta', persistently refers to him – with 'elegant terseness', as Emma sarcastically puts it – as 'Mr E.' For unmarried, and unrelated, men and women to use one another's Christian name is almost unknown. The Dashwood sisters and Edward Ferrars do so in *Sense and Sensibility* because they are connected by marriage; Fanny and Edmund, in *Mansfield Park*, are on first-name terms, as cousins. Fanny is, however, deeply offended when her unwelcome suitor Henry Crawford and his sister claim the same intimate privilege. It sounds a note of warning to the reader, as it should to hot-headed Marianne Dashwood, that the bold charmer Willoughby familiarly addresses her as 'Marianne' without becoming formally engaged to her. But she is ruled by her feelings, rather than any respect for social custom, in this – just as she is when Willoughby daringly shows her round his future estate, Allenham, without first introducing her to its current owner and resident, his benefactress Mrs Smith. In thus displaying a 'most shamefully unguarded affection', and 'slighting', so recklessly, 'the forms of worldly propriety', Marianne is putting at risk her whole future happiness – as her more prudent, and conventional, elder sister, Elinor, is unhappily aware.

Throughout her novels, Jane Austen continually demonstrates how many of the codes of early nineteenth-century conduct were not mere empty rituals, but offered safeguards for the individual – and for vulnerable young women in particular. She was never blind to the 'follies and nonsense' of social intercourse: the vapid life of Bath, with its public round of dull promenades and pointless engagements depressed her intensely; and she complained, throughout her life, of such irritations as 'the trouble of liking people' in general, and the 'elegant stupidity' of small parties in particular. 'We met nobody but ourselves, played at vingt-un, and were very cross', she told Cassandra, after an evening with Steventon neighbours in 1801; after a similar gathering in Southampton, she wrote, in 1808, 'The Miss Ms. were as civil and as silly as usual'; describing a party in Bath, in 1805, she recorded, 'There was a monstrous deal of stupid quizzing, & common-place nonsense talked, but scarcely any wit.' Writing in *Sense and Sensibility* of Marianne Dashwood's contempt for small-talk, she observes acidly, 'Upon Elinor, therefore, the whole task of telling lies when politeness required it, always fell.' Nevertheless, those rules of conduct which were based on precepts of courtesy and duty had her whole-hearted endorsement. Courtesy dictated the conventional niceties of social behaviour – the rules of introduction, the etiquette of paying and returning calls, the observing of rights of precedence, and so on. Duty, with its far greater implications, underpinned the whole structure of society – from the child's duty to a parent, as exemplified by the heroine's tireless ministering to her fretful father, in *Emma*, and Jane Austen's own loyal care for her hypochondriac mother, to the soldier's or sailor's ultimate duty to King and country, immortally summed up in Admiral Nelson's historic signal to the British fleet before the Battle of Trafalgar: 'England Expects That Every Man Will Do His Duty'.

It was a point of courtesy that a gentleman should not greet a lady in public until she had acknowledged him first, if she chose: as Frank Churchill points out in *Emma*, 'It is always the lady's right to decide upon the degree of acquaintance.' When Emma Woodhouse and Harriet Smith meet the respectable tenant-farmer Robert Martin while out walking, Emma pointedly does not invite Harriet to introduce him to her, but stands aloof and silent throughout the ensuing scene. Odious Mrs Elton, in the same novel, wishes it to seem that she is bestowing a favour when, speaking to Mr Weston of his son Frank Churchill, she graciously remarks, 'I shall be very happy in his acquaintance'. No 'acquaintance', of any degree, could begin without a formal introduction, by a suitable third party. After a ball at the seaside resort of Lyme, in 1804, Jane Austen reported with amusement that an 'odd-looking man, who had been eyeing me for some time . . . without any introduction, asked me if I meant to dance again', concluding charitably, 'I think he must be Irish, by his ease.' Such untoward 'ease' is not, however, permitted to the characters in her novels. Catherine Morland, making her debut at Bath's Upper Rooms, in *Northanger Abbey*, 'longed to dance', but as 'she had not an acquaintance in the room', remains a frustrated spectator. Only on her second appearance, at the Lower Rooms, is she introduced to a suitable partner by the Master of Ceremonies, Mr King. (A real person, a successor to the great 'Beau Nash', who had first established Bath as a social centre, in the 1720s, Mr King presided over the city's public assemblies until 1805, and would thus have been known to Jane Austen while she lived there.) 'If you find she does not want much Talking to, you may introduce me bye & bye', young Lord Osborne condescendingly tells a friend, after noticing Emma Watson in *The Watsons*; in *Pride and Prejudice* Mr Darcy, still more disdainfully, declines at first to be introduced to Elizabeth Bennet, on the insulting grounds that she is 'not handsome enough to tempt *me*'. Though Elizabeth, with characteristic wit and spirit, treats the snub as a good joke, she is aware enough of its implications to seek to dissuade her foolish clergyman cousin, Mr Collins, from risking the 'impertinent freedom' of introducing himself, uninvited, to Mr Darcy. As she urgently, but vainly, warns him, 'It must belong to Mr Darcy, the superior in consequence, to begin the acquaintance.' It was such points as these which Jane Austen would stress in her correspondence with her aspiring novelist niece. 'I have scratched out the introduction between Lord P. & his Brother, & Mr Griffin', she told Anna in August 1814, adding, in explanation, 'A Country Surgeon ... would not be introduced to Men of their rank.'

The classic guide to the British peerage, *Debrett's Peerage and Baronetage*, which first appeared in 1802, might have been the source which Jane consulted, in August 1814, in order to re-assure Anna that a title which she had used in her novel did not actually exist, 'either among the Dukes, Marquesses, Earls, Viscounts or Barons'. Such concern for the details of title, form and precedence did not mean, however, that Jane Austen was in any way impressed by aristocrats: quite the reverse. Few portraits in her fiction are more scathing than that of Sir Walter Elliot, in *Persuasion*, constantly re-reading his own entry in the *Baronetage*, and convinced that the 'blessing of a baronetcy' – the lowest form of hereditary title, bearing with it no seat in the House of Lords – made him innately superior to others. She frequently pokes fun at the pretensions of baronets: the servant of Sir Walter Elliot's reprobate heir makes it known at every inn that his master 'would be a baronight some day'; scheming Isabella Thorpe, in *Northanger Abbey*, will – Henry Tilney predicts – continue her pursuit of his eligible brother 'unless a baronet should come in her way'; while in a letter of 26 October, 1813, having mentioned 'Mr Deedes & Sir Brook', Jane wrote flippantly, 'I do not care for Sir Brook's being a Baronet I will put Mr Deedes first because I like him a great deal the best.' Behind the joke about social precedence lies a truth which pervades all her novels: Jane Austen decidedly did not 'care for' titles, of any degree.

Few comic characters in English literature are more entertainingly unpleasant than Mr Darcy's aunt Lady Catherine de Bourgh, in *Pride and Prejudice*. Unlike the over-affable and courtly Sir William Lucas in the same novel, who has merely had the (non-hereditary) honour of a knighthood bestowed on him for civic service, Lady Catherine is genuinely of noble blood: the fact that her title accompanies her Christian name, not her surname, shows that it is hers by birth, and not by marriage. (Sir William Lucas's wife is merely 'Lady Lucas'.) Despite her high lineage, however, Lady Catherine is portrayed as an ill-mannered woman, who believes that her rank exempts her from the normal demands of politeness to others. 'Mr Darcy', Jane Austen notes, after one instance of her rudeness, 'looked a little ashamed of his aunt's ill-breeding'. It is part of Mr Darcy's process of education in the course of this novel that he overcomes both family pride and social prejudice, to recognize that his own aristocratic aunt is ignorant and embarrassing, while Elizabeth Bennet's city-merchant uncle – who lives and trades in an unfashionable part of London, 'within view of his own warehouses' – is a man of intelligence, taste and good manners. 'She derives part of her abilities from her rank and fortune' is Mr Wickham's sarcastic comment on Lady Catherine's reputation for cleverness; in the same vein, a character in *The Watsons* observes that the presence of the titled Osbornes 'gives a credit to our Assemblies' which is 'more than they deserve . . . but Great People have always their charm'. Emma Watson, the heroine, goes further, declaring that young Lord Osborne might be 'better bred' if he 'were *not* a Lord'. Anne Elliot, in *Persuasion*, is downright ashamed of her father and sister for pursuing so avidly their grand relations, the Dowager Viscountess Dalrymple and her daughter, who, apart from their hereditary titles, 'were nothing', possessing 'no superiority of manner, accomplishment or understanding' to justify such pride in the connection. The word 'snobbery' would not enter the English language until the 1830s, over fifteen years after Jane Austen's death, but snobbery, with all its folly and false values, is as much her target as it would later be Thackeray's, in his great Regency historical novel of 1846, *Vanity Fair*.

As 'a gentleman's daughter', like Lizzy Bennet, Jane Austen was socially eligible to mix with the aristocracy as well as the gentry. In youth, she and Cassandra were frequent guests at the summer balls given by their father's former pupil Lord

Portsmouth, at Hurstbourne Park, and were well-enough acquainted with another local peer, Lord Bolton, not only to receive invitations to his family seat, Hackwood Park, but also to be asked to dance at neighbourhood Assemblies by his heir. 'One of my gayest actions', Jane reported flippantly after a Basingstoke ball in 1799, 'was sitting down two dances in preference to having Lord Bolton's eldest son for my partner, who danced too ill to be endured.' Partners would always dance two dances together; it was a point of courtesy that if a lady refused a gentleman's invitation she could not then accept another – however preferable – but must sit out the two dances in question. Nor could she change her mind, after accepting; it is ill-bred, and unkind, of Lord Osborne's sister, in *The Watsons*, to renege on her engagement to dance with Master Charles Blake – the more so because he is only 10 years old, and the nephew of her brother's former tutor. As a gentlewoman, though she had not been presented at Court, Jane was of sufficient status to be granted a private visit to the Prince Regent's London palace, Carlton House, where, in the Prince's absence, she was received 'with many flattering attentions' by his librarian, and given a conducted tour of the library and apartments. Yet, while she was conscious of her own social acceptability, she was also well aware of the limitations of her position in society, and was quick to make mock of herself, or her family, for any hint of putting on airs – real or imagined. Having visited Carlton House, and received a letter of congratulation on *Emma* from the Countess of Morley, her response was to write jokingly to Cassandra of 'my near Connections – beginning with the P.R. & ending with Countess Morley'. A year earlier, when their brother Henry attended a ball given by White's, the most exclusive and influential of the gentlemen's clubs in St James's, where membership was limited to aristocrats, politicians and notables such as the Duke of Devonshire, William Pitt and Beau Brummell, Jane had teased, 'Henry at Whites! Oh what a Henry!'

She took the same tone when describing her own occasional forays into the world of *ton*ish living. In 1813, while staying with Henry in London, she had been driven about town in his smart open barouche:'I liked my solitary elegance very much', she wrote, '& was ready to laugh all the time, at my being where I was. – I could not but feel that I had naturally small right to be parading about London in a Barouche.' While she had every right, as the heir's sister, to be a house-guest at Godmersham, the great country estate which her brother Edward inherited from his adoptive parents, she constantly revealed in her letters her awareness of the gulf between life in the Austens' cottage at Chawton and the 'Elegance & Ease & Luxury' of her existence at Godmersham. 'At this present time I have five Tables, Eight and twenty Chairs & two fires all to myself', she marvelled, in a letter of November 1813; three days later, she dashed off another before breakfast, which began, 'very snug, in my own room, lovely morn^g, excellent fire, fancy me'. An earlier visit, in 1808, had culminated in a dinner-party, at which, with anticipatory pleasure, she wrote, 'I shall eat Ice & drink French wine, & be above vulgar Economy.'All that stood between the luxury of her life at Godmersham and the 'vulgar Economy' of Chawton was money; which is why the 'possession of a good fortune' is a subject of such intense interest and importance throughout her fiction.

Contrary to some modern misapprehensions, Jane Austen's attitudes to wealth are not mercenary, but rather, analytical and practical. None of her heroines is remotely influenced by the worldly prospects which marriage to the hero would open up. 'Oh my sweetest Lizzy!' exclaims Mrs Bennet in *Pride and Prejudice*, on hearing of her daughter's match with Mr Darcy (who has £10,000 a year); 'What pin-money, what jewels, what carriages you will have! . . . A house in town!' Yet, unknown to her mother, Elizabeth Bennet has previously turned down these glittering prizes, not only without a thought, but with downright contempt, on receiving Darcy's first, 'ungentlemanlike' proposal of marriage. The only aspect of his vast possessions which she later hints – jokingly – at coveting is his country estate of Pemberley, with its 'beautiful grounds' and loyal, well-managed household. Fanny Price's revulsion at Henry Crawford's suit, in *Mansfield Park*, is no whit lessened by his wealth and position, – though by accepting him she would not only free herself from all deprivations, but also bring the benefits of his influence and income to her naval-officer brothers and down-at-heel family at Portsmouth. And Anne Elliot in *Persuasion* bitterly regrets her decision, under misplaced moral pressure, to give up the man she loves, solely because of his apparent lack of financial prospects. The simple, hardy sailor's life – as exemplified in Captain and Mrs Harville's cheerful cottage, with its home-made bookshelves, and even Admiral and Mrs Croft's more affluent, but equally unpretentious, domesticity – is shown, in Anne's eyes, as infinitely preferable to the empty parade of the Viscountess Dalrymple's world, with its meaningless social rituals and sham, self-seeking relationships. Fortune-hunting is a hallmark of the unworthy in Jane Austen's works; and just as Elinor Dashwood, in *Sense and Sensibility*, will not stoop to court Mrs Ferrars, her rich future mother-in-law, as does her mercenary rival Lucy Steele, so Elizabeth Bennet in *Pride and Prejudice* – unlike grovelling Mr Collins – refuses to curry favour with Lady Catherine de Bourgh, for all her wealth and influence. Money is never treated as an end in itself; it is, however, 'universally acknowledged' as necessary, in moderation, for a comfortable life.

Jane Austen regularly provides precise details of incomes because, to her contemporary readers, such information would have given an instant guide to a character's social situation and spending power. An income of £4,000 or more would provide the house in town for the London social season which is the goal of spoilt, worldly women such as Maria

Bertram and Mary Crawford; at the other end of the scale, £100 a year would be the minimum on which a servant could be afforded. Since even the impoverished Miss Bates and her mother, in *Emma*, can maintain a servant, the overworked Patty, the plight of Anne Elliot's friend Mrs Smith, in *Persuasion*, who is dependent on a communal lodging-house maid and the occasional care of a visiting nurse, is clearly dire. On £400 a year Fanny Price's mother, in *Mansfield Park*, is able to employ two slatternly servant-girls; on £500 per annum – the same income as the Austens had at Chawton – Mrs Dashwood and her daughters in *Sense and Sensibility* can just afford 'two maids and a man'. The fact that the Dashwoods regarded themselves as living modestly – in a borrowed cottage, without a horse or carriage – on this sum puts a perspective on Willoughby's extravagance: with his country establishment, his hunters, groom and gundogs, his fine curricle and fashionable amusements on an estimated £600 or £700 a year, he is clearly heading for a fall. It is understandable that a man of his luxurious tastes, and moral weakness, would be tempted by the 'smart and stilish' heiress Miss Grey, with her £50,000 (which, if invested at 5 per cent in government stock, would yield some £2,500 per annum). Mr Wickham, in *Pride and Prejudice*, is willing to settle for a great deal less, in courting Miss King – 'a nasty little freckled thing', according to Lydia Bennet, but nevertheless the possessor of £10,000, representing £500 of annual income. Wickham, as the son of a steward, with no inheritance, is of course a far less eligible suitor than Willoughby: in Jane Austen's world such points could be assessed with some precision. 'Pray, what is the usual price of an Earl's younger son?' Elizabeth Bennet asks Colonel Fitzwilliam, adding jokingly, yet meaningfully, 'Unless the elder brother is very sickly, I suppose you would not ask above fifty thousand pounds.' There is a similar calculation in the opening paragraphs of *Mansfield Park*: whatever her beauty, Jane Austen observes, (at her most ironic), a woman with only

£7,000 to her portion might be reckoned 'at least three thousand pounds short' of 'any equitable claim' to marry a baronet with 'a handsome house and large income'.

A key factor in assessing a character's wealth is his or her ability to keep a carriage. Jane Austen's father, on quitting Steventon Rectory for lodgings in Bath, was obliged to give up his – as is the widowed Mrs Dashwood, on leaving Norland Park for Barton Cottage. About £700 was the lowest income on which a carriage might be maintained; and from Willoughby's dashing open two-seater curricle to the sleek barouche-landau belonging to her sister Selina, with which Mrs Elton hopes to impress her new acquaintances at Highbury, carriages play a significant role in all Jane Austen's novels. The contrast between loutish John Thorpe's mishandling of his second-hand, one-horse gig and the skill of Henry Tilney's driving, in his elegant curricle and pair, vividly illustrates the gulf between them. Mrs Bennet witholds the use of the family carriage from Jane to ensure that she will be marooned at Netherfield, with Mr Bingley; Emma Woodhouse, trapped alone with Mr Elton in the swaying, cushioned intimacy of her father's carriage, finds herself subjected to his unwanted advances. An important strand of plot in *Emma* hinges upon the local apothecary Mr Perry's plan to 'set up his carriage' – indicating his advancement in the world; which underlines the cool social confidence of the rich and well-bred hero Mr Knightley, who chooses to walk whenever possible, rather than use his carriage. New to the carriage-owning classes, Mrs Elton – who claims exultantly, 'I believe we drive faster than anyone else' – is predictably excited by her sister's barouche-landau; the word 'barouche' only entered the English lexicon in 1813, two years before *Emma* was written, and this four-horse equipage, with its two retractable hoods, front and back, was the latest in what the would-be 'gentleman coachman' John Thorpe might have termed 'bang-up' conveyances. Among Mr Knightley's inferiors a certain competitiveness over carriages is often in evidence; and while young Charles Musgrove, breakfasting at an inn in *Persuasion*, jumps up eagerly to look at a passing curricle, 'that he might compare it with his own', General Tilney in *Northanger Abbey* can be in no doubt that his splendid chaise, with its 'postilions handsomely liveried, rising so regularly in their stirrups' and 'outriders, properly mounted', must inspire respect in other road-users. If the design, newness and expense of a vehicle were not proof enough of status, the custom of painting the owner's coat-of-arms on the door would proclaim his or her identity to the world; only the unlucky chance of a great-coat having been draped out of the window, obscuring the panel, prevents the Musgrove and Elliot party in *Persuasion* from recognizing the passing curricle as belonging to their kinsman, Mr William Walter Elliot.

Showing consideration for the coachman and horses is a mark of good breeding which comes naturally to Mr Knightley, though not, apparently, to Mrs Elton. Even spiteful Mrs Norris, in *Mansfield Park*, knows enough of proper behaviour to pretend to pity the rheumatic old family coachman whom she has forced to drive her in the depths of slippery winter, protesting, 'My heart quite ached for him at every jolt!' – adding 'The poor horses too! To see them straining away!' She claims credit for having walked a little way uphill, to spare 'those noble animals', but this was normal practice: approaching London in 1811, Jane told Cassandra, 'the Horse actually gibbed' on reaching Hyde Park Gate, and she and her sister-in-law Eliza got out, '& were detained in the even^g air several minutes', which gave Eliza a cold on the chest. Such genuine concern for the welfare of both horses and servants is taken to an extreme by querulous old Mr Woodhouse, in *Emma*, who hardly wishes his carriage to be used at all, for fear of troubling the coachman – till his daughter Emma artfully points out that their driver, James, will be only too happy to take them to the house in question, since she has procured his daughter a place there, as a maid. 'I only doubt whether he will ever take us any-where else', she concludes, with coaxing wit.

In *Emma*, more than any of her other novels, Jane Austen examines the structure and interactions of English society in the early part of the nineteenth century. There are no titled characters (baronets or otherwise); but in the Knightleys of Donwell Abbey she depicts a microcosm of the ancient, Domesday-Book-listed, landed families which formed the backbone of the British establishment; and below them she paints in, with her fine brush, a miniature spectrum of country characters of almost every social and financial shade, from the well-born, and/or wealthy, inhabitants of Highbury, through the rising ranks of the newly well-to-do, and the sturdy yeo-man Martins, down to the outcast gypsies who waylay and threaten Harriet. Old Mrs and Miss Bates are poor, but they are gentlewomen; Mrs Elton, by contrast, has a fortune of £10,000, but she is the daughter of a Bristol merchant (one implication being that he has made his money in the slave trade), and the sister-in-law of a man whose family have acquired their country estate through recent purchase, not inheritance. 'A little upstart, vulgar being', in Emma's angry description, with her 'pert pretentiousness and under-bred finery', Mrs Elton is a very different newcomer to the moneyed middle classes from the worthy Cole family, who, though 'only moderately genteel', are now – having prospered in trade – 'in fortune and style of living, second only to the family at Hartfield'. They indeed show many of the attributes of the old rich, with their interest in improving their house, pleasure in entertaining their neighbours, and charming, unas-suming courtesy to Emma and her father. Emma's attempts to 'cut' the Coles leave her, not them, isolated; and Mr Knightley, the arbiter of rational values in this novel, makes it plain that he has no patience with her silly snobberies. As he reminds her, and Jane Austen reminds the reader, good principles and a good heart count for more than any worldly 'distinction of rank'. Emma may dismiss the decent farmer Robert Martin as not merely 'illiterate and coarse', but 'clownish'; but in Mr Knightley's clearer judgement he is a man of 'sense, sincerity and good-humour', who displays 'true gentility'.

A sure test of 'true gentility' in Jane Austen's novels is a character's treatment of servants. Accustomed from birth to being waited on herself, even when she and Cassandra and their mother were living on the relatively meagre income of £500 a year, she would seem, from the many passing references in her letters, to have been a good mistress. A manservant at Southampton named Cholles had to be dismissed, in 1803, because 'he grew so very drunken and negligent'; but a successor, James, was 'the delight of our lives . . . attentive, handy, quick and quiet', while another was 'my own dear Thomas', and one of the last, William, was praised as 'a good-looking lad, civil and quiet'. There was a (perhaps inevitable) whiff of patronage in her attitude: before moving to Bath, in 1801, Jane wrote jauntily, 'We plan having a steady Cook, & a young giddy Housemaid, with a sedate, middle-aged Man, who is to undertake the double office of Husband to the former & sweetheart to the latter. No Children of course to be allowed on either side.' But in her life, as in her novels, the relationship was expected to be one of mutual respect. If Mr Knightley, in *Emma*, represents the best style of master–servant dealings in his cordial, almost comradely, treatment of his bailiff William Larkins, Mrs Norris in *Mansfield Park* exemplifies the worst; while she fulsomely flatters the housekeeper at grand Sotherton Court, and patronizes the gardener, cadging pheasants' eggs and a cream cheese from one and a rare plant from the other in the process, back at Mansfield Park she bullies the staff, giving 'troublesome directions' to the housekeeper, and chivvying the butler and footmen with unnecessary 'injunctions of despatch'. She even mocks the working-class speech of the estate carpenter's child – 'a great lubberly fellow of ten years old' – mimicking, 'Father had bid him bring up them two bits of board for he could not nohow do without them.' (The fact that Sir Thomas Bertram subsequently refers to the carpenter, courteously, as 'my friend Christopher Jackson', and praises his workmanship, underlines the nastiness of Mrs Norris's attitude.) Though servants play almost no part in the action, they are so skilfully etched in as to have distinct personalities and – Jane Austen hints – perspectives. The reader can infer that the 'two elegant ladies' who wait on Miss Bingley and her sisters look askance at Elizabeth Bennet, with her windblown hair and muddy ankles; Fanny Price certainly seems to be in awe of Lady Bertram's personal maid, Mrs Chapman. The 'half-smile' on the face of Baddeley, the butler, when Fanny, rather than Mrs Norris, is summoned to meet Mr Crawford in the drawing-room suggests that those below stairs at Mansfield Park know all that is going on; certainly the household staff at Longbourn, in *Pride and Prejudice*, are not fooled by Mrs Bennet's joy, and promises of a bowl of punch at the wedding, into thinking of Miss Lydia as anything but a fallen woman, and they smirk at her patched-up marriage. By contrast, the devotion of a servant to a good employer is no less telling: having heard Mrs Reynolds, the housekeeper at Pemberley, extolling Mr Darcy as 'good-natured' and 'affable', Elizabeth Bennet reflects gratefully, 'What praise is more valuable than the praise of an intelligent servant?'

While incivility to employees is always unacceptable, so is over-familiarity, in any form. There is never any hint of sexual involvement between master or mistress and servant in Jane Austen's fiction, unlike in the works of her favourite novelists Richardson and Fielding; even the worst of her rakes, Wickham and Willoughby, set out to seduce young women of their own class, or – in the case of 15-year-old Georgiana Darcy – above it. (Mr Wickham, in *Pride and Prejudice*, is the son of the Darcy family's steward, but with a Cambridge University education and an officer's rank he is 'a gentleman', and not to be equated with a lowly footman such as Henry Fielding's Joseph

Andrews.) Responsible characters do not share confidences with servants, for fear they may tattle among themselves, or to other households – or, worst of all, to the newspapers, which then, as now, thrived on titbits of society gossip. 'Putting herself in the power of a servant' is mentioned as a key factor in Maria Rushworth's downfall, in *Mansfield Park*; certainly it is from a newspaper report that Fanny Price learns of 'the beautiful Mrs R.' having 'quitted her husband's roof' in the company of the 'captivating Mr C.' In *Sense and Sensibility*, Mrs Jennings's vulgarity is underlined by the fact that she conspires with her maid and a groom to find out about Marianne's and Willoughby's activities; ironically, at the climax of the novel, it is a servant who proffers the dramatic news of Lucy Steele's marriage (which he has learned at an inn) – and even the reticent and dignified heroine, Elinor, cannot resist pressing him for details. Inns, where the gentry would stop to change horses and take refreshment, were ideal breeding-grounds for gossip, in stables and dining-rooms alike. In *Persuasion* it is a waiter at an inn who informs the Elliots' party that the owner of the curricle which caught Charles Musgrove's eye is none other than their cousin, Mr William Walter Elliot; in *Pride and Prejudice*, Elizabeth Bennet hastily dismisses the waiter when, at an inn, her indiscreet sister Lydia announces that she has some 'excellent news' to impart. 'I dare say he often hears worse things than I am going to say' is Lydia's careless, and ungrateful, retort.

It may have been a coincidence that the Dashwoods' servant is named Thomas, as was the Austens' manservant at the time when she was writing *Sense and Sensibility*. Certainly Jane could be idiosyncratic in her choice of characters' names. It is rare for an author, in any period, to give his or her own Christian name to a leading character, yet two of the most elegant, attractive and accomplished women in Jane Austen's novels – Miss Bennet in *Pride and Prejudice* and Miss Fairfax in *Emma* – are called 'Jane'. Her most ungenteel female, the man-hungry spinster Anne Steele in *Sense and Sensibility*, has the same first name as one of the most sensitive and appealing of all her heroines, Anne Elliot in *Persuasion*; in *Pride and Prejudice*, Darcy's haughty, aristocratic aunt Lady Catherine shares hers with the heroine's giddy younger sister Kitty. Occasionally Jane Austen betrays a preference: she evidently disliked 'Richard', commenting that Catherine Morland's father in *Northanger Abbey* was 'a very respectable man, though his name was Richard', and giving the name of 'Dick' to Mrs Musgrove's worthless and little-lamented late son in *Persuasion*. By contrast, 'Henry', after her beloved brother, was clearly associated with good looks and wit, and was given alike to the charming hero of *Northanger Abbey*, Henry Tilney, and the charming villain of *Mansfield Park*, Henry Crawford. On a visit to Godmersham, in 1813, she wrote of a fellow-guest, Mr Wigram, 'They say his name is Henry. A proof how unequally the gifts of Fortune are bestowed. – I have seen many a John & Thomas more agreable [*sic*].' Social criteria seemed to play scant part in her choice. While Mr Darcy's sister is 'Georgiana', in echo of such Georgian and Regency society leaders as Georgiana, Duchess of Devonshire and Georgiana, Duchess of Bedford, this is also the name of a middle-class girl in Jane's juvenile fragment, *The Three Sisters*; and she uses 'Thomas' both for the Dashwoods' manservant and Fanny Price's rich, imposing uncle, Sir Thomas Bertram. Only rarely did she state a direct opinion on the naming of characters. 'The name of Rachael is more than I can bear', she told her would-be novelist niece Anna, after reading an instalment of her manuscript; in 1813, having praised the 'Sagacity & Taste' and 'large dark eyes' of a family friend, Charlotte Williams, she declared, 'I will compliment her, by naming a Heroine after her.' It is tempting to surmise that she had this promise in mind when, embarking on her last, unfinished novel *Sanditon*, in 1817, she called the heroine 'Charlotte Heywood'. It is certainly possible that the high-minded heroine of *Mansfield Park* is named in tribute to her adored niece Fanny Knight – though Jane wrote with amusement, in June 1814, that a Chawton friend, Miss Dusautoy, 'has a great idea of being Fanny Price – she and her youngest sister together, who is named Fanny'.

Although, as she was at pains to point out, Jane Austen's characters (if not their names) were drawn from imagination, rather than from real people, her deeply sympathetic portrayals of governesses may have been in part inspired by her affection for a former governess at Godmersham, Anne Sharp, whom, by the end of her life, she addressed as 'dearest Anne'. From the 'genteel, agreeable-looking' Mrs Annesley, Georgiana Darcy's governess in *Pride and Prejudice*, to Emma Woodhouse's beloved former teacher and mentor, Mrs Weston, in *Emma*, such women are almost invariably depicted as 'more truly well-bred' than any of their employers and supposed social superiors. Of Miss Sharp's successor at Godmersham, Miss Allen, Jane wrote in 1811, 'I suppose she is hard at it, governing away – poor creature! I pity her, tho' they *are* my nieces.' This is very much Emma Woodhouse's sentiment on hearing that Jane Fairfax has reluctantly accepted a position as governess with a friend of vulgar Mrs Elton. For all Miss Bates's protestations that 'it will be nothing but pleasure, a life of pleasure' for her niece, and references to 'great sums' by way of salary, Emma can only respond, 'I should think five times the amount . . . on such occasions, dearly earned.' Yet, in the absence of a tolerable marriage, or (in rare cases, such as Fanny Burney's and Maria Edgeworth's), a successful writing career, the only option for a respectable, educated woman without family or private means was to become a teacher in a school – 'and I can think of nothing worse!' exclaims the heroine of *The Watsons* – or a governess in a respectable household. The personal columns of newspapers such as *The Times* during this period were full of poignant advertisements from females such as 'E.C.', 'a young Lady, of respectable connections and amiable disposition', desiring a post 'in which salary not so much as comfort is her object', or 'E.B.', who, 'qualified by accomplishments and education', wished for 'a SITUATION, as GOVERNESS'; and could be contacted via 'Mr Hatchard's Piccadilly' – the famous London bookshop, still thriving today. There is unusual passion, for both Jane Austen and Jane Fairfax, in Miss Fairfax's outburst about 'the sale – not quite of human flesh – but of human intellect'; crassly, Mrs Elton responds with a reference to the slave trade, to which Jane replies forcefully, 'Governess-trade, I assure you, was all that I had in view,' adding, 'but as to the greater misery of the victims, I do not know where it lies.' It is one of the most heartfelt passages in all Jane Austen's fiction.

When Mrs Elton tries to patronize Emma's former governess, calling her 'quite the gentlewoman', Emma answers coolly that for 'propriety, simplicity and elegance', Mrs Weston's manners are a 'model for any young woman'. Georgiana Darcy's governess displays similar good manners, introducing polite small-talk to cover an awkward moment in *Pride and Prejudice*. For all Jane Austen's dislike of banality, she approved entirely of any gambit which would smooth the path of social intercourse – even if it meant resorting to that traditional British ploy, talking about the weather. Insipid Lady Middleton, in *Sense and Sensibility*, provides welcome relief for Elinor when she turns an embarrassing conversation by observing that 'it rained very hard', a topic on which she is joined by Colonel Brandon – 'who was on every occasion mindful of the feelings of others', as Jane Austen significantly states – 'and much was said on the subject of rain by both of them'. In *Emma*, no less a hero than Mr Knightley averts a difficult situation by asking Mrs Weston, 'What does Weston think of the weather: shall we have rain?' And on a similar note, when Darcy and Elizabeth meet unexpectedly at Pemberley, in *Pride and Prejudice*, they cover their confusion (and deeper feelings) by exchanging nervous platitudes about the local scenery: as

Jane Austen puts it, 'They talked of Matlock and Dove Dale with great perseverance.' To be 'mindful of the feelings of others' is the essence of good manners, even to the extent of 'telling lies when politeness required it'.

For Fanny Price's 14-year-old sister Susan, the prospect of her first visit to Mansfield Park conjures up alarming visions of 'silver forks, napkins and finger glasses'. Yet, despite her fears of social inadequacy, her innate good nature and intelligence quickly establish her as a favourite with the grand Lady Bertram. Susan Price, like Fanny, is clearly destined to rise above the world into which she was born – in the Prices' case, a world based in a cramped, shabby Portsmouth household filled with rowdy, ill-disciplined children, a coarse, blasphem-ing father and waited on by a 'trollopy-looking maidservant' and her underling. Social mobility is a constant underlying theme of Jane Austen's novels, from *Sense and Sensibility*, in which the predatory Lucy Steele so far ingratiates herself with her betters as to marry one of the rich Ferrars sons, to *Persuasion*, in which the old-fashioned, unambitious country squire, Mr Musgrove, and his wife, who are 'not much edu-cated, and not at all elegant', have seen their eldest children, with their 'more modern minds and manners', take their place in polite Bath and country-house circles – the son, Charles, having married a baronet's daughter, the girls 'living to be fashionable, happy and merry'. Education is seen as a major factor in social advancement, for women in particular. The Musgrove girls have 'brought from a school in Exeter', all the usual 'accomplishments'; after an expensive education, the ill-bred Mrs Jennings's daughters, in *Sense and Sensibility*, are married to a baronet and a propertied, prospective Member of Parliament; the tenant-farmer Robert Martin's sisters, in *Emma*, as pupils at Mrs Goddard's, are considered, even by snobbish Emma Woodhouse, to have risen in the world. 'Like other young ladies, she is considerably genteeler than her parents', Jane Austen wrote of an acquaintance at the seaside resort of Lyme, in 1804. Where her fictional gentlemen are concerned, Jane matches, with subtle precision, the school to the character: thus well-bred Edmund Bertram in *Mansfield Park* has been at Eton, the grandest British public school, then as now, while middle-class Isabella Thorpe's younger brother, in *Northanger Abbey*, is at Merchant Taylors', a well-respected, but less socially elevated foundation, then based in the City of London. Worldly Henry Crawford and foppish Robert Ferrars are both products of Westminster, the most famous and fashionable of the London public schools – but subtly tainted, Jane Austen seems to hint, by its associations with the temptations of the town. She may have had mixed feelings about the practice of sending boys to be educated at a public school, rather than in the household of a private tutor such as her father; certainly there is heavy irony in the passage in which fatuous Robert Ferrars congratulates himself on being 'well fitted to mix in the world', through having had 'the advantage of a public school', rather than suffering 'the misfortune of a private education', to which he attributes his brother Edward's 'gaucherie'. Where the villainous Mr Wickham was taught before going up to Cambridge University – all paid for by Mr Darcy's father – is not stated; but his 'gentlemen's education' and 'social powers' have equipped him not only to hold an officer's commission in Wellington's army, but to move in the same circles as Darcy himself. By a finely observed double irony, when Elizabeth Bennet is first warned against him, she attributes the slur to snobbery, saying angrily to his accuser, Miss Bingley, 'His guilt and his descent appear by your account to be the same.' In fact, in seeking to oppose one form of prejudice she is guilty of another – that in favour of good looks and a glib tongue.

Too much social polish is almost invariably a warning sign in a Jane Austen character. From plausible Mr Wickham and the 'coxcomb' Robert Ferrars to Mr Elton in *Emma*, 'spruce, black and smiling' in his evening-dress, and treacherous Mr

William Walter Elliot in *Persuasion*, such males are the antithesis of the 'nice, gentlemanlike, unaffected sort of young man' whom she wished her niece Fanny to marry. Just as the 'emptiness and conceit' of Robert Ferrars contrast ill with the 'modesty and worth' of his honourable brother Edward, who is willing to marry a woman he no longer loves rather than break his word, so the shallow charm of sly Mr Elton is shown up by the honest, unassuming decency of Robert Martin, who courts Harriet Smith not with riddles and flattery, in the Elton style, but by 'going three miles round' to get walnuts for her, and bringing a shepherd boy into his parlour to sing for her. Mrs Jennings in *Sense and Sensibility* is cheerfully 'ill-bred', with an embarrassing disregard for the social proprieties, but her warm heart and kindness to young people increasingly endear her to Elinor Dashwood; Mrs Musgrove in *Persuasion*, though 'not much educated, and not at all elegant', shows Anne Elliot a motherly welcome which – in contrast to the cold vanity of her own family and the snobbery of her friend Lady Russell – Anne is grateful for. And yet too great a neglect of the rituals of polite behaviour was never to Jane Austen's liking. The insistence of Anne Elliot's sister Mary, wife of the Musgroves' son Charles, on taking precedence over her mother-in-law because, as a baronet's daughter, she outranks Mrs Musgrove, is shown as petty and undignified; but Anne herself is disconcerted by the casual way in which the different generations of the Musgrove family dispense with the usual formalities of paying visits, by calling at each other's houses at will, without regard for ceremony. To Anne, 'such a style of intercourse' seems 'highly imprudent', since it gives rise to 'continual subjects of offence'.

The accepted early nineteenth-century system of paying, and receiving, morning calls was highly codified. Most women of leisure, whether in town or country, Bath or Brighton, would regard it as part of their daily routine to visit friends and acquaintances, bearing 'calling cards' printed with the visitor's name, which the servant who answered the door would duly present to the mistress of the house. If she were out, or indisposed, cards would be left on a salver in the hall, as witness to the intended courtesy; if she were at home, and 'receiving', the caller would be ushered by the servant into her presence, to spend 'the full half-hour' which politeness required, taking refreshment and exchanging news and small-talk. The potential for offence on either side (as Anne Elliot is acutely aware) was considerable. Old Mr Woodhouse, in *Emma*, is anxious about paying the newly-wed Mrs Elton the visit which was her due, fretting 'Not to wait upon a bride is very remiss'; Catherine Morland in *Northanger Abbey*, having been told that Miss Tilney is not at home, only to see her leave the house soon after, fears that she is being shown 'angry incivility' for having somehow 'broken the laws of worldly politeness'. No lady could visit an unmarried man, which is why even the unconventional Marianne Dashwood in *Sense and Sensibility* has to wait, agonizingly, for Willoughby to come to her on her arrival in London; and why Mr Bennet, in the famous opening chapter of *Pride and Prejudice*, is pressed by his wife to 'wait upon' their eligible new bachelor neighbour Mr Bingley, since she cannot go herself. Once cards had been left, or a visit paid, the call had to be returned promptly or the acquaintance might lapse; even the trusting Jane Bennet, while staying in London, accepts that the belatedness and brevity of Miss Bingley's overdue visit must represent a deliberate put-down, and resolves to end their threadbare friendship by not returning it. In a letter of advice on her niece Anna's novel, Jane followed some comments on character and dialogue with the point, 'Your G.M.' (Grandmother) 'is more disturbed at Mrs F.'s not returning the Egertons' visit sooner, than anything else. They ought to have called at the Parsonage before Sunday.' The rules of repaying dinner-party invitations were still more strictly observed. In *Sense and Sensibility*, when Sir John Middleton asks why certain friends might not be asked to dinner, his wife replies frostily, 'it could not be done', since 'They dined with us last.' To the reply from his mother-in-law, jolly Mrs Jennings, 'You and I, Sir John, should not stand upon such ceremony', her other son-in-law, the abrasive Mr Palmer, replies cuttingly, 'Then you would be very ill-bred.'

In the context of the Regency social world that comment is, undeniably, true. Yet when, later in the novel, Mrs Jennings exclaims, with homely good sense, 'I have no notion of people's making such a to-do about money and greatness', she has the author's evident sympathy. All the honourable characters in Jane Austen's fiction place Christian values above 'the distinction of rank', and points of etiquette. Even when Emma Woodhouse's self-deluding meddling is at its height, in *Emma*, she is shown taking food and comfort to the poor of the village; and for all Miss Bates's tedious garrulity, she is an admirable character, praised for her cheerful outlook and willingness, in her poverty, to share all she has with those poorer than herself. It is, ultimately, Anne Elliot in *Persuasion* – the heroine whom one acquaintance thought most like Jane herself – who demonstrates the author's ideal of social conduct, when she is described as 'an elegant little woman', with 'manners as consciously right as they were invariably gentle'.

It is surely no coincidence that Jane Austen, who once promised to compliment a friend by 'naming a heroine after her' should have called this most delightful character Anne Elliot. *Persuasion* was written for publication by John Murray – and John Murray's wife, before her marriage, had been Miss Anne Elliot.

8

'Politics and Public Events'

'What weather! & what news!'
Jane Austen, letter to Cassandra, 1813

'How horrible it is to have so many people killed! And what a blessing that one cares for none of them!' Jane Austen wrote to her sister Cassandra, on 31 May, 1811. There was nothing heartless, or ironic, in the comment. To the Austen sisters and their contemporaries, the phrase 'to care for' was used to signify deep feeling; and in Jane's response to the first news of the British victory at Albuera, one of the bloodiest battles of the Peninsular War, she was expressing heartfelt relief that on this occasion neither she nor her immediate family and friends had lost a husband, brother, son or suitor in the action. 'Let other pens dwell on guilt and misery', she would write at the conclusion of *Mansfield Park*; and her reference to the dead of Albuera was sandwiched between family news of Anna's cold, the progress of her patchwork, and the Chawton cook's 'deficiency' at pastry-making. Nevertheless, this novelist whose brothers were engaged in the war at sea against Napoleon, whose kinsman by marriage was guillotined in the French Revolution, and whose life was lived under the shadow of foreign invasion, was intensely aware of the historic events unfolding around her, and her novels are suffused with a sense of the political and social upheavals of the time.

'The politics of the day occupied very little of her attention', her nephew would claim in his *Memoir* of 1870; yet Jane

216

Austen clearly believed that, although they might not have the vote, or be represented in Parliament, women should be informed about politics. The heroine of her juvenile work *Catharine* (written in 1792) is shocked to find that her new friend Camilla is so empty-headed as to confuse history and politics: in *Mansfield Park*, even frivolous Mary Crawford takes it for granted that Fanny Price is aware of current affairs, writing from London, 'I have no news for you. You have politics of course.' As part of Henry Tilney's half-humorous, half-serious attempts to educate and inform sweet young Catherine Morland, in *Northanger Abbey*, he gives her a 'short disquisition on the state of the nation'; and though on this occasion Jane Austen notes, 'from politics it was an easy step to silence', the reader can infer that, once they are married, her political (as well as cultural) education will continue. Intelligent and well-read as Elizabeth Bennet is, she anticipates such a process as a result of her 'union' with Mr Darcy, in *Pride and Prejudice*, reflecting that 'by her ease and liveliness, his mind might have been softened', while 'from his judgement, information and knowledge of the world, she must have received benefit of greater importance'.

The comical misunderstanding which ensues when Catherine Morland – speaking of a new horror-novel – warns the Tilneys that 'something very shocking will soon come out in London' underlines the constant fear of political instability and violence which lurked behind the apparent serenity of Jane Austen's world. Clever Miss Tilney instantly assumes she must be speaking of some threatened insurrection: as Henry explains, his sister has envisaged 'a mob of three thousand men assembling . . . the Bank attacked, the Tower threatened, the streets of London flowing with blood', and their brother Captain Tilney sent to quell the insurgents, with the 12th Light Dragoons. His description evokes the Gordon Riots of 1780, when anti-Catholic protestors, incited by Lord George Gordon, brought vicious fighting to the London streets, besieging the Bank of England, looting and burning, till put down by the army, with the loss of several hundred lives. Jane Austen was only 4 years old at the time, but the events left a deep impression on the propertied classes – an impression reinforced, at the end of that decade, by the lurid example, just across the Channel, of the French Revolution.

The American War of Independence, which began in the year of her birth, 1775, had done much to foster a new spirit of radicalism among the British. The prominent libertarian Member of Parliament John Wilkes was joined in his support for the rebel colonists by a growing number of intellectuals, acknowledging the justice of the American rallying-cry, 'No taxation without representation'; and rather than fight for King George III, who was implacable in his belief that 'America must be a colony of England or treated as an enemy', numbers of army officers resigned their commissions. In 1783, under the Treaty of Versailles, the great military, as well as moral, victory of the newly formed United States was formally conceded by Britain. Six years later, on 6 October 1789, a mob of French citizens stormed the gates of the Palace of Versailles itself, and King Louis XVI, with Queen Marie-Antoinette and their children, was escorted forcibly back to Paris – to become, officially, a constitutional monarch: in truth, a prisoner. The ideals of the French Revolution, summed up in Jean-Jacques Rousseau's immortal slogan *'Liberté, Egalité, Fraternité'*, were noble, and in Britain there were many men and women, of all classes, who hailed with joy the apparent overthrow of a decadent, oppressive and unjust old regime in favour of a new and enlightened era. 'Bliss was it in that dawn to be alive, / But to be young was very Heaven', wrote the young Romantic William Wordsworth. When the Irish statesman Edmund Burke, in 1790, published an opposing view in *Reflections on the Revolution in France*, urging a more cautious response, and warning of the likely rise of a French dictator, and a long war, the feminist intellectual Mary

Wollstonecraft countered, eloquently, with her support for the Revolution and its principles, in her well-received *A Vindication of the Rights of Men*. Yet she, like Wordsworth, the Whig leader Charles James Fox, and so many other radicals, would become disillusioned as the initial idealism of 'that dawn' gave way to the state-sponsored bloodshed of 'the Terror', when, between 1792 and 1795, massacres and the work of the efficient new public Guillotine accounted for the deaths of thousands of men, women and children. Among them were the King and Queen – and Jane Austen's cousin by marriage, an aristocratic French army officer named Count Jean Capot de Feuillide.

For Jane, who was just 19 when news of this relation's execution arrived, it must have been a shocking, and perhaps formative, event. The Count's wife, her cousin Eliza, née Hancock, had stayed frequently at Steventon when in England, and had become a favourite with Jane's father, as well as with her brothers James and Henry, who – despite her married status – had vied ardently for her attentions. Eliza was pretty, pleasure-loving and worldly-wise; and on first meeting her the 11-year-old Jane must have been fascinated by her accounts of theatres, balls and fashions, and the tales of her travels, from exotic India (where she was born) to pre-Revolutionary Paris. It may have been Eliza's influence which caused the smitten Henry to abandon his initial plans of becoming a clergyman, and join the Oxfordshire Militia, when Britain went to war with France in 1793; certainly she described him with pleasure as 'Captain, Paymaster & Adjutant', when finally agreeing to marry him, in 1797. Even as a girl Jane would have been well aware of Eliza's faults and failings, and she surely incorporated some of them into such flawed characters as Isabella Thorpe and Mary Crawford. Yet she was fond of this giddy cousin and sister-in-law, and seemed wholly to share her attitudes to the politics and people of France. The only reference to revolutionary ideals in her fiction is a joking nod in *Emma*, when, describing the preparations for a party, she writes, 'A private dance, without sitting down to a supper, was pronounced an infamous fraud upon the rights of men and women.' A year after Napoleon's final defeat at Waterloo, she reported that her brother Edward had returned from a trip to Paris, 'thinking of the French as one could wish, disappointed in everything'; of another recent traveller, Henry's and Eliza's French servant Mme Périgord, Jane noted, 'She speaks of France as a scene of general poverty & Misery, – no Money, no Trade – nothing to be got but by the Innkeepers.' She expressed an equal lack of sympathy towards the nation whose Declaration of Independence, in the year after her birth, had formally enshrined the concept of the 'Rights of Man': in 1814, when the United States and Britain were once again at war, she wrote gloomily, 'If we are to be ruined, it cannot be helped – but I place my hope of better things on a claim to the protection of Heaven, as a Religious Nation, a Nation in spite of much Evil improving in Religion, which I cannot believe the Americans to possess.'

If much of Jane's attitude towards foreigners was the product of fierce and genuine patriotism, there was, too, a certain self-mockery in her professed xenophobia. Writing in 1817 of letters from abroad, she declared, 'They would not be satisfactory to *me*, I confess, unless they breathed a strong spirit of regret for not being in England.' After reading aloud, 'by candlelight', the radical poet Robert Southey's *Letters from England by Don Manuel Alvarez Espriella*, a purported account of a Spanish gentleman's travels through, and opinions of, contemporary England, she noted, 'The Man . . . is horribly anti-English. He deserves to be the foreigner he assumes.' She could laugh at her own zeal; nevertheless, this staunch 'Hampshire-born Austen' set a high store by loyalty – to country, to county, to family and friends. When one of the most dramatic events of her youth, the trial of Warren

Hastings, took place in the late 1780s, dividing public opinion, there could be no doubt where the Austens' allegiances lay. As Governor of Bengal, Hastings had been a close friend of the Revd George Austen's sister Philadelphia and brother-in-law, Tysoe Saul Hancock. Through this connection, the Hastings's little son was sent to be educated in the Austens' household; and though, tragically, the child died, the warm relationship between his parents and Jane's survived – to be further strengthened by the visits of Eliza Hancock at Steventon. Officially the intriguing Eliza was Warren Hastings's god-daughter, but privately many believed her to be his daughter, and certainly the bond between her and her mother, and the celebrated Mr Hastings, was unusually strong. Eliza was among the spectators who flocked to see the historic trial in progress; and no doubt her descriptions of the proceedings, and opinions on the state of affairs in India which lay behind it, would have made a considerable impact at the Steventon dinner-table.

Hastings had had a brilliant career, rising steadily up the ranks of the mercantile East India Company, which, through settlements in the provinces of Bombay, Madras and Bengal, traded in such precious commodities as silks, cotton and spices. The British Raj had yet to come into being; but as trade expanded, so, too, did the East India Company's role in administration and defence, for the advancement of its own (and Britain's) interests, and protection against the constant threats from France's rival colonial ambitions and the opposition of native overlords. As Governor of Bengal, in the early 1770s, Hastings proved so able that he was appointed as Britain's first Governor-General of India; and during the next ten years his achievements included setting up a civil service and creating a postal system, codifying Hindu law, and tackling famine relief, as well as improving methods of tax-collection and overthrowing opponents as formidable as Hyder Ali, the ruler of Mysore. He made enemies in England as well as India, however; and on his return in 1785 he was impeached and put on trial, on twenty-two charges which ranged from cruelty, extortion and bribery to illegal self-enrichment. Among his accusers were such eminent figures as Edmund Burke, Charles James Fox and the great playwright and politician Richard Sheridan, whose oratory drew crowds to the proceedings as though to a theatre. Eventually, after almost eight years, Warren Hastings was acquitted on all charges. Among those who expressed their delight at the verdict was Henry Austen, who wrote, in a somewhat fulsome letter, 'Permit me to congratulate my country & myself as an Englishman.' Jane's own opinion could be deduced from the warmth which she recorded Hastings's praise of *Pride and Prejudice*, on its publication in 1813. 'I am quite delighted with what such a man writes about it', she told Cassandra – and later, reverting to the subject, added, 'I long to have you hear Mr. H's opinion of *P. and P.*'

Hastings had been fortunate, as a young Company man, to escape the horrors of the 'Black Hole of Calcutta', an atrocity which occurred in 1756 when the Nawab, determined to curb the growing power of the British in Bengal, attacked Calcutta and confined 146 civilians in a tiny, stifling cell, where almost all suffocated. The incident left a grim impression in Britain, and Jane Austen (though not born at the time) learned of it as she grew up: in 1796, writing of the granddaughter of one of the few survivors, she referred to her, somewhat flippantly, as 'Miss Holwell, who belongs to the Black Hole at Calcutta'. Though Jane never journeyed beyond the borders of England herself, and could be dismissive of fashionable European travel – as when she wrote lightly of a friend's absence, 'We shall not have Miss Bigg, she being frisked off like half England, into Switzerland' – she seemed, like several of her heroines, intrigued by reading, and hearing, of more exotic places. Elinor Dashwood in *Sense and Sensibility* enjoys talking to Colonel Brandon, who has served with his regiment in the West Indies, partly because 'he has seen a great deal of the world; has been abroad'. Her sister's and Willoughby's replies reveal their shallowness: Marianne 'contemptuously' responds, 'He has told you that in the East Indies the climate is hot, and the mosquitoes are troublesome', while Willoughby sneers, 'His observations may have extended to the existence of nabobs, gold mohrs, and palanquins.' It is tempting to imagine that Jane's cousin Eliza peppered her conversation with talk of 'nabobs' (Indian grandees), 'mohrs', or mohurs (gold coins, worth 15 rupees), and 'palanquins' (splendid litters, for luxurious transport); and since this novel was apparently conceived in the early 1790s and begun in earnest in 1797, the year of Eliza's and Henry's wedding, it may be that Colonel Brandon's character and career were planned at a time when Indian affairs were much discussed at Steventon. As *Sense and Sensibility* unfolds, and the true drama and romance of the 'sensible' Colonel's life-story emerge, his soldiering in faraway India adds to the reader's growing awareness that he is an impressive, as well as 'well-informed' and 'amiable' man. Because of the novel's uncertain chronology, and (presumably) major revisions between its inception and its eventual publication in 1811, it is impossible to establish when Brandon's Indian service took place; but given the stated 13-year time-lapse since his return, if Jane Austen's original version stood it would have been during Hastings's Governor-Generalship. Coincidentally, perhaps, Warren Hastings fought a duel in 1780 against a political adversary; in *Sense and Sensibility* Colonel Brandon breaks the law to fight a duel against the dishonourable Willoughby.

The well-worn criticism that her novels are merely 'light and bright and sparkling', and take no account of the great events of the times, was one which Jane herself anticipated. On receiving her first copy of *Pride and Prejudice*, in 1813, her pleasure was tempered with the anxiety familiar to almost every author, in every age, as to how it would be received by critics. 'It wants shade', she mused; 'a long chapter of sense', or

else of 'solemn specious nonsense, about something unconnected with the story' – such as 'the history of Buonaparté'.
In fact, though he is never mentioned by name in her novels,
and only appears on this one occasion in her letters, the
history of Napoleon Bonaparte would be integral to her
novels, as to her life. Regency readers of *Pride and Prejudice*
needed no telling that Mr Wickham's militia regiment was
quartered at Meryton, in readiness to defend the nation from
French invasion, any more than Cassandra could doubt that
Jane's passing comment, 'What weather! & what news!', in her
letter of 6 November 1813, referred to the future Duke of
Wellington's latest victory in the Peninsular War, at Vittoria.
From 1796, when Jane Austen was almost 21, until 1815, two
years before her death, when he was vanquished at Waterloo,
the figure of Napoleon loomed over the lives of the British
people almost continually; and all her novels, in some degree,
are touched by his shadow.

The militia – regiments embodied in wartime for the
nation's defence – provided employment for her own charming, but volatile, brother Henry, as for the charming, but
reprobate, Mr Wickham. Having joined the Oxfordshire
Militia after the outbreak of war between Britain and
Revolutionary France in 1793, Henry was sufficiently taken
with the military life to consider joining the Regulars – the
full-time regular army, with whom he might have earned
battle-honours abroad. In the event, like Mr Weston in *Emma*,
he 'satisfied an active cheerful mind and social temper' by
remaining in the auxiliary forces, in which (again like Mr
Weston), he became a Captain. As *Pride and Prejudice* makes
plain, the social side of army life, in Jane Austen's day, was alluring. In contrast to modest, thoughtful Edward Ferrars, in *Sense
and Sensibility*, who has rejected joining the army, as 'much too
smart for me', Mr Wickham admits cheerfully that the prospect of 'society, and good society' was his 'chief inducement'
for seeking a commission in the militia. There is no mention

of manoeuvres, drill, or dispatches from battle-fronts in Jane Austen's fiction; but at every ball there is the predictable group of gorgeously uniformed Regency officers to catch the eye of susceptible local young ladies. (On one occasion Jane herself seemed flattered to learn that a good-looking young officer had apparently wanted to dance with her, but as he did not wish it enough to effect an introduction, nothing came of it.) The closest she comes to touching on military duties is in such references as Mr Bennet's promise to take his daughter Kitty 'to a review' (a grand parade of troops) if she behaves in future; and Lydia Bennet's fantasy of herself, at Brighton Camp – 'Its tents stretched forth in beauteous uniformity of lines ... dazzling with scarlet' and 'herself seated beneath a tent, tenderly flirting with at least six officers at once'. The famous encampments on the Downs outside Brighton, where the Prince Regent, Colonel-in-Chief of the 10th Light Dragoons, held court at his fabulous seaside palace, were well-known in fashionable soldiering circles, and even enshrined in a popular song of the eighteenth and nineteenth centuries, 'The Girl I Left behind Me', with its lilting words, 'And now I'm bound for Brighton Camp / Kind heaven then pray guide me.' There was more than a hint of laughing in the face of danger in the attitude of this generation of young men and women towards the threat of overthrow by a foreign tyrant; and Jane Austen's apparently light-hearted treatment of military matters reflects both the Regency dandy approach to hardship and unpleasantness of all kinds, and the 'business as usual' philosophy of Britain's response, some 130 years later, to another European dictator's vaunting dreams of conquest. At the same time, however, the dark realities of Bonaparte's activities could not be ignored. They struck at the heart of Jane Austen's family – and, however subtly, found their way into her novels. Captain Weston, in *Emma*, may profit from his militia career by rising in the world and marrying an heiress; but Jane Fairfax, in the same novel, has lost her father, a gallant Lieutenant in the regular army, on active service in the Napoleonic Wars, and is left impoverished, to contemplate a future as a governess. Reality is never far below the surface in Jane Austen's outwardly escapist, playful fiction.

Under the brilliant generalship of Bonaparte, demonstrated in the Italian campaign of the mid-1790s, France became an ever-more menacing enemy. As Britain's valuable territories in the West Indies – which included Jamaica, Barbados, the Bermudas and Antigua – faced the threat of French aggression, a connection of the Austen family, Lord Craven, was one of many patriotic young men who joined up to be sent abroad in search of adventure and honour in the service of their country. Having purchased a Colonelcy in the 3rd Line Infantry, Craven invited Cassandra Austen's beloved fiancé, the Revd Thomas Fowle, to accompany his regiment as Chaplain. Eager to make money, in order to marry Jane's sister, Tom Fowle agreed, only to become one of some 80,000 victims of the dreadful tropical disease Yellow Fever, among the British forces. It was a blow from which Cassandra never recovered. All the letters between her and Jane, which must have touched on the subject, for the year 1797 were evidently destroyed; and Cassandra, for all her beauty and (if Jane is to be believed) brilliance, never married. There may have been some shred of comfort for the sisters in the fact that, nine years later, their beloved brother Francis would earn enough reputation and reward in the naval action of Santo Domingo to return home in triumph and marry his fiancée, Mary Gibson, with whom he set up house, along with Mrs Austen, Cassandra and Jane, in Southampton, in 1806. And the West Indies were preserved as British, rather than French, colonies for generations to come.

By 1802, when Jane Austen was living, unhappily and unproductively, at Bath, both nations were weary of the long war, and, under the Peace of Amiens, hostilities temporarily ceased. Napoleon's Egyptian incursions, both at sea and on land, had threatened British India; but his triumph at the Battle of the Pyramids had been undermined by Britain's reassertion of supremacy at sea, in Horatio Nelson's glorious victory at the Battle of the Nile, in 1798 – an event which would be popularly reflected, back at home, in women's fashions and trends in furniture design alike. Back in France, Napoleon consolidated his successes by taking power on the domestic front, bringing order and unity to the nation as First Consul – and then, in 1804, being created hereditary Emperor, during a lavish ceremony in which he took the imperial diadem from the grasp of the presiding Pope, to crown, with his own hands, both himself and his consort, the ageing Empress Josephine. The marriage did not last; and nor did the peace. By 1810 Napoleon I had divorced Josephine, and remarried a new Empress, the nubile Marie-Louise of Austria – whose library would later include a copy of the 1815 translation of *Sense and Sensibility*, entitled *Raison et Sensibilité, Ou les deux manières d'aimer*, published in Paris by A. Bertrand, and stamped with the crown and gold cypher of the young Empress. It was an ironic culmination to a decade in which, with France and Britain once again at war, military invasion of England, rather than her own literary invasion of France, would be on Jane Austen's mind. In August 1805 she reported on troop movements in the locality of Goodnestone, the Kent home of her brother Edward's adoptive mother, commenting – tongue-in-cheek – that 'on the matter of game', the 'evil intentions of the Guards are certain'. It was a moment when, with the partridge-shooting season about to open, officers and men of all three regiments of foot-guards would be marching by, en route to and from their barracks and the coast, at Chatham and Deal; and landowners might justifiably fear for their game-birds, at risk from expert poaching and pot-shots. There would be many such topical asides among the mundane 'minutiae' of Jane's day-to-day correspondence.

It was against a background of renewed war with France

that Jane's first-completed novel, the future *Northanger Abbey*, was accepted by a publisher, in 1803. To the author's concern, it did not appear; when this work was finally published in 1817, by the far more distinguished firm of John Murray, the edition included a posthumous note from the author, explaining that, since its inception, 'places, manners, books and opinions' had 'undergone considerable changes'. In 1803, there would have been a special weight to General Tilney's patriotic choice of English breakfast-china, as he 'thought it right to encourage the manufacture of his country'. As the war intensified, Napoleon adopted the strategy known as the 'Continental System', whereby the European nations blockaded Britain, to limit her imports of supplies and restrict her all-important foreign trade. Portugal – the oldest British ally – stood apart; the upshot was the invasion of the Iberian peninsula by France, and the long-drawn-out struggle for supremacy of the Peninsular War, from 1808 to 1814. Fierce resistance by local partisans, and the brilliant leadership of the future Duke of Wellington (who had come to prominence in India, in the 1790s), eventually secured a series of historic victories, and the downfall of Napoleon, but at a terrible price in human life. Jane Austen and her family were deeply struck by the death of General Sir John Moore at Corunna, in 1809 – an event which captured the popular imagination, and was commemorated in verses beginning, 'Not a drum was heard, not a funeral note', by the young contemporary poet Charles Wolfe. On the retreat, seeking to rescue his force of some 25,000 against vastly superior French opposition, Moore fought a desperate battle – defeating the enemy, but dying in the action. Jane Austen had anticipated that her brother Frank's ship, the *St Albans*, might be involved in evacuating troops: on 10 January, she had written, 'The "St Albans" perhaps may soon be off to help bring home what may remain by this time of our poor army, whose state seems dreadfully critical.' As news of the British victory filtered through, her thoughts were with the dead hero's family. Late in January, she wrote soberly, 'This is grievous news from Spain. It is well that Dr Moore was spared the knowledge of such a son's death.' When Sir John's deathbed words were made public, her tone changed somewhat, however: reacting, perhaps, to his last reference to his mistress Lady Hester Stanhope, and hopes of great reputation in England, in a speech which apparently made little mention of religion, she observed, a touch tartly, 'I wish Sir John had united something of the Christian with the hero in his death.' It was always Jane Austen's way to make light of life, whenever possible – and even major world events could be treated by her with a hint of humour. In 1814, when the ghastly war seemed to be at an end, and the former Napoleon I, now abdicated, was apparently safe in exile on the island of Elba, the Emperor of Russia (Britain's great ally) visited London, along with other major representatives of foreign powers, in the triumphant 'Summer of the Tsars'. Amid the atmosphere of general festivities and rejoicing, Jane teased her sister Cassandra, then staying with Henry in London, 'Take care of yourself, and do not be trampled to death in running after the Emperor.' For their niece Fanny Knight she had a still sterner message: 'I hope Fanny has seen the Emperor, and then I may fairly wish them all away.'

There was, however, nothing dismissive in her tone when she wrote about the navy – either in real life, or in her fiction. For all her reservations about the death of Sir John Moore, she reflected after Corunna, with heartfelt relief, 'Thank Heaven! we have had no one to care for particularly among the Troops.' She was thinking, clearly, of the risks that her brother Francis might have run, had his ship the *St Albans* been involved in the action. 'I hope I never ridicule what is wise or good', states Elizabeth Bennet in *Pride and Prejudice*; and though Jane Austen is happy to poke fun at such institutions as marriage, the monarchy and even the clergy, she never laughs at her brothers' activities at sea, in the King's service. She seems, on the contrary, to have been fascinated and moved by every detail of their naval experiences, from her childhood years when they were sent to the Royal Naval Academy at Portsmouth, to emerge (like Fanny Price's adored brother William, in *Mansfield Park*) as dedicated young midshipmen, to the end of her life. She loved to be beside the sea, whether lodging at Southampton, or staying, on holiday, at Lyme; and the *Mansfield Park* scenes set at Portsmouth, when Fanny Price is visiting the dockyard, or gazing out at the ships at Spithead, across a 'sea now at high water, dancing in its glee and dashing against the ramparts', are among the most evocative passages Jane Austen ever wrote.

Her advice to her would-be novelist niece Anna, to write only of settings where she would be 'quite at home', was reflected in her own fiction: though she never attempts to depict life on board ship, she deals expertly with the characters and conversations of naval officers on land, with their families and wives, and such technical terms as she uses are carefully researched. (In 1804, somewhat scornfully, she mentioned her aunt Mrs Leigh-Perrot talking of 'a sloop, which my aunt calls a Frigate'. It was not a mistake which Jane would have made.) She knew that Fanny Price's father, a retired Lieutenant of Marines, in a few moments' conversation with Mr Crawford, would instantly 'begin upon the last naval regulations, or settle the number of three-deckers now in commission'. Mr Price, unlike any of Jane's other sea-going officers, is allowed by her to be 'dirty and gross', hard-drinking and hard-swearing – because, as a Marine, or ship-board soldier, he has served in a separate corps and not the Austens' beloved navy. Though a gallant and highly respected body, the Royal Marines (as they became in 1802, in recognition of their valour) were considered of lower social status than their naval counterparts – which is why, in part, Fanny Price's mother is said to have 'married to disoblige her family', and why influential Sir Thomas Bertram has no connections in the profession, through whom to assist his brother-in-law's career. The importance of friends and patrons in high places is emphasized, later in the novel, when young William Price gets his promotion from lowly midshipman to naval Lieutenant through Henry Crawford's request for help from his uncle, the dissolute (but powerful) Admiral – who had influence with the Board of Admiralty, in charge of the Royal Navy's entire administration. Of all the family news with which Jane filled her letters, none seemed to give her greater pleasure than relating the news that Francis or Charles had received promotion. It was one of the tragedies of her early death that she did not live to see her elder brother's eventual rise to the splendid rank of Sir Francis Austen, KCB, Admiral of the Fleet.

A prime source of nautical information with which Jane Austen was evidently well acquainted was the Navy List, a John Murray publication, regularly updated, which provided details of officers' careers, and the ships they served in. Anne Elliot, as the ex-fiancée of Captain Frederick Wentworth, is amused to see, in *Persuasion*, that the Musgrove girls, fired with new-found interest, have acquired 'their own navy list', and, together, 'pore over it with the professed view of finding out the ships which Captain Wentworth had commanded'. In writing her great novels involving Regency naval life, Jane was (as ever) scrupulous in her research. In 1813, while working on *Mansfield Park*, she wrote to Frank, then serving in the Baltic, in HMS *Elephant*, 'shall you object to my mentioning the Elephant in it, and two or three other of your old ships?' – adding, anxiously, 'I have done it, but it shall not stay, to make you angry. They are only just mentioned.' Frank's permission was evidently forthcoming; and in after-years he would claim that there was more of himself than just the names of his ships in his sister's fiction. An upright, devout, and generally respected man, he had much in common with the hero's friend, Captain Harville, including a talent for making household objects: while the amiable Harville 'Made toys for the children' and 'fashioned new netting-needles and pins with improvements', Captain Austen is mentioned in Jane's letters as ever-busy, whittling wooden playthings, or knotting 'very nice fringe for the Drawing-room Curtains'. The impassioned little speech which Captain Wentworth delivers in *Persuasion* on the unseaworthiness of some ships, in which 'the admiralty', as he puts it, 'entertain themselves now and then with sending a few hundred men to sea', heedless of risk, has the ring of a real conversation, overheard by Jane between her brothers and their friends – particularly when it ends with a cheery rebuttal from kindly Admiral Croft, and Wentworth's conclusion, 'Ah! she was a dear old *Asp* to me . . . I knew that we should either go to the bottom together, or she would be the making of me.' In a rare mention of actual combat with Napoleon's fleet – 'our touch with the Great Nation', in his phrase – he mentions taking a French frigate: to the listening Anne's horror, he clearly might have lost his life in the action, or the storm which followed.

To the modern reader it may seem surprising that, with two brothers constantly at sea during such a dramatic period of naval warfare Jane makes no reference to great historic engagements – such as the Battle of Aboukir Bay in 1798 (the Battle of the Nile), during which one of Frank's future ships, the *Canopus*, was captured from the French, or, most crucial of all, the glorious victory of Admiral Lord Nelson at Trafalgar in 1805, which ensured Britain's vital sea-supremacy in the long-drawn-out war. Though Captain Austen (of whom Nelson had a high opinion) would see action off Santo Domingo a year later, he expressed deep regret at having missed Trafalgar. Yet full-scale battles were, in fact, relatively rare during this era. Much of the danger faced by Britain's sailors involved smaller engagements, between single ships – such as Captain Wentworth's encounter with the French frigate – or 'boat actions' and raids, whereby the Royal Navy attacked the French in harbour, or on shore. The day-to-day challenges of achieving victory – as Jane Austen was well aware – involved patrolling coastal waters; harrying the enemy away to the West Indies; running the gauntlet to fetch supplies from Gibraltar; blockading ports friendly to France. Grim and dangerous as the life often was, its potential rewards were great. One was social status: as snobbish Mary Crawford remarks, in *Mansfield Park*, 'Soldiers and sailors are always acceptable in society. Nobody can wonder that men are soldiers and sailors.' Another, still more important, was wealth. Through the capture of enemy ships, fortunes could be earned in 'prize money', divided out by seniority among officers and crew. 'A French schooner laden with sugar' taken by Charles Austen's ship, in 1809, during a 'cruize', or tour of duty, would have been a fine addition to Charles's pay, 'but Bad weather parted them'. For taking a privateer, in 1801, he had received £30, with hopes of a further £10 – part of which he laid out on buying topaz crosses on gold chains for his sisters. 'He must be well scolded', Jane protested fondly; some twelve years later she would use of this act of brotherly affection when creating the character of charming young midshipman William Price, in *Mansfield Park*. In *Persuasion*, Frederick Wentworth is said to have accrued the considerable fortune of £20,000 in prize money – though, as he ruefully points out, but for a good measure of luck, 'I should only have been a gallant Captain Wentworth, in a small paragraph at one corner of the news-papers; and being lost only in a sloop, nobody would have thought about me'.

Learning of her brothers' exploits was endlessly fascinating to Jane. Even she could have enough of the hero-worship which surrounded Lord Nelson, after his great victory and gallant death at Trafalgar: in 1813, she wrote crisply, 'I am tired of Lives of Nelson, being that I never read any' – but added, 'I will read this however, if Frank is mentioned in it.' Unlike many of her contemporaries, she did not have to bear the pain of seeing her brothers listed in the press among those killed in action; on the contrary, in 1800 she had the satisfaction of finding in a neighbour's newspaper a reference to Captain Austen, in the *Petterel*, having captured a Turkish ship from the French. 'You will see the account in the *Sun* I dare say', she told Cassandra. The *Sun* was then an evening newspaper, printed in London: with its pro-government views it would have been an obvious choice for Edward Knight and his moderate Tory circle at Godmersham. There was a wide choice of newspapers in Jane Austen's day, and she mentions, in passing, various different ones, both national and local, from the *Sun* and the equally pro-Tory *Courier* to 'the Bath paper' and 'the Portsmouth paper'. Though her nephew would later claim in his *Memoir* that Jane Austen's letters pay scant attention to 'politics or public events', she clearly believed it important for gentlemen and ladies alike to keep abreast of the news. There is usually a newspaper to hand in the country houses of which she writes: both Mr Darcy in *Pride and Prejudice* and Tom Bertram in *Mansfield Park* glance at a paper when needing a way out of a difficult conversation; and sending his newspaper to Mrs Dashwood and her daughters each day is one of the kindnesses which Sir John Middleton thoughtfully shows them, along with presents of fruit and game, in *Sense and Sensibility*. Closely printed in the 'broadsheet' format, consisting of a large single sheet folded at the centre to create four pages, a newspaper such as *The Times* – which cost 6½d in 1815 – covered a variety of subjects, from war news and parliamentary reporting, to announcements of charity events and theatre performances, fashion notes, and a wealth of advertisements, for property, situations vacant, schools, carriages, and goods for sale. Gossip about the aristocracy was an ever-popular feature of the press. Fanny Price's father, in *Mansfield Park*, clearly enjoys the titbits of scandal; on reading the thinly veiled revelation of Mrs Rushworth's adultery, he comments coarsely that 'so many fine ladies were going to the devil now-a-days that way' – adding, in a crude reference to harsh navy discipline, 'A little flogging for man and woman too, would be the best way of preventing such things.' While clearly recoiling from such talk, Jane Austen herself took note of society reports and scandal. When an acquaintance, Mrs Powlett, eloped with 'A Noble Viscount' in 1808, Jane read about it in the press, telling Cassandra, 'A hint of it, with Initials, was in yesterday's *Courier.*' Another London paper, the *Morning Post*, gave the salacious detail, 'Mrs P.'s *faux pas* with Lord S----e took place at an inn near Winchester.' Then as now, the public had an insatiable appetite for such revelations about the rich, titled and famous; and when royal figures were involved the papers had a field day.

King George III, who was on the British throne throughout Jane Austen's life, was in many ways a model of propriety: the father of fifteen children, devoted to his plain wife, Queen Charlotte, and drawn to simple, respectable pursuits such as music and farming. He had, however, a regrettably reactionary and paternalistic political outlook, which, no matter how benevolent in its intentions, was to have heavy consequences both abroad and at home – contributing to the loss of America, and to the rebellious, extravagant, debaucheries of his son and heir the Prince of Wales. Like his father, the Prince had many good qualities; but where the King was responsible and dutiful, the Prince, despite his undoubted charm, taste and talents, was self-indulgent, frivolous and weak – and, in the opinion of many, unsuited to rule, at a time when republican sentiment was in the air. When George III was taken violently ill, in 1788, with the frenzied symptoms now judged to have been caused by the disease Porphyria, a national crisis threatened. On this occasion, despite barbaric medical treatments, His Majesty recovered – but there would be several more such bouts before incurable insanity set in, and the Prince of Wales was appointed Regent, in 1811. Believing the King to be dying, several of Jane Austen's female relations ordered mourning-clothes: outwardly, at least, a show of respect for the monarchy had to be maintained, for the sake of national stability. Even the death of a relatively minor royal personage, the old Duke of Gloucester, in 1805, caused Jane to ask, 'I suppose everybody will be black for the D. of G. Must we buy lace, or will ribbon do?' Despite her air of detachment, however, she seemed to have had a certain sneaking interest in royal goings-on, and she certainly followed the battle for public sympathy which the Prince and Princess of Wales fought out in the newspapers, following the collapse of their façade of a marriage.

At the time of the Prince's wedding to his blonde, buxom German cousin, Princess Caroline of Brunswick, in 1795, he was secretly already married, to a Catholic widow, Maria Fitzherbert. But the lack of the King's consent, and her Catholicism, made this ceremony invalid. The reckless, extravagant Prince needed an heir; most of all, with his debts for buildings, clothes, jewels and frivolities running into hundreds of thousands of pounds, he needed money, which Parliament agreed to grant him, once he had found a wife. The royal marriage, which took place in 1795, ended, unofficially, almost as soon as it began; after conceiving a honeymoon baby – the heiress-presumptive Princess Charlotte – the couple parted. Thereafter they carried on a lively war of words, in which the public sentimentally supported the unstable, attention-seeking, but crowd-pleasing, Princess of Wales. When, in 1813, the Regent banned her from seeing their daughter, Caroline sent him an impassioned letter, which he returned unread; her response was to leak its entire contents to the *Morning Chronicle*. Its publication caused a furore. Such pursuit of publicity did not entirely suit Jane Austen's sense of delicacy: reflectively, she wrote to her friend Martha Lloyd, 'I suppose all the World is sitting in Judgement upon the Princess of Wales's Letter.' Revealingly, she added, 'Poor woman, I shall support her as long as I can, because she *is* a Woman, & because

I hate her husband – but I can hardly forgive her for calling herself "attached & Affectionate" to a Man she must detest.' She concluded, 'If I must give up the Princess, I am resolved at least always to think that she would have been respectable, if the Prince had behaved only tolerably by her at first.' By the time the Prince, as King George IV, attempted to divorce Queen Caroline in 1820, Jane Austen had been dead for four years. It is tempting to speculate as to what her thoughts might have been on that shocking turn of royal affairs.

Though the Prince Regent changed his political opinions with age, in youth he had been an ardent Whig, which may have contributed to Jane's detestation of him. The clear-cut distinctions of modern parliamentary politics had yet to emerge; and while the Whigs in the House of Commons tended to represent the interests of the aristocracy and upper classes, as well as expressing liberal ideals, the Tories – with their broad adherence to the more traditionally middle-class principles of upholding the Crown and keeping disaffection in check – were more identified with the landed gentry, and educated, but modestly situated, families such as the Austens. There were profound injustices in the political system: while heads of titled families, from Barons upwards, automatically held a seat in the House of Lords (from whom most officers of state were provided), members of the House of Commons were elected with little regard to the size of constituencies, or the needs of the population – among whom only about one in eight men, and no women, were entitled to vote, on qualifications which varied widely throughout the kingdom. Many MPs virtually bought their seats; and even a man as patently stupid as Mr Rushworth, in *Mansfield Park*, could be 'in for some Borough', in the certainty of winning in a local election which might even be uncontested. Mrs Palmer in *Sense and Sensibility* finds it vastly amusing that her taciturn husband is 'forced to make everybody like him', while standing for election – but she is in no doubt as to the outcome. 'How

charming it will be', she exclaims, 'when he is in Parliament!
. . . How I shall laugh!' Though he insisted in his *Memoir* that
Jane Austen took little interest in politics, her nephew sur-
mised that she probably 'shared that moderate Toryism which
prevailed in her family', and there is nothing in her writings
to suggest otherwise. A marginal note in her juvenile spoof–
History of England declares proudly, 'Spoken like a Tory!'; years
later, her niece Caroline would decline to kiss the Whig Prime
Minister Lord Palmerston, as a gesture of protest, when he
came canvassing in their area. The cool, pragmatic, upright and
clever Tory, William Pitt the Younger, who was Britain's Prime
Minister during much of Jane's adult life, was far more to her
liking than a swaggering, flamboyant populist such as the brilliant Whig leader Charles James Fox; and as the French
Revolution disintegrated into misgovernment and bloodshed,
in the early 1790s, she would have had no sympathy with the
outlandish views of a crusading MP such as Thomas Paine,
whose work *The Rights of Man* advocated votes for all adult
males, an end to wars, and the setting up of a system of welfare
benefits and free state education.

Yet there was no lack of social conscience in Jane Austen's
attitudes; and her compassion towards others – in particular,
such downtrodden groups as single women, the infirm and
the poor – is constantly demonstrated in her writings. On the
contentious issue of slavery, she leaves the reader in no doubt
as to her views. By the time *Mansfield Park* was published, in
1815, the slave trade had been illegal, under British law, for
eight years, and British subjects were forbidden to take part
any longer in the dreadful commerce in human life – which
at its height had involved the shipping of some 75,000
men, women and children from Africa to America and the
West Indies, almost half in British vessels, under conditions
of appalling cruelty. Banning such a lucrative traffic, which
had contributed greatly to the wealth of major ports such
as Bristol and Liverpool, had involved a hard-fought, long

crusade by men and women of conscience: among them, the industrialist Josiah Wedgwood, who helped to raise funds – and public awareness – by producing an earthenware medallion, bearing the cameo of a kneeling, chained African, with the inscription, 'Am I not a man, and a brother?' Leading the movement was the celebrated William Wilberforce, a devout, teetotal, Tory MP, whom the Austens would surely have admired. The 1807 Anti-Slavery Act was only one step in a long struggle for freedom, and equality, however: in the year of *Mansfield Park*'s publication an advertisement for an anniversary dinner of the African and Asiatic Society, to be chaired by Wilberforce himself, could announce baldly, 'About 100 Africans and Asiatics are expected to dine in an adjoining room.' And those slaves already in bondage overseas were not free – which is why Fanny Price's timid attempt to converse with her uncle, Sir Thomas Bertram, about the slave trade, on his return from Antigua, is greeted by 'a dead silence'. As always, Jane Austen is artfully non-committal on a potentially controversial topic: what Sir Thomas's stance would have been is never disclosed. But the inference is that, as a rich Englishman whose wealth derives partly from 'business' in Antigua, he owns sugar plantations, still manned by slave workers. Certainly, it was a delicate subject, at a moment when British seamen were mounting patrols to stop and search foreign ships suspected of still carrying captured Africans, and public opinion in Britain had largely swung behind the 'abolitionists'. When Jane Fairfax mentions 'the sale . . . of human intellect', in *Emma*, published in 1815, Mrs Elton (whose father, suspiciously, made his fortune as a 'Bristol merchant') is quick to fire up, 'If you mean a fling at the slave-trade, I assure you Mr Suckling was always rather a friend to the abolition.' Jane Fairfax's response is poignant: explaining that she spoke merely of 'the governess-trade', she draws a distinction between the degrees of guilt involved, but cannot resist, bitterly, comparing the miseries of the respective 'victims'. Jane Austen would surely have been proud to know that, in the 1820s, her brother Charles was to play a part in the suppression of the slave trade by the British navy – and would be presented with a ceremonial sword by no less a personage than Simon Bolivar, the great campaigner for South America's freedom from Spanish rule.

Ultimately, Jane Austen's moral attitudes were dictated, not by political ideology, but by her conscience as a committed, practising Christian. Brought up in the Church of England, she would die in it; yet though her own faith apparently never wavered, she constantly explored, through her novels, attitudes to belief and religious observance – and she could be as critical of foolish or unworthy clergymen, such as Mr Collins and Dr Grant, as of worldly sceptics, such as Mary Crawford. There was, indeed, much to criticize in Church affairs in her day, when taking orders could be seen more as entering a respectable profession than obeying a genuine vocation. The clergymen who feature in all her major novels range from honourable, desirable heroes (Henry Tilney, Edward Ferrars, Edmund Bertram), to comic anti-heroes (Mr Collins, Mr Elton); but even among the former, their career- and marriage-prospects play a far greater part in the narrative than any questions of faith. And while parish work is scarcely mentioned, the agreeable tasks of redecorating and 'improving' their respective vicarages are discussed in some detail.

In her cynical, subtle, portrait of Mary Crawford, Fanny Price's 'elegant' rival in *Mansfield Park*, Jane Austen provides an eloquent mouthpiece for criticisms of the Church. As she wrote in 1813, this was to be a novel with 'ordination' as its central theme: and the dangerously attractive Miss Crawford's serpentine temptings of Edmund to abandon his desire for the ministry, in favour of his desire for her, put his resolve to an almost Biblical test. Articulate and intelligent as well as seductive, Mary makes a good case for scorning the Regency clergy: 'A clergyman has nothing to do but be slovenly and selfish –

read the newspaper, watch the weather, and quarrel with his wife. His curate does all the work, and the business of his own life is to dine.' She has before her the example of her own brother-in-law, Dr Grant. 'An indolent, selfish bon vivant', in Jane Austen's description, he nevertheless rises higher in the Church than any other cleric in her novels, having eventually 'succeeded to a stall in Westminster Abbey', which denotes his elevation to the position of a canon at fashionable Westminster, 'with an increase of income', as well as status. Dr Grant achieves this through 'interest', meaning 'influence' – and patronage, as Jane Austen consistently shows, was all-important for an aspiring clergyman. Younger sons of wealthy families, such as Henry Tilney in *Northanger Abbey*, might have an inherited 'living', or parish, kept for them – sometimes with a less fortunate, temporary incumbent installed until the inheritor should be ordained; others, like Edward Ferrars in *Sense and Sensibility*, disowned by his mother and seeking a 'living', would be grateful for the good offices of a wealthy person such as Colonel Brandon, with a living to bestow. Brandon apologizes to Edward and Elinor for the small income at Delaford – a mere £200 per annum: but Jane's own brother Henry, after taking orders, was obliged to accept the curacy of Chawton in 1818 at less than £55 a year. To increase their earnings many clergymen took on more than one living, to the detriment, presumably, of their parishioners' spiritual needs. Odious as Mr Collins's grovelling to his rich, influential patroness Lady Catherine de Bourgh in *Pride and Prejudice* may be, it is – perhaps – understandable.

The importance of genuine spirituality in such times became a subject of increasing interest to Jane Austen as she grew older. The example which a good clergyman might set was evidently much on her mind, in creating her fictional clerics. Emma Watson in her unfinished novel *The Watsons* is deeply moved by hearing a description of the hero, Mr Howard, preaching, 'with great propriety, and in a very impressive manner; and at the same time without any Theatrical grimace or violence'. The speaker, Emma's father, adds, 'I do not like the studied air and artificial inflexions of voice, which your very popular and most admired Preachers generally have.' Here, devotional style, theatrical style and reading style come together, as expressions of Jane Austen's taste which Fanny Price, with her simple faith, and Elizabeth Bennet, with her lucid wit, would surely have shared. Such attitudes would be integral to Jane's growing attraction to the Evangelical movement, which, by the end of the eighteenth century, was attracting a considerable following, with its emphasis on personal worship and Bible reading, family prayers twice daily, and Sunday observance, as well as ardent preaching, and the rooting out of corrupt and indulgent practices from the Church. 'I do not like the Evangelicals', Jane had commented in 1809, after being recommended the devout Miss Hannah More's proselytizing work *Coelebs in Search of a Wife*; but by the end of 1814 she was in a more receptive frame of mind. 'I cannot suppose we differ in our ideas of the Christian Religion', she told her niece Fanny Knight: 'We only affix a different meaning to the word Evangelical.' A month before, she had mused, 'I am by no means convinced that we ought not all to be Evangelicals, & am at least persuaded that they who are so from Reason and Feeling, must be happiest & safest.' It was, she suggested, all a question of '*Goodness*'.

Few authors in the history of English literature can have had a better claim to '*Goodness*' than Jane Austen. A product of the great Georgian and Regency ages, she had Reason and Feeling in abundance, along with brilliant wit; but most of all, in her combination of exquisitely ironic comic powers with a profound and compassionate understanding of human nature, she had 'Goodness'. 'I *have* lost a treasure, such a Sister, such a friend as never can have been surpassed – She was the sun of my life', wrote her sister Cassandra on her death in

1817. Today, nearly two centuries later, Jane Austen continues to bring sun into the lives of readers throughout the world. Through her immortal works she remains, as she was to those who knew her, a unique, and treasured, companion.

Further Reading

The vast, and diverse, range of sources available to the student of Jane Austen is, of course, almost limitless. The following list is merely a brief guide to some recommended further reading.

THE NOVELS

Chapman, R. W. (ed.), *The Works of Jane Austen*, 5 vols. (Oxford, Oxford University Press, 1993–4)

THE LETTERS

Chapman, R. W. (ed.), *Jane Austen's Letters* (Oxford, Oxford University Press, 1979)

Le Faye, Deirdre (ed.), *Jane Austen's Letters* (Oxford, Oxford University Press, 1995)

BIOGRAPHIES AND MEMOIRS

Austen-Leigh, James Edward, *A Memoir of Jane Austen* (London, Folio Society, 1997)

Cecil, David, *A Portrait of Jane Austen* (London, Constable, 1978)

Fergus, Jan, *Jane Austen: A Literary Life* (New York, St Martin's Press, 1991)

Honan, Park, *Jane Austen: Her Life* (London, Weidenfeld & Nicolson, 1987)

Jenkins, Elizabeth, *Jane Austen: A Life* (London, Victor Gollancz, 1938)

Lane, Maggie, *Jane Austen's Family* (Robert Hale, 1984)

Laski, Marghanita, *Jane Austen and Her World* (London, Thames & Hudson, 1997)

Nokes, David, *Jane Austen: A Life* (London, Fourth Estate, 1997)

Shields, Carol, *Jane Austen* (London, Weidenfeld & Nicolson, 2001)

Tomalin, Claire, *Jane Austen: A Life* (London, Viking, 1997)

Further Reading

GENERAL STUDIES

Grey, J. David, *The Jane Austen Handbook* (London, Athlone, 1986)
Copeland, Edward and McMaster, Juliet (eds), *The Cambridge Companion to Jane Austen* (Cambridge, Cambridge University Press, 1997)

SPECIALIZED STUDIES

Butler, Marilyn, *Jane Austen and the War of Ideas* (Oxford, Oxford University Press, 1975)
Collins, Irene, *Jane Austen and the Clergy* (London, Hambledon, 1995)
Edwards, Anne-Marie, *In the Footsteps of Jane Austen* (London, BBC Publications, 1979)
Haythornethwaite, Philip, *Uniforms of Waterloo* (London, Blandford Press, 1984)
Hubback, J. M. and Hubback, Edith, *Jane Austen's Sailor Brothers* (London, Bodley Head, 1904)
Lane, Maggie, *Jane Austen and Food* (London, Hambledon, 1995)
Laver, James, *Costume and Fashion* (London, Thames & Hudson, 1995)
Parissien, Steven, *Regency Style* (London, Phaidon, 1992)
Plumb, J. G., *Georgian Delights* (London, Weidenfeld & Nicolson, 1980)
Southam, Brian, *Jane Austen: The Critical Heritage* (London, Routledge, 1968)
Stone, Lawrence, *The Family, Sex and Marriage in England, 1500–1800* (Harmondsworth, Penguin, 1990)
Thornton, Peter, *Authentic Decor, 1620–1920* (London, Weidenfeld & Nicolson, 1985)
Tompkins, J. M. G., *The Popular Novel in England, 1770–1800* (London, Methuen, 1969)
Watkins, Susan, *Jane Austen in Style* (London, Thames & Hudson, 1990)

Index

Index

Index

Austen, Henry (JA's brother), 6; attachment to family, 29; bankruptcy, 39; 'Biographical Notice' in *Northanger Abbey*, 41; career, 94, 219, 224, 241; character, 5, 33–4, 112, 224; education, 10, 13; on JA, 113, 117; JA on, 33–4; as JA's agent, 31, 36–7; and JA's visit to Carlton House, 37; in London, 184, 185, 198, 199; marriage to Eliza, 15, 16, 21–2, 219; opinion of JA's novels, 33, 125; preface to *Persuasion*, 117; on Warren Hastings, 222

Austen, James (JA's brother), 6; attraction to Eliza, 15, 16; character and tastes, 13, 112; education, 10; JA's relationship with, 13, 23, 39, 99; legacy, 42; second marriage, 21; as Steventon clergyman, 24

Austen, Jane:
life: 1–44; background, 99; birth, 5; childhood, 5, 8; daily routine, 51; education, 9, 10, 99–100; move to Bath, 24; move to Chawton, 29; romantic attachments, 18–19, 23–4, 25–6, 128–31, 134, 155; illness and death, 40, 42–3, 56; funeral, 43; grave, 1, 43, 44
appearance: 18, 75, 88, 90, 141–2; portrait by sister, 12
character and characteristics: 18, 22–3; codes of conduct, 189, 190–1, 193–4; dislike of pretentiousness, 60, 84, 98, 124, 139–40, 185–6, 196–7, 204; dislike of town and love of nature, 160, 164–5, 184–5; importance of religion and spirituality, 215, 240, 241–2; love of children, 149–53; love of the sea, 230; morality, 117–18, 215; sense of duty, 194; wit *see* wit
interests and activities: book buying, 123; dancing, 61–3; fashion, 25, 80, 81, 84–5, 96; food and drink, 46–7, 50, 53–5; games, 64; history, 102, 122–3; housekeeping, 46–8; music, 59–61, 164; reading, 98–102, 105, 106, 107, 122–3; sewing, 78–9; Shakespeare, 115–16; shopping, 93; theatre, 115–16; word-play, 64, 99, 113, 114
views: acting, 116–17; affectation of accomplishments, 139–40; architecture, 173–4; aristocrats, 196; Bath, 24, 161; education, 139,

140–1; foreigners, 220; fortune-hunting, 200; hypochondria, 55–6; interference in others' lives, 142, 145–6; London, 161, 185–6; marriage, 138, 140, 143–4, 147; politics, 216–17, 237; royalty, 236–7; sexual freedom, 134, 136; travel and transport, 222; wealth, 126, 199–200
writings: accuracy in novels, 119, 188–9, 190; anonymity of authorship, 20, 31, 34, 43; attitude to criticism, 124–5, 190, 222, 223–4; Christianity and Christian values in, 105, 215, 240–1; code of conduct in, 190–1, 193–4; controversial topics, 239; criticism of Anna Austen's writing, 35, 113, 120, 188–9, 190, 208, 214, 230; defence of popular novels, 119–20; detractors, 44; dramatic pieces, 15; early writings, 12–13, 15, 74, 100–4, 113–14, 117; earnings, 44, 126–7, 199–200; French translation, 227; JA's attachment to her characters, 33, 156; letters, 18, 19, 66, 74; literary discussion in, 109; novels as her children, 155–6; poetry, 113–14; political reference, 168; as professional writer, 30–1; religion in, 105, 240; reviews of her novels, 33, 36, 37, 125–6, 223–4; snobbery as target, 197; style, 99, 112, 189–90; writing habits, 174
titles: NB references to individual characters can be found under their names; *The Adventures of Mr Harley*, 12; *The Beautifull Cassandra*, 12; *Catharine, or The Bower*, 58, 105, 107, 138, 217; *A Collection of Letters*, 104; *Elinor and Marianne*, 20, 30; *Emma*, 6, 33, 36–7, 38, 44, 61–2, 114, 118, 125, 126, 141, 156, 160, 167, 174–5, 186, 191, 204, 220; *First Impressions* (original working-title for *Pride and Prejudice*), 19–20, 21, 31–2, 172; *Frederic and Elfrida*, 100; *The History of England* (JA's), 101–2, 104, 111, 238; *Jack and Alice*, 12, 54, 100; *Juvenilia*, 13, 100–4, 113, 117; *Lady Susan*, 145; *Love and Freindship*, 12, 16, 46, 101, 102–4, 111; *Mansfield Park*, 15, 32, 33, 36–7, 51, 63, 69, 91, 125, 144–5, 191, 193, 201–2, 216, 230; *The Mystery*, 15; *Northanger*

Index

Index

Index

Index

Index

Index

Index